The Primordial Mind in ...

The universal quest to create cosmologies – to comprehend the relationship between mind and world - is inevitably limited by the social, cultural and historical perspective of the observer, in this instance western psycho-analysis. In this book Michael Robbins attempts to transcend such contextual limitations by putting forward a primordial form of mental activity that co-exists alongside thought and is of equal importance in human affairs.

This book challenges the western assumption that knowledge is synonymous with rational thought and that the aspect of mind that is not thought is immature, irrational, regressive and pathological. Robbins illustrates the central role of primordial mental activity in spiritual cultures analogous to that of thought in western culture as well as its significant contributions to numerous other phenomena including dreaming, language, creativity, shamanism and psychosis.

In addition to his extensive clinical experience as a psychoanalyst Robbins draws on first-hand contact with Maori and other shamanistic cultures. Vividly illustrated by first and second hand accounts, this book will be of great interest to psychoanalysts, those with a psychological interest in spiritual cultures as well as those in the fields of developmental psychology, cultural anthropology, neuroscience, aesthetics and linguistics.

Michael Robbins has practiced psychoanalysis for four decades. He has held professorships on the faculties of the Harvard and UCSF medical schools and is currently a member of the Boston and International Psychoanalytic Societies. He lives and practices in Amherst, Massachusetts.

The Primordial Mind in Health and Illness

A Cross-Cultural Perspective

Michael Robbins

Routledge
Taylor & Francis Group

LONDON AND NEW YORK

First published 2011 by Routledge
27 Church Road, Hove, East Sussex BN3 2FA

Simultaneously published in the USA and Canada
by Routledge
711 Third Avenue, New York 10017

Routledge is an imprint of the Taylor & Francis Group, an Informa business

Typeset in Times by Garfield Morgan, Swansea, West Glamorgan
Printed and bound in Great Britain by TJ International Ltd, Padstow,
Cornwall
Paperback cover design by Andrew Ward

British Library Cataloguing in Publication Data
A catalogue record for this book is available from the British Library

Library of Congress Cataloging-in-Publication Data
Robbins, Michael, M.D.
  The primordial mind in health and illness : a cross-cultural perspective /
Michael Robbins.
    p. cm.
  Includes bibliographical references and index.
  ISBN 978-0-415-45460-5 (hbk.) – ISBN 978-0-415-45461-2 (pbk.) 1.
Subconsciousness. 2. Cognition. 3. Ethnopsychology. 4. Psychoanalysis.
I. Title.
  BF315.R58 2011
  150–dc22

                                                              2010040393

ISBN: 978-0-415-45460-5 (hbk)
ISBN: 978-0-415-45461-2 (pbk)

Contents

Tables

Preface

Where does a book come from? My interest in the history of ideas has increased as I have noticed the changes and transformations of my own thinking in the course of my personal odyssey from student to clinician and then to erstwhile creator of ideas, and as I have become aware of how theories come and go in my own field of psychoanalysis. Ideas become popular and are embraced as truths (in "scientific" terms, validated) and even develop a cult-like following, only to be dismissed as outmoded or even as quackery or illusion when the pendulum of belief swings the other way, and they are more or less forgotten. In a generation or two they may be resurrected and christened under new names and in new guises by ostensible creators who are seemingly unaware of the precedents and prior incarnations of these ideas. In this respect western culture is very different from spiritual cultures that honor elders, ancestors, and the continuity of knowledge. One of the first things I do when I read is to look at the reference list and ask where the author's ideas came from. Sometimes this bit of intellectual archeology leads in fascinating directions and at other times it seems that the author is unaware that his or her contribution is not original. I do not mean to point fingers, as I have been guilty of this kind of naivete earlier in my career. I can only hope I have learned from it.

I am a psychoanalyst. I became interested in the field in the romantic era of psychoanalysis, influenced by books like *The Fifty Minute Hour* and *I Never Promised You a Rose Garden* and movies like *Spellbound*. It was then generally believed that psychoanalysis could cure all mental ills. But pride cometh before the fall, and with the advent of neuroscience, the ascent to power of psychopharmacology and the movement away from finding meaning in the mind and toward finding it in pathological material processes in the brain, psychoanalysis has been marginalized in many parts of the world.

My training in psychoanalysis took place at the old Massachusetts Mental Health Center in the early 1960s, when psychopharmacology was in its infancy and lengthy hospitalization and intensive psychodynamic therapy for psychotic persons was the treatment of choice for serious mental ills. My mentor was Elvin Semrad, whose vast influence on a generation of psychiatrists and psychoanalysts was generated by personal contact and charisma rather than the written word. He taught in an era when it was socially sanctioned to work intensively and psychologically with individual persons. He taught that one learns, understands and helps by sitting with psychotic patients hour after hour, and that bearing and helping them bear hitherto unbearable feelings and the ideas related to them is the crux of the work. His ideas had a significant impact on my own development. Such work is no longer possible in an era in which organic factors are believed to cause mental illness, psychotic manifestations are considered meaningless epiphenomena of a pathological brain, and treatment consists of medicating people to bring about rapid symptom relief, with very brief hospitalization only when essential. Therapy based on intensive and extensive human relationship that focuses on feelings is considered wasteful of resources if not actually regressive and harmful. As a result psychotherapy is no longer taught in most psychiatric training programs. Semrad never wrote about his work although perhaps he wanted to for he amassed an enormous collection of recorded consultations and therapy sessions. The basic idea he proposed, that primordial mental states do not enable bearing and thinking about painful emotions and related subjects, is something I have tried to understand and formulate in various ways, including the writing of this book.

During the latter stages of my psychiatric residency I began psychoanalytic training. After completing residency training I took a hospital job and became a psychiatrist in charge of a ward at McLean Hospital, in the Harvard system. I remained there for many years, involved in treatment, administration, teaching and consulting. It turned out to be a serendipitous association insofar as I began to integrate my psychoanalytic insights with my work with psychotic persons, an interest I maintain to this day, and I gradually developed a broader interest in the way mind works, especially in its primordial aspects.

As my personal psychoanalytically informed interest doing intensive work with psychotic patients developed, and I began to experience some success in my work, the social pendulum with regard to mental ills in general, and more serious psychotic ones in particular, shifted from the study of mind to materialism, the study of brain. No doubt psychoanalytic claims to understanding and treatment were exaggerated, as I believe those of neuroscience are today, but the pendulum swung far in the other direction and the idea that psychosis is, as Sullivan put it, a human condition and that the psychological manifestations of such illnesses are meaningful expressions of personality has become endangered.

My psychiatric training emphasized learning directly from my disturbed patients rather than from reading books about theory. I learned a certain attitude – irreverence, perhaps contempt – for book learning. Probably some of my attitude was defensive, as theory often seemed arcane and difficult to comprehend. So I came late to theory and to the history of ideas. When I should have been intrigued with Freud and other giants of psychoanalytic history I read what I had to mostly in a *pro forma* way. I still believe that learning about human mind and therapy cannot take place like learning to cook using a cookbook. In today's anti-psychotherapy climate, where people in training do not have the opportunity to relate in an intensive and extensive way to patients, they cannot learn, no matter how good the written primer.

I have had a longstanding interest in creativity, one of the themes of this book. As time permitted I have done some wood sculpting. In 1969 I published my first psychoanalytic paper, which was on the subject of artistic creativity. In retrospect I think the ideas were naive and trivial, but for some reason they got the enthusiastic support of Phyllis Greenacre, one of the pioneers in the field.

Gradually, in the late 1960s and early 1970s, I became interested in how mind works and how psychoanalytic theory might help me to better understand what I was doing. This was before the work of Melanie Klein, which had already made a substantial impact in the UK and South America, was widely known in the United States, which was a bastion of more classical "Freudian" thinking. One of the first theorists who made an impression on me was Otto Kernberg, a dynamic, charismatic, thoughtful person who was trying to work with seriously ill persons and formulate theory about it. His early papers on borderline personality organization made a substantial impact on me. Only later did I realize Kernberg, who had trained in a Kleinian institute in South America, was struggling to reconcile those ideas with others. On the surface he was critical of Klein, and believed himself to be aligned with Fairbairn, whose ideas are very different. Yet, as it took me some time to discover, his theory of borderline personality is a thinly disguised presentation of Kleinian theory. Although he would have denied it at the time, I credit him for introducing Kleinian theory to an orthodox Freudian American audience.

I slowly learned about the work of Klein, Fairbairn, Mahler, Kohut and others and began to develop some ideas that in retrospect were not so original as I thought. I did not yet appreciate the profundity of Klein's contribution, perhaps because of her "unscientific" personalized conceptual language as well as the negative way in which I was introduced to it. My first paper on what I now think of as primordial mind (1976) was a critical response to Kernberg's ideas. In retrospect I was more focused on what I opposed than what I proposed, which I hardly yet knew. I wonder if I was repeating with Kernberg what he had done with Klein and her ideas. In any case, just as I owe Elvin Semrad a debt of gratitude for teaching me how to work with patients and learn from them, I owe Otto Kernberg a similar debt for teaching me the importance of theory and for directing me toward the fascinating subject that this book is about. In 1980 I began approaching primordial mind more directly and wrote a paper comparing and contrasting Fairbairn, Klein and Kohut. I was still in the early stages of learning.

Over the decade of the 1980s I wrote a number of papers, some from a developmental perspective using observational data from my own children. I compared the concepts of Klein, Fairbairn, Mahler and Kohut and tried to formulate a theory of my own about what I chose to call the primitive personality disorders. Combining Mahler's concept of symbiosis and Klein's concept of projective identification, I proposed what I called possession configurations – pathological symbiotic bondings. The concept was an attempt to incorporate Klein's intrapsychic theory with Mahler's interpersonal model of separation and individuation. My ideas have changed a great deal since then and I look upon many of the earlier ones as trials or beginnings.

In the whirlwind of the ascendency of neuroscientific reductionism and related mechanistic treatment of psychosis with drugs and re-education, the belief that psychosis is a disturbance of personality and that in some instances psychoanalytically informed treatment can bring about results far beyond these newer and "more scientific" methods has been obliterated. I am a fast typist and for many years after the end of my own training I took elaborate notes on therapy with patients in the ten minutes between sessions. Often I wrote as much as a single-spaced page. It was a form of self-supervision as well as an effort to improve the accuracy of my memory by comparing the notes with tape recordings of sessions from time to time. I gradually realized I was creating an archive of evidence of the potential value of psychoanalytically informed psychotherapy of psychosis at a time when, in a sense, the libraries were burning down and wisdom was being lost, perhaps forever.

In the late 1980s, and with what I hope was an adequate degree of humility, I decided to write a book that Semrad, who had by that time died, might have written had he been able. It was to be a clinically oriented book. Believing that there are very few really detailed reports of therapies from start to finish, nor any that detailed failures as well as successes, I went through successive condensations of my notes and came up with five lengthy reports of entire treatments. Later, in the writing of *Experiences of Schizophrenia* (1993), I decided to append a section on theory of psychotic mind and its treatment. I did this ambivalently, because I knew my own ideas on the subject of psychoanalysis and psychosis were still not thoroughly crystallized.

In the ensuing years I have been influenced by the philosophy of science and cultural anthropology. In the late 1980s and early 1990s, under the sway of postmodernism, I became aware of General Systems Theory and then of Chaos or Complexity Theory. I began to think of human personality in terms of a hierarchy of systems from microscopic to macroscopic, related by principles of analogy and transformation: brain, the individual psyche, the familial and interpersonal field, society, and, at the macroscopic end, one's culture. The beginning of cultural awareness in turn led me to realize that psychoanalytic theory is in some respects indigenous rather than being so universally applicable as I had believed. In *Experiences of Schizophrenia* I proposed what I called a hierarchical systems theory, and in 1996 I published *Conceiving of Personality*, in which I examined various systems that comprise personality and the disciplines appropriate to understanding each, including but not exclusive to psychoanalysis. I proposed the concept of self-centric (western) and socio-centric (spiritual) cultures. In that book I also wrote a bit about the history of ideas in psychoanalysis and how much of the accepted wisdom of the moment is influenced by fad and fashion.

Over the ensuing years I have continued to study cultural anthropology. In the last couple years I have been fortunate enough to make the acquaintance of two shamans, and to be welcomed into a community of Maori healers. These experiences have served to de-center me in a way that has been disconcerting but also eye-opening.

I cannot conclude this personal odyssey without commenting on what has remained constant in the face of all the changes I have described. It is the idea that Semrad taught me, that one learns about how mind works through intensive experience with other human beings, mostly one's patients. Important as my reading of other people's theories has become, in the "last analysis" my patients have been my teachers, and what I have learned about how the mind works I owe to them.

Acknowledgments

I would like to express gratitude to colleagues and patients of mine who kindly and generously contributed time, effort and personal material, and to family members whose critical readings helped to improve the quality of the manuscript.

To my patients who have taught me most of what I know about primordial mind. I owe special thanks to Jacob, Kay, Lisabeth and Caroline, who bridged the worlds of personal psychosis and thoughtful understanding to provide me with their retrospective understanding, and were courageous enough to give me written permission to publish what they wrote. You know who you are even though respect for your privacy precludes me from disclosing your real names.

To a remarkable Maori shaman, Egan Bidois, who has become a friend during the course of preparing the book, and whose unsparingly honest and detailed account of his life in the context of his culture has helped me to bridge the worlds of western and spiritual cultures, of shamanism and psychosis, and of western medicine and spiritual healing. He has challenged my limited western cultural perspective and I hope his contribution will have a similar impact on you, the reader.

To Warren Colman, Editor in Chief of the Journal of Analytical Psychology, for a scholarly reading and some very helpful criticisms.

My gratitude to Michelle Robbins for her hard work on an early version of the manuscript.

My gratitude to the editorial staff at Routledge for their hard work and support, both those behind the scenes whose names I do not know, and those who have worked directly with me including Kate Hawes, Sarah Gibson, Kathryn Russel and Sally Mesner Lyons.

Most important, my love and appreciation to Karen Sheingold. Your devotion and support, your editorial efforts, and most of all our dialogues about the ideas on which the book is based that helped me to clarify my own thinking, have made this a better book.

Chapter 1

The big picture

There is a *whakatauaki*, or proverb, in Maori culture that states
"Nga hiahia ai ki te timata aa ka kite ai tatou te mutunga"
(You must understand the beginning if you wish to see the end)

In the pages to come I present the thesis that there is a normal primordial form of mental activity that operates continuously from the inception of life alongside and in relation to thought. It accounts for a rich diversity of human phenomena ranging from the unremarkable to the extraordinary, from things looked upon as "normal" to others labeled pathological. Often its activity is undetectable unless we are trained to look for it, but its most obvious manifestations include dreaming, the mind of infancy and early childhood, the bonding behavior of infants and their caregivers, the modal mental activity in spiritually based cultures, some kinds of creativity, and the psychotic spectrum of illness.

At first glance this may not seem like a new idea. After all, psychoanalysis is based on theories about the relationship between a conscious, thoughtful, symbol-using part of mind and a repressed or otherwise defended against unconscious part. However, these theories were created from the perspective of western rational thought, which is equated with psychic consciousness or awareness. From that perspective the primordial aspects of mind are looked upon as inferior – *un*-conscious, irrational, immature and primitive. I argue and illustrate that a new model of primordial mind in relationship to thought is necessary – one that appreciates both that and how it is different from thought and not inferior to it, and that in complex interactions with thought it contributes in significant ways all the time to all our lives.

Origins of the western view of mind

As western culture evolved out of its tribal and spiritual roots it has come to value change and progress, and to put its infancy behind it. Objectivity and rationality are among its cherished goals and science and technology are at the apex of its accomplishments. Ontogeny recapitulates phylogeny, and the evolution of the culture has been repeated in the development and maturation of each of its members. Western cosmology – one might even say western mythology – believes that it is normal to expect development of a relatively self-sufficient individual who adapts to a world of separate others and external reality. This individual self or psyche has internal complexity or stratification. "Within" it rational logical thought and related moral sense or conscience are looked upon as the highest or most mature strata. The "lower" stratum of self, which is related to our tribal origins and to infancy, is believed to consist of unconscious forces that are immature, irrational and uncivilized, and to have the potential to be disruptive to the social order and the community.

The conception of a self stratified into conscious and unconscious components originated with the birth of western culture in ancient Greece and subsequently was elaborated by Kant. Plato (1927) envisioned the *psyche* as a spectrum ranging from reason to impulse, divided into rational, spirited or affective, and appetitive parts. The appetitive part was believed to emerge while the rational part sleeps, and was said to be characteristic of children and responsible for dreaming. It is described as sensory-perceptual, somatic, sensual, concrete and unbounded; a realm of shadow and illusion where meanings are in a state of flux or oscillation and contradiction abounds.

Kant (1781, 1798) postulated a tripartite mind model consisting of reason, understanding and sensibility, which resembles Freud's superego, ego and id respectively (Brook, 1997). Kant believed that much of the mind's operation is unconscious. The conscious world is phenomenal and the unconscious, which one can never know directly, is *noumenal*. In his view the process of becoming conscious involves abstraction and conversion of intuitions from the sensory-perceptual or phenomenal world into representations by a process of understanding. These representations possess the quality of reason, the dimensions of time and externality/ internality, and can be expressed in language and remembered.

Freud gave these ideas contemporary credibility. His study on hysteria (Breuer and Freud, 1893) was the basis for what in 1895 he called a "scientific" psychology, a "topographic" model of consciousness and unconsciousness modeled after the neuroscience of his time. His study of dreaming (1900) led him to expand on his model and postulate primary and secondary mental processes. The lower or irrational appetitive part of the Platonic mental spectrum Freud called unconscious – *das es* or the "it." In Strachey's effort to lend scientific credibility to Freud's work it is translated into science-like terminology, the *id*. The *id* is the unconscious "place" or aspect of mind ruled by the primary process, a set of operations that produce hallucinatory or dreamlike phenomena; experiences that seem quite real to the subject. Freud believed that the primary process accounts not only for dreaming, but for the mental activity of infancy and early childhood, and for schizophrenia, but he never explored the subject of psychosis.

Being and knowing in spiritual cultures

Because the western view of person and cosmos is indigenous and not universal, models that iterate its assumptions need to be reconsidered. Whereas science, based on objectification, is the ideal product of western culture, spiritual cultures specialize in other ways of knowing and healing. Beliefs and perspectives in the world's many spiritual cultures are quite different. Most of us know what is meant by western industrialized culture, but spiritual cultures are more difficult to categorize. Mostly they are indigenous tribal cultures that practice shamanism, of which there remain an astounding number in the world (Bourguignon, 1973). However, there are important ways in which spirituality has determined mind and social behavior in large eastern cultures that are based on Buddhism and Hinduism as well.

Western and spiritual cultures have very different perspectives on the nature of the cosmos and the relation of the person to the world. Spiritual cultures are socio-centric (Robbins, 1996); they are based on the spatial or existential idea of a unitary collective consciousness, consisting of the animate and natural worlds and the ancestral world. Members of such cultures appear self-effacing to western eyes but they are not. They do not aggrandize themselves as individuals or stand out in relation to others because they believe that it is the timeless eternal collective of which they are a part that is important. What is stratified vertically within a separate self in western culture is conceived of existentially or laterally in the spiritual cosmos. While they distinguish between the corporeal body and the soul, distinctions between inner self (subjectivity) and outer world (objectivity), internal layers of mind, waking and dreaming, past and present time, are not made in the same way as in western culture; these are simply different realms of a unitary experience that have equivalent "reality" value. In western culture passions, rages, conflicted impulses and wishes to be repressed are believed to exist mostly in a suppressed unconscious part of the psyche and to emerge in disguise in nocturnal dreaming. In spiritual cultures such things are perceived as good and evil forces existing in the natural and social (spiritual) world, a cosmos that is animated as a geographical underworld in which the person journeys or travels and struggles in waking life. The dream state is not distinguished in terms of waking and sleeping, rationality and irrationality, but is considered an essential source of information about individual and community. What in the western psyche are conceived of as memories are similarly distributed in the cosmos; the ancestral world is alive and active. While death of the body is accepted, ancestors continue to exist in spirit as audible and visible presences, voices and visions that are just as real and present as any other experience. The disciplined awareness and use of these primordial mental processes is considered the highest form of development in such spiritually based cultures; something that enables and enriches community life.

All the existing models of primordial mental activity are of necessity constructed through the epistemological lens and bias of western rational thought – which is assumed to be *the* way of knowing about self and world – some more than others. The generally accepted western model of thought and the unconscious, with its implicit devaluation of primordial mind, does not seem adequate. Jung's perspective, which was heavily influenced by his hospital work with psychotic persons at the Burghölzli clinic, is less judgmental though impressionistic. Perhaps because he himself struggled with psychosis (Jung, 2009) and came to have respect for the potential richness and creativity of primordial mind he did not judge it according to conventional western ideas. He believed that mind has two qualitatively different manifestations that are in continuous dialectical relationship throughout life; a rational realistic aspect and a creative, fantastic mythopoetic one (Jung, 1956). He anticipated relating mind and culture with his belief that western mind's mythic aspect is the residue of human evolution from tribal-spiritual origins. More recently Matte-Blanco (1975, 1988) addressed the limitations inherent in the necessity of viewing mind through the lens of logical thought. He made the bold assertion that primordial mind is not lesser and irrational. He proposed that mind uses two qualitatively different kinds of logic in a variety of dialectical permutations. He concluded that it is not possible to know primordial mind directly, only through the ways in which it perturbs what he described as the asymmetric logical mode that is the predominant element of ordinary thought. The concept of logic, however, still carries implicit connotations of thought. When all is said and done it is not clear that it is possible to adequately and fairly conceive of a fundamental way of knowing oneself and the cosmos through an epistemological lens that is qualitatively different.

Pathological bias in existing models of mind

The western cultural bias inherent in theories of primordial mind is reinforced by another bias related to the clinical psychoanalytic background of most of the theorists. Freud formulated his model of normal mind for the most part from his clinical work with mentally ill adults, including a theory about infant mind and about normal development. Melanie Klein, the other theoretical giant in this area, derived her model of primordial mind from work with persons she believed to be psychotic. A quarter century after Freud described the primary process and seemingly without awareness of its relationship to her work, Klein formulated her model of the paranoid-schizoid position and phantasy, in dialectical relationship with the more mature depressive position. Other than my own work (2004, 2008) and a couple of peripheral references that I note in Chapter 2, there has been no direct comparison in the literature between Freud's model of the primary process and Klein's of the paranoid-schizoid position and phantasy. Their striking similarities have gone unrecognized. One of the similarities that is not surprising in light of their common data source is that both models portray the "normal" infant as psychotic, at war with its own impulses and with reality, and development as a kind of therapeutic process.

Confusion between thought and primordial mental activity and problems of conceptual language

There is a further source of confusion that pervades these and other efforts to model primordial mind. In his formulation of the primary process it is not clear whether Freud intended a single model of unconscious mind or two. In some places he describes repressed thoughts or memories which are a symbolic part of the thought system, and in others he outlines a mental process of sensory-perceptual actualization or hallucination which is entirely different from thought. A similar confusion between normality and psychosis pervades Klein's model of the phantasy-dominated paranoid-schizoid position and Kleinian clinical practice.

Significant contributions to the nature of primordial mind have been made by developmental psychologists, most notably Werner (1948) and Piaget (1936). Their work is limited because it is based entirely on the study of normal individuals. There are more recent contributions by observers of infancy and proponents of attachment theory as well, both psychoanalysts and psychologists, but they have yet to be woven into a comprehensive theory of primordial mind.

For the most part these important contributions seem to be efforts to describe a common primordial phenomenology. However, the models are difficult to compare and to reconcile because each theorist has adopted an idiosyncratic conceptual language that has little or no connection to any of the others. Werner and Piaget have gone furthest toward formulating concepts that are widely understood and readily shared.

A preview: Primordial mental activity and thought

The authors whose work I have mentioned have achieved major insights into the workings of primordial mind. My reasons for proposing yet another model rather than elaborating on one of those are addressed in detail in the first part of the book. For now I should like to make a brief introduction to some of the characteristics of what I call primordial mental activity (PMA), which I shall be referring to throughout the book. Thought is the aspect of mind that represents and reflects about itself and about the body, and that represents specific emotions. PMA is the body's mind. It is driven by raw affect and is sensory-perceptual and except in dreaming, involves motor activity. It makes and receives deep impressions. As it is a concrete operation it communicates not by exchanging meaning but by pressure and induction; acting on or feeling acted upon. It is not a modality of expressing and receiving meaning but rather of expressing and assimilating belief and certainty. Primordial mind is holistic and does not differentiate what in western cosmology is within the self from what is in the external world. It creates a sense of actuality that we call belief rather than mental event. Perception and narration is in sequences determined by inner affective states rather than logic or rationality, so from the standpoint of thought it is not integrated. Experience is immediate and stimulus-bound, without a sense of time and memory. It does not observe thoughtful or logical distinctions involving time, space and causality. PMA is readily confused with thought because it has access to and utilizes whatever content the person may have learned, including language and socio-cultural experience, albeit in their concrete forms rather than the abstract, symbolic, representational way that characterizes thought.

PMA operates continuously from the inception of life, both when awake and asleep, and in a variety of permutations related to thought ranging from dissociation to different forms of integration, it accounts for such disparate phenomena as I have enumerated, including infant mind, attachment behavior, dreaming, creativity, cultural differences and psychosis. The labels we give to the manifest phenomenology and the judgments we make about them depend on a number of variables: the context in which they occur (waking or sleeping, interpersonal, social and cultural); their adaptive or maladaptive function in that context; and whether they are under the control of thoughtful mind or are dissociated from it.

PMA is the mental adaptation of infancy because thought, which develops separately, is rudimentary and matures slowly over the first decade of life. PMA is not transformed into thought; however, in the ordinary course of development thought gradually plays an increasingly prominent role. PMA comes under the regulation of thought with regard to the times, places and purposes for which it is employed. A complex set of variables – including constitutional factors, the nature of the infant attachment experience and related interpersonal processes of infancy and early childhood, the degree of integration or dissociation between PMA and thought, and the personal, social and cultural context within and outside of the primary family – determines whether the ultimate behavioural outcome for a given individual is adaptive or maladaptive, or considered normal or abnormal.

In spiritual cultures there is much more recognition and reinforcement early in life for manifestations of PMA, which are looked upon as ways of knowing and communicating that are beneficial to the community. Although thought, as we know it in western culture, is less valued, it is still relied upon to control the time and place for using PMA and the purpose to which it is put. When members of spiritual cultures are required to function in western culture, which not only does not offer a supportive community role for PMA, but actually defines some of its manifestations as psychotic, disaster can ensue (see Chapters 13–15).

There is evidence to suggest a more or less common neural substrate to the diverse phenomena I have noted and hence for primordial mind. I present possible constitutional elements in Chapter 11, and in Chapter 16 turn to contemporary neuroscience and findings based on newer technologies such as functional neuroimaging. These investigations are as yet in an early stage and differences in the phenomena under investigation and the methodology and language used in various studies make the results difficult to interpret, but the evidence is both suggestive and exciting.

The organization of the book reflects a tension between theory and exemplification. The first part of the book is weighty with theory. Especially during the twentieth century and beginning with Freud a number of important models of primordial mind have been proposed by persons including Klein, Bion, Matte-Blanco, Jung, theorists of attachment, relationship and implicit knowledge, and developmental psychologists, including Piaget and Werner. In highlighting their strengths and limitations I provide the rationale for proposing the model of primordial mental activity that is the foundation for understanding the examples that are presented in the latter part of the book. The remainder of the book has theory as well, but much more in the way of illustration. This includes biographical and autobiographical accounts, numerous examples from my clinical practice with psychotic and less severely ill persons, dreams of my own and of my patients, and remarkable, thoughtful first-person reflections about the nature of their psychoses from patients in advanced stages of therapy. There is an extraordinary account written for this book by a Maori shaman who left the family and culture in which he grew up in order to get a western education. He developed symptoms which were diagnosed by the western mental health system as psychosis and was treated unsuccessfully with western medical methods. Eventually he was healed by Maori methods and has gone on to achieve a remarkable degree of maturity. He holds a position as cultural counselor to Maori patients in a clinic which uses western medicine and is an advocate for the preservation of Maori culture.

I have had misgivings about the order of the book but I think the theory is necessary in order to fully appreciate the examples. I anticipate the book may be of interest to two kinds of readers, some for whom theory is very important, who realize that significant attempts have been made to model primordial mind and wish to understand why I believe these models are not adequate and another model is necessary; and some who are more interested in phenomenology and are willing to consider the model I propose on its own merits. For the first group the first section of the book, through Chapter 4, will be essential, whereas the latter group might wish to begin with Chapter 5, in which I propose the model of primordial mental activity (PMA) and contrast it with thought, and then move on to the illustrations.

Chapter 2

Western models of primordial mind I: Freud and Klein

In Chapter 1 I noted that conceiving of a person as a separate individual psyche stratified in layers ranging from psychological consciousness to unconsciousness is an artifact of western self-centric thought. In western culture knowledge and the epistemological perspective from which it is attained is defined in terms of conscious logical objectification, and aspects of mind and behavior whose meanings and significance are not thoughtfully evident are presumed to have unconscious correlates. Such phenomena are labeled "irrational" and "unrealistic." Spiritually based cultures do not distinguish the individual from an external world, reality from fantasy, and rationality from irrationality, nor do they conceive of a psyche that has both conscious and unconscious aspects. What needs to be known relates to meanings that reside in the natural, spiritual and ancestral worlds, not in the self, and it is to be known by expert interpretation, not scientific objectification.

It is important not to overlook the implications of the fact that this book is written from my perspective as an embedded member of western culture, specifically scientific culture. Since ancient Greece western thinkers have attempted to conceive of primordial mental activity. During the twentieth century and especially following Freud's groundbreaking contributions such efforts have intensified and taken on increasingly scientific attributes of exemplification, objectification and verification. In this section of the book I explore the major western models of primordial unconscious mind, including those of Jung, Freud, Klein, Bion and Matte-Blanco, theorists of attachment and implicit knowledge, and the developmental psychologists Piaget and Werner. I try to highlight their similarities, differences, strengths and weaknesses in order to show why I believe another model is necessary.

A western observer who is attempting an objective "scientific" con-ceptualization of primordial unconscious mind encounters a barrier that is serious precisely because it is relatively invisible, not readily apparent. What is viewed as unconscious from the perspective of western thought may also be seen as a way that mind experiences, knows, and expresses itself that is qualitatively different from thought. The "scientific" observer cannot conceive of it directly precisely because he or she is confined by another, thoughtful way of knowing. Even if it were possible to shift perspective and abandon rational scientific thought the result would be a different experience and not a thoughtful conception. A book written from such a perspective might make interesting reading as an illustration of the workings of other minds but would contribute little to an understanding of what is going on. Further along in the book I have included first-person illustrations, but only after proposing a conceptual framework in which to understand them. As a consequence of this cultural myopia it is easy to get the two mental activities confused and to speak of primordial mind in the language that gives thoughtful mind a pride of place and unwittingly implies that this other process is deficient because it "lacks" some of the essential aspects of thought; it is labeled un-conscious rather than different-conscious. It is important to try to find a way to think about a mental activity that is not thoughtful without confusing the way one thinks about the process with the process itself. This confusion permeates most psychoanalytic theories. It can be illustrated by the difficulty distinguishing the dream *experience* from the product that remains when it has been re-cast in thought in order to contemplate and talk about it. Another example that is elaborated in Chapter 15 is the tendency when talking with a schizophrenic person to "make sense" of strange utterances by means of projection of the inter-preter's thoughtful mind; that is, assuming the productions are thoughts that the person intends but is unable to articulate clearly rather than a quali-tatively different form of expression. As I elaborate in Chapter 3, Matte-Blanco was the only western theorist who directly recognized and struggled with this seemingly insoluble epistemological conundrum.

A few words about the nature of psychic consciousness and uncon-sciousness will serve as a preamble. It is necessary to understand what is meant by consciousness in order to comprehend unconsciousness, for it is only through the lens of conscious thought that we can contemplate what is unconscious. Psychic consciousness is a state of self-awareness that presupposes an organizing or integrating self and the capacity to think and to reflect. In western culture one of the subjects for reflection may be "interior" mental states that seem different or unusual and whose signi-ficance may not readily be apparent; in spiritual cultures similar phenomena are looked upon as existential relationships with the cosmos. While psychic consciousness can only occur in a waking state it is not synonymous with being awake. People who have recovered from psychotic states or emerged from trances have been conscious in the physical sense, but often talk about the experience of "waking up," implying a retrospective sense that they were unconscious. Persons in such "altered" states have the illusion or belief that they are conscious.

In the psychoanalytic situation that Freud devised it is assumed that symptoms and states of distress whose causes are not understood, and observed behaviors that from the perspective of a presumed rational objective observer seem extraordinary or abnormal, are unconsciously determined. This requires postulating objectivity in the observer, an assumption that the postmodern perspective of relativity, context and relationship has taught us is questionable. Evidence to confirm the hypothesis of unconscious motivation and meaning is retrospective and consists of such things as uncovering of new meaning through free association, an "aha" experience on the part of the analysand, or subsequent information about ensuing life change that implies the efficacy of an interpretation. This inferential process is not hard science and there is much room for the play of other unconscious factors that comprise the biases of subjectivity. As a result many psychoanalysts now maintain that it is not possible to reach objectively reliable conclusions about the unconscious components of an individual mind, and have relegated the concept of individual unconsciousness to the status of convenient heuristic fiction, like the concept of infinity in mathematics.

Freud

Freud was the first psychoanalyst to model primordial mental activity and psychic unconsciousness, and his insights laid the groundwork for the developments and contributions that have followed, including my own. His model of the primary process was his initial attempt to explain unconscious mind. Although it is not generally recognized, he entertained two very different conceptions of the primary process. He vacillated between describing it as a qualitatively unique form of mental activity and conceiving of it as a variant of thought. One model of unconscious and primary process involves repression of consciously unacceptable thoughts and feelings in a way that preserves their unique quality as representational symbolic thoughts and emotions; another is a primary reflexive avoidance of affective-instinctual excitation and over-stimulation and transformation of such excitation into a qualitatively unique form of mental activity that is concrete, undifferentiated and unintegrated, and sensory-perceptual-motor in quality. Finally there are attempts to model a transformational process by which unacceptable thoughts and memories are qualitatively transformed into sensory-perceptual-motor experiences.

The primary process as a qualitatively distinctive mental activity

Freud described the primary process and the characteristics that distinguish it from the mature thought that he called the secondary process in a series of papers on aphasia (1891, 1895); as part of his neuro-psychological theory entitled *Project for a scientific psychology* (1895/1950); in his *The Interpretation of Dreams* (1900), especially Chapter 7; and in *Formulations on the two principles of mental functioning* (1911a). It is the mind's attempt to process somatic-affective experience that he called instinctual tension. At first he called the regulating factor the unpleasure principle but subsequently (1911a) renamed it the pleasure principle.

The primary process is ontologically primary. Freud writes:

> When I described one of the psychical processes occurring in the mental apparatus as the 'primary' one, what I had in mind was not merely considerations of relative importance and efficiency; I intended also to choose a name which would give an indication of its chronological priority. It is true that, so far as we know, no psychical apparatus exists which possesses a primary process only and that such an apparatus is to that extent a theoretical fiction. But this much is a fact: the primary processes are present in the mental apparatus from the first, while it is only during the course of life that the secondary processes unfold, and come to inhibit and overlay the primary ones.
>
> (Freud, 1900, p. 602)

The primary process is said to result from repression of an accumulation of what Freud variously called excitation, affect, instinct and anxiety, which the immature infant is helpless to satisfy or cope with (1895, 1915a). It transforms this state of excitation into a state of satisfaction or tension-relief by creating a sensory-perceptual-motor experience that Freud called wish-fulfillment. Freud writes that:

> The infant. . . probably hallucinates the fulfillment of its internal needs; it betrays its unpleasure, when there is an increase of stimulus and an absence of satisfaction, by the motor discharge of screaming and beating about with its arms and legs, and it then experiences the satisfaction it has hallucinated. Later, as an older child, it learns to employ these manifestations of discharge intentionally as methods of expressing its feelings. Since the later care of children is modeled on the care of infants, the dominance of the pleasure principle can really come to an end only when a child has achieved complete psychical detachment from its parents.
>
> (1911a, p. 218f)

At night the primary process preserves sleep by forming dreams or "hallucinatory" experiences, avoiding disturbing thoughts that would keep the subject awake. In the waking adult state in which motor discharge is possible the result is kinds of actions and expressions that Freud called acting out, which have a delusional flavor and characterize the psychoanalytic transference.

Freud modeled the process of wish-fulfillment after an electrical current flowing from negative to positive:

> A current of this kind in the apparatus, starting from unpleasure and aiming at pleasure, we have termed a 'wish'; and we have asserted that only a wish is able to set the apparatus in motion and that the course of the excitation in it is automatically regulated by feelings of pleasure and unpleasure.
>
> (Freud, 1900, p. 597)

In his earliest description of the primary process Freud writes that "it is a question of an indication to distinguish between a perception and a memory (idea)" (1895, p. 325). In *The Interpretation of Dreams* (1900) he states this distinction in a number of places, for example, "The primary process endeavors to bring about a discharge of excitation in order that. . . it may establish a 'perceptual identity.' The secondary process, however, has abandoned this intention and taken on another in its place – the establishment of a 'thought identity'" (1900, p. 602). He describes the characteristics that distinguish the primary process, which in this formulation is synonymous with unconscious, as follows: "exemption from mutual contradiction, primary process (mobility of cathexis), timelessness, and replacement of external by psychical reality – these are the characteristics which we may expect to find in processes belonging to the system Ucs" (1915a, pp. 186–187). He writes that

> The strangest characteristic of unconscious (repressed) processes, to which no investigator can become accustomed without the exercise of great self-discipline, is due to their entire disregard of reality-testing; *they equate reality of thought with external actuality*, and wishes with their fulfillment – with the event – just as happens automatically under the dominance of the ancient pleasure principle.
>
> (1923, p. 225, italics mine)

He describes "a complete hallucinatory cathexis of the perceptual systems" (1900, p. 547) and adds that "the dream. . . represented. . . a situation which was actually present and which could be perceived through the senses like a waking experience" (ibid., p. 533). He further states that the "dream-work proper diverges further from our picture of waking thought than has been supposed. . . it is completely different from it qualitatively and for that reason not immediately comparable with it" (ibid., p. 507). In elaborating the differences he writes that: "One is the fact that the thought is represented as an immediate situation with the 'perhaps' omitted, and the other is the fact that the thought is transformed into visual images and speech" (ibid., p. 533).

In the primary process there is an instinctual current and a trans-formation process. In addition to the aforementioned repression Freud postulates two other "mechanisms" of the primary process – condensation and displacement – which serve to transform potentially disturbing mental elements that might otherwise be thoughts into an experience of immediate sensory-perceptual reality or actualization – which he called hallucinatory – that serves to fulfill a disguised version of the repressed wish. Freud's descriptions of condensation and displacement include such adjectives as "plastic" and "ambiguous," and his synonyms for them include *com-pression, replacement, exchange, transformation* and *reduction*. Freud writes: "By the process of displacement one idea may surrender to another its whole quota of cathexis; by the process of condensation it may appropriate the whole cathexis of several other ideas" (1915b, p. 186). LaPlanche and Pontalis describe it as follows: "Displacement is closely connected with the other mechanism of the dream-work. . . condensation in so far as displace-ment along two chains of associations leads eventually to ideas or verbal expressions formed at the intersection of these two paths" (1973, pp. 122–123). Condensation has the common sense implication of unification of two or more distinct ideas, and displacement the rather similar implication of separate pathways merging with one another. Both seem to describe the wishful unification or fusion of affect-laden ideas that are unrelated in meaning but share a common formal or superficial characteristic. Freud's economic distinction between the free or mobile energy cathexis char-acteristic of the primary process and the binding of energy cathexis charac-teristic of the secondary process seems to have a similar connotation of undifferentiation. In all, this primary process formulation of unconscious-ness describes an *absence of psychological differentiation or boundaries*, in which things are not thought *about* but through mobilization of somatic-sensory-perceptual processes are experienced and expressed as actual happenings.

Dreaming as the product of a qualitatively distinctive mental process

Freud describes language in primary process dreaming as concrete rather than representational and symbolic (1900, p. 295; 1915b; 1917). The sub-jective experience of the dreamer is not one of thought but is hallucinatory/delusional, "a complete hallucinatory cathexis of the perceptual systems" (1900, p. 548). He adds that "the dream. . . represented. . . a situation which was actually present and which could be perceived through the senses like a waking experience (ibid., p. 572)," and states that the "dream-work proper diverges further from our picture of waking thought than has been supposed. . . it is completely different from it qualitatively and for that reason not immediately comparable with it" (ibid., p. 507). Silberer, a major contributor to the study of dreaming who was also influenced by Freud, writes that the manifest dream "is characterized by a tendency to replace the abstract by the concrete" (1951, p. 208). Writing about the non-symbolic element of dreaming Freud asserts that "it is true in general that words are treated in dreams as though they were concrete things" (1900, p. 295). Influenced by Freud's work, Kraepelin (1906, translated by Heynick in 1993 and also noted by Engels, Heynick and Stack in 2003) made a decade-long study of his own dreams and reached a similar conclusion. In their glossary of psychoanalytic terms and concepts Moore and Fine (1990) define the primary process as "the most primitive form of mentation; it seeks immediate and complete discharge, by. . . hallucinatory wish fulfillment"; the secondary process "operates with bound cathexis and verbal, denotative symbols" (ibid., p. 148).

Although Freud is generally associated with the idea that dreams are symbolic vehicles, in practice he not infrequently conceived of them as gestalt analogical presentations of a person's intrapsychic *weltanschauung*. For example, in describing his interpretation of one of his patient's dreams he remarks: "And after reflecting a little I was able to give her the correct interpretation of the dream, which she afterwards confirmed. I was able to do so because I was familiar with the whole of the dreamer's previous history" (1900, p. 152). While he discovered the technique of free association to uncover repressed symbolic meanings, he also stated that: "As a rule the technique of interpreting according to the dreamer's free associations leaves us in the lurch when we come to the symbolic elements in the dream-content" (1900, p. 353).

Others outside of psychoanalysis have also argued that dreaming, and hence the primary process, is not symbolic. In their influential treatise on symbol formation the cognitive psychologists Werner and Kaplan (1963) comment that things, images, body postures, and sensations are substituted in dreams for words, yielding a concrete product. They cite examples from Freud's dreams, in one of which the concept of superfluity becomes something overflowing, while in another the concept of being manipulated literally becomes having one's hand shaken. They use a variety of terms to describe this process, including condensation, but do not consider the product to be symbolic. Writing about the imagery of dreaming from a literary perspective Bert States (1992) cites Gertrude Stein:

This is rather like saying a rose is a rose is a rose; but what Gertrude Stein was trying to express in this famous tautology is the non-referentiality of rose-ness. It is an immanently phenomenological piece of poetry designed to prevent our seeing a rose as a sign, or as having a significance that is outside of its being. . . the dream is the instantiation of a felt meaning. . . and what meaning one gets out of it on the waking side by way of interpretation is itself a new meaning (because a new symbolization).

(States, 1992, pp. 10–11)

The primary process as a variant of thought

Within the same set of writings that I have been quoting Freud also describes psychic unconsciousness and the primary process very differently, as a thought-related symbolic activity – a defensive process of sequestration, disguise and distortion of consciously unacceptable thoughts, feelings and memories resulting in the formation of arcane symbols that can be decoded by an associative process guided by appropriate interpretation of defenses. Freud derived the hypothesis of the unconscious as a hidden aspect of thoughtful mind from his studies of hysterical patients (Breuer and Freud, 1893). Thumbing through *The Intepretation of Dreams* (1900) we read that dreams and the primary process arise from repressed thoughts or memories: "The latent dream-content is concerned with forbidden wishes that have fallen victim to repression. . . they are based upon memories from earliest childhood" (1900, p. 244). In his discussion of dreaming he writes that "a thought becomes repressed" (1900, p. 546f). His technical recommendations for dream interpretation are based on the assumption that dreams are a symbolically meaningful variant of thought whose hidden meaning can be linearly uncovered or decoded by the method of free association and interpretation of resistance:

> The dream-thoughts and the dream-content are presented to us like two versions of the same subject-matter in two different languages. Or, more properly, the dream-content seems like a transcript of the dream-thoughts into another mode of expression, whose characters and syntactic laws it is our business to discover by comparing the original and the translation. The dream-thoughts are immediately comprehensible, as soon as we have learnt them. The dream-content, on the other hand, is expressed as it were in a pictographic script, the characters of which have to be transposed individually into the language of the dream-thoughts.
>
> (1900, p. 277)

Freud notes that "the productions of the dream-work, which, it must be remembered, are not made with the intention of being understood, present no greater difficulties to their translators than do the ancient hieroglyphic scripts to those who seek to read them" and that "the keys are generally known and laid down by firmly established linguistic usage" (1900, pp. 341–342). This amounts to a secondary process model in which the dream is a variant of thought, a symbolic enactment of a drama whose script resides in the repressed unconscious awaiting decoding by the wakeful subject. To put it another way, dreaming and waking "languages" might well be looked upon as manifestations of secondary process thought that employs symbolism both to reveal and to conceal meaning.

In Section D of Chapter 6 of *The Interpretation of Dreams* (1900), "Conditions of Representability," Freud refers to the sensory-perceptual happenings of the primary process as representational, claiming that the mind chooses images and even words in the dream according to their potential for carrying or representing unconscious wishes. In this different description of the primary process repression is defined as a mechanism deployed against thoughts and feelings that are unacceptable to the conscious mind, "things which the patient wished to forget, and therefore intentionally repressed from his conscious thought and inhibited and suppressed" (Breuer and Freud, 1893, p. 9). He describes a process of disassociation and reassembly of the thoughts and affects to produce a distortion or arcane symbolization that holds the meaning of the transference relationship as well as other phenomena (Breuer and Freud, 1895, pp. 302–303; Makari, 1994). Repression and dissociation–reassembly do not seem to change the status of the content as a potentially recoverable aspect of thought; they simply place it under symbolic disguise. Seven years later, in *The Interpretation of Dreams*, Freud writes: "This effortless and regular avoidance by the psychical process of the memory of anything that had once been distressing affords us the prototype and first example of psychical repression" (1900, pp. 597–599).

Freud's belief that the primary process is a symbolic language was elaborated by Ernest Jones (1916), who wrote a treatise on primary process symbolism. He was perhaps the first of a number of analysts, both adherents of Freud and of Klein, to attempt to explain (or perhaps to try to rationalize) how symbolization and concretion can be more or less identical: "A symbol is characteristically sensorial and concrete, whereas the idea represented may be a relatively abstract and complex one" (Jones, 1916, p. 89); "Symbolism is always concrete. . . substituting a concrete sensorial image for a more difficult idea" (p. 137). When he writes that "the basal feature in all forms of symbolism is identification" (ibid., p. 138), he means that a process of fusion leads to the formation of a concrete product or identity. The thing becomes identical to the idea and replaces it. *As* or *like* becomes *is*. Jones implies that symbolization is actually a regressive process: "The over-profuse use of metaphors, as that of slang – which fulfills the same psycholinguistic function – is well known to be the mark of expressional incapacity; the person belongs to what, in association work, is called the predicate type" (ibid.). Of course words often concretely designate things. And they can also be used as symbols (Freud's famous cigar, the "White House"), but the two uses are not identical. Words that designate objects or things (for example "shit") can be used referentially, to designate objects, metaphorically, to symbolize concepts or ideas, or concretely as objects of action in swearing, like throwing something. Other authoritative voices have also asserted that dreams employ symbolic processes, including the psychoanalyst Lacan (1968) and the eminent linguist Roman Jakobson (1956).

One reason dreaming (and primary process) has been confused with symbolic thought is that dreams are *experienced* as happenings but contemplated and talked about as thoughts. In the process of such a rendition the dream proper is readily confused with the waking thoughtful state in which it is recalled and cast into thoughtful language. Dreams are *experienced* as happenings, but unlike real happenings in waking life they were not simultaneously encoded into language and thought, so that there is no thoughtful memory of an event available to the waking subject who has dreamed. It takes a significant effort to capture fleeting traces of experience and cast them into language and thought. The potentially symbolic verbal product is not the essence of the dream, as Freud pointed out when he made the distinction between manifest and latent content. However, he was referring to symbolic disguise and I am referring to the fact that the meaning of the dream is inherent in the action or experience itself, and the thoughtful re-casting is another kind of activity entirely, as is witnessed by the feeling of futility students of their dreams experience in ever being able to cast the richness of experience into language. States describes the problem as follows: it "is difficult to talk about precisely because it consists of having such experiences, and talking about them in almost any manner tends to draw one into a conceptual mode of thought" (1992, p. 5).

Attempts to reconcile and connect primary process and thought

Freud struggled to relate the primary and secondary processes. If the primary process is truly distinctive how might conscious thought be transformed into primary process activity? Following some of his thoughts chronologically he writes in *The Interpretation of Dreams*:

> But from the moment at which the repressed thoughts are strongly cathected by the unconscious wishful impulse and, on the other hand, abandoned by the preconscious cathexis, they become subject to the primary psychical process and their one aim is motor discharge or, if the path is open, hallucinatory revival of the desired perceptual identity. We have already found empirically that the irrational processes we have described are only carried out with thoughts that are under repression.
>
> (1900, p. 604)

A decade later he says:

> In the realm of phantasy, repression remains all-powerful; it brings about the inhibition of ideas in statu nascendi before they can be noticed by consciousness, if their cathexis is likely to occasion a release of unpleasure. This is the weak spot in our psychical organization; and it can be employed to bring back under the dominance of the pleasure principle thought-processes which had already become rational.
>
> (1911a, p. 222)

Fifteen years later he writes:

> Psycho-analytic observation of the transference neuroses, moreover, leads us to conclude that repression is not a defensive mechanism which is present from the very beginning, and that it cannot arise until a sharp cleavage has occurred between conscious and unconscious mental activity – that the essence of repression lies simply in turning something away, and keeping it at a distance, from the conscious. . . . The second stage of repression, repression proper, affects mental derivatives of the repressed representative, or such trains of thought as, originating elsewhere, have come into associative connection with it. On account of this association, these ideas experience the same fate as what was primally repressed. Repression proper, therefore, is actually an after-pressure. Moreover, it is a mistake to emphasize only the repulsion which operates from the direction of the conscious upon what is to be repressed; quite as important is the attraction exercised by what was primally repressed upon everything with which it can establish a connection. Probably the trend towards repression would fail in its purpose if these two forces did not cooperate, if there were not something previously repressed ready to receive what is repelled by the conscious.
>
> (1915a, pp. 146–147)

He also writes that: "The cathexis that has taken flight attaches itself to a substitutive idea which, on the one hand, is connected by association with the rejected idea, and, on the other, has escaped repression by reason of its remoteness from that idea" (1915b, p. 181). In the section of his 1915b paper entitled "Communication between the two systems" Freud makes his most direct attempt to relate conscious thought and his conception of the unconscious as a primary process system. He states that the primary process remains active throughout life during wakefulness as well as sleep. His effort to explain the relationship between the two is labored and convoluted, however, and illustrates aspects of his metapsychology that many have criticized, involving three layers of mind, the complex interplay of forces, counter-forces, transformations, amalgamations and substitutions, and a conception of displacement that is not clearly defined.

The primary process since Freud

Freud vacillated between seeing the primary process as either a qualitatively unique mental activity or an arcane variant of thought. He never revised the primary process model to take into account his 1920 addition of a death instinct. While he maintained that the primary process is the basic mental activity of infancy and early childhood and the substrate of psychosis as well, he did not pursue these promising lines of investigation. Later in his life when he summarized his work in the *New Introductory Lectures on Psychoanalysis* (1933), there is no mention of the primary process and his description of unconscious phenomena is entirely structural-dynamic, referring to repression of conflicted thoughts. Subsequently there has been relative neglect of this profoundly important contribution, but it seems to reflect Freud's ultimate reluctance to struggle further with the complexities it poses.

Because of Freud's vacillation as to whether he was describing an aspect of symbolic thought or a qualitatively distinctive mental activity, both dreaming and unconscious mind nowadays tend to be looked upon as aspects of symbolic thought – arcane in the instance of dreaming and repressed or sequestered so as to be invisible to conscious awareness in the case of unconscious mind. Nowadays references to unconscious usually refer to repressed or sequestered thoughts and feelings. When the term is used in a more primary sense it usually denotes experience that has never been encoded into thought. Concepts such as implicit or procedural knowledge and process have been developed to describe this aspect of mind (see Chapter 4).

Most psychoanalysts have found it easier to accept Freud's depiction of dreams as symbolic variants of thought than to conceive of them as products of an entirely different form of mental activity. As a result, dreams are usually interpreted as symbolic vehicles, hence the dream has lost the unique status Freud accorded it when he made the oft-quoted remark "The interpretation of dreams is the royal road to a knowledge of the unconscious activities of the mind" (1900, p. 609). Dreams are now generally looked upon as but one among many ways to decode repressed, symbolically disguised unconscious meaning (Waldhorn, 1967).

Freud predicted the relevance of the primary process model to psychosis. Klein discovered the phenomenology he had written about in her work with psychotic children. However, she did not relate her work to his and developed an entirely different conceptual schema, the paranoid-schizoid position and phantasy, that disrupted continuity with Freud's work.

Another group of experimentally oriented analysts began a series of psychological experiments to validate its phenomenological manifestations in everyday life. Some experimentally oriented analysts have attempted to validate the existence of a primary process activity. The 1917 experiment by Poetzl using subliminal stimulation and subsequent analysis of dreams, mentioned in a 1919 footnote to *The Interpretation of Dreams* (1900, p. 181), may be the first of such efforts. Fisher repeated the experiment with similar success, and along with Paul and Shevrin has done extensive additional research (Fisher, 1956; Fisher and Paul, 1959; Shevrin and Fisher, 1967). Subjects are exposed to subliminal perceptual stimuli and encouraged to recall subsequent dreams. Elements of the imagery that the person had not been conscious of perceiving during the waking experiment are discovered to have been incorporated into and to distort subsequent manifest content. Fisher found that the transformations or distortions of perception occur at the time of perception itself, and are consistent with the principles of primary process. Conscious thought is never involved. Brakel and associates (Brakel *et al.*, 2002; Brakel, 2004) conducted studies using supraliminal and subliminal stimulation in normal adults, adults under stress, and children. She concludes that there is a primary mental process that is qualitatively different from secondary process and continues to express itself throughout life, and that "perhaps it is the basic mental organization in many nonhuman mammals" (2004, p. 1131). These researchers conclude that a process of attribution in which subsequent perceptions are colored by what was learned subliminally is involved. This seems similar to what is described in Freud's formulation of the primary process as condensation and displacement and Klein's mechanism of projective identification.

During two decades – the 1960s and 1970s – a group of cognitively and developmentally oriented analysts grounded in the structural model and the concept of ego functioning began to explore the idea that the primary process is an ego function or a function regulated by the ego that expresses itself in many ways, including language, creativity and psychosis (Rapaport, 1960, 1961; Holt, 1967, 1976; Noy, 1969).

Noy proposed that there are two systems of mind that do not stand in any kind of hierarchical relationship to one another, "one equipped to deal with reality, and another equipped to deal with the self" (1969, p. 174). He and Holt (1976) were among the first to challenge the belief that the primary process is primitive, regressive and static. Noy wrote:

In prevailing theory, the primary processes are regarded as more primitive than the secondary ones. This seems like a very one-sided judgement. One can say that operating with word presentations, using abstract concepts, or considering the time factor is a more developed function than operating without them is regarded to be. But this is a "superiority" only if the function is evaluated from the viewpoint of reality. If the viewpoint is shifted to the self and its needs, then the contrary is true: the ability to represent a full experience, including all the feelings and ideas involved, is a higher achievement than merely operating with abstract concepts and words, and the ability to transcend time limits and organize past experiences with present ones is a higher ability than being confined to the limitations of time and space. Would it not be better to leave all this discussion of primitiveness or higher developmental rank and say simply that the difference between the primary and secondary processes is in their function and not in their degree of development?

(1969, p. 175)

French and Fromm (1964) and Holt (1967) asserted that the dream, hence the primary process, is a different kind of mental activity than thought, but one that is also related to learning, integration and synthesis, and problem-solving.

Further reference will be made to some of this work in Chapter 5, and in the chapters on creativity (Chapter 12) and language (Chapter 15).

Summary of Freud's contribution to understanding primordial mind

In situating primordial mind in the realm of "unconscious" processes Freud adopted the western perspective that everything is relative to rational thought and the idea that primordial mind, being different, is in some important aspect unknown and mysterious, rather than being an equal, observable, but different way that mind works. Freud's theory is one of nature and biology; interpersonal relationships and the environment are secondary. Mental activity is driven by a desire to obtain relief from vaguely defined affective or instinctual tension. The mental activity itself is qualitatively distinctive from thought – or at least that is a part of what Freud believed. In the difference model of primary process such activity is discontinuous, concrete and actualized in that it is sensory-perceptual-motor and immediate. It is undifferentiated with regard to mind and world and does not distinguish wish from reality. Hence, in Freud's understanding, such activity is psychotic; hallucinatory and delusional. Freud was not clear about the relationship of primordial mind and thought, however, and continued to articulate without realizing it an alternative model in which it is an arcane variant of symbolic thought. In the difference model of primary process, then, it is a psychotic defensive activity the infant engages in directed against its own affects and unacceptable reality. There is no distinction between "normal" infancy and early childhood and psychosis, hence development is a kind of therapeutic process, or to say it more clearly, the source of Freud's ideas, namely his work with disturbed patients, was not clearly differentiated from his understanding of infancy and child development.

Klein

Writing a quarter century after Freud's study of dreaming led him to conceptualize the primary and secondary processes, Melanie Klein (1930, 1935, 1937, 1946) formulated another dualistic model of mind – the paranoid-schizoid and depressive positions – and the mental activities she called splitting, projective identification and phantasy. With this model she did for the understanding of psychosis what Freud had done in elucidating the significance of dreaming.

Whereas Freud's models of unconscious mind are abstracted from his study of dreaming and from clinical psychoanalysis involving verbal communication with what he believed to be neurotic adult patients (retrospective readings of his reports have suggested some of these may have been psychotic), Melanie Klein's theory is derived from analysis of disturbed children that involved play accompanied by whatever verbal description they were capable of. Conceptual formulations were abstracted by using the analyst's imagination or fantasy about what was going on in the child's mind.

Klein's model begins with the unconscious paranoid-schizoid position that predominates in infancy and early childhood and its characteristic mental operations of phantasy, splitting and projective identification. She called the more mature aspect of mind that includes a conscious component as well as a dynamic (repressed) unconscious component the depressive position. These positions remain in dialectical relationship throughout life (Steiner, 1987; Ogden, 1989). She writes of the paranoid-schizoid (PS) position that "in this early phase splitting, denial and omnipotence play a role similar to that of repression at a later stage of ego-development" (Klein, 1946, p. 102). What is repressed in the more mature depressive (D) position includes both the primary material of phantasy and the more developed and psychically represented thoughts and feelings that are unacceptable and distressing. She adds: "In repression the more highly organized ego divides itself off against the unconscious thoughts, impulses, and terrifying figures more effectively" (1958, p. 88).

In the paranoid-schizoid position instinctual rage, heightened by experiences of frustration of basic need gratification, is a critical motivational element. Klein postulates that the psychological survival of the infant depends on construction of a positive ego feeling in the face of this rage. Her model describes a mind much like what Freud described as primary process, which is concrete rather than symbolic, sensory-perceptual-somatic-motor, undifferentiated and unintegrated, and creates a kind of hallucinatory-delusional sense of actualization. Defined as different from thought, it is in a primary sense unconscious. Mind is gastrointestinal and uro-genital, based on the belief that what is "good" can be ingested and what is "bad" can be excreted or eliminated. Need is experienced orally as somatic tropism toward the mother (breast) that is undifferentiated from a state of satisfaction (good), and frustration elicits somatic-psychic excretory responses that are equally undifferentiated from parts of the object (bad). States of incipient and actual satisfaction are experienced as an omnipotent (or undifferentiated) phantasy that Klein named the "good" or ideal breast, while states of frustration and rage are projectively identified as phantasies of a destroyed/destroying (persecutory, bad) breast. The undifferentiated subjective experience is of ridding oneself of unwanted parts and putting them inside another person, and incorporating concrete "good" aspects of the other person into the self. Klein viewed the activity of the paranoid-schizoid position as defensive rather than as a reflection of a mental process that does not integrate or have narrative continuity. It is this absence of integration and continuity that Freud noted in the primary process characteristics of timelessness and absence of contradiction.

The relationship of infancy and psychosis in Klein's theory is vividly illustrated in a statement made by Money-Kyrle in a 1969 paper titled *On the fear of insanity* – that "we are born mad and become sane" (quoted by Spillius in her introduction to *Melanie Klein Today*, 1988, p. 198). It is of interest that Klein goes on to describe the more mature "depressive" position as though it, too, were pathological. Distortions characteristic of the paranoid-schizoid position give way to a more mature defensive distortion involving a need to make reparation to a mother who is delusionally and concretely believed to have been damaged by the infant's hatred during the preceding phase.

Klein (1930), Isaacs (1948) and Segal (1957, 1978) all assert that phantasy is a concrete rather than a symbolic process. Isaacs says: "In the unconscious mind. . . everything remains concrete, sensorial or imaginal" (King and Steiner, 1991, p. 275). However, they seemed reluctant to give up the idea that phantasy is not symbolic, perhaps because of difficulties such a conclusion might pose for the process of clinical interpretation. Klein came up with the term "symbolic equation," which enables the theorist to believe that products of phantasy are simultaneously concrete things and abstract symbols: "Symbolism is the foundation of all phantasy, sublimation, and of every talent, since it is by way of symbolic equation that the things, activities, and interests become the subject of libidinal phantasies" (1930, p. 220). Hannah Segal (1957, 1978) popularized the term "symbolic equation" in two papers much as Ernest Jones had done for Freud. While maintaining that phantasy is concrete she nonetheless offers the following comment about a clinical vignette: "From the start [of the analysis of a schizophrenic man], however, some of his delusions could be recognised as phantasies familiar to every analyst. But I found there was no point interpreting them out of context" (1950, p. 270). However, she also observes that her patient consistently rejected her interpretations of his phantasies and her efforts to make conscious what she believed was the repressed unconscious but symbolized content. She apparently construed this failure as resistance rather than as reflecting a fundamental difference between his concrete "it is what it is" mentation and her symbolic "it is something to think about because it is something other than what it seems" interpretive stance. Ironically these efforts at explanation of phantasy or primary process seem more like enactments of phantasy insofar as the law of contradiction between concreteness and symbolism has been abridged and opposites have become identical. Abundant published vignettes suggest that despite Kleinian belief that phantasy is concrete many Kleinian analysts interpret to their patients as though it were symbolic thought or fantasy. In practice Kleinian analysts tend to rely heavily on their subjective responses to their analysands, which they understand as projective identifications, and then cast the result into body language as a *fantasy*, a symbolic presentation of oral and anal issues, rage, envy and the like, that can be interpreted to the patient in a way that he or she is capable of thinking about. They are deriving meaning by analogy rather than decoding of symbolism by following patients' associations. This form of mental activity is different from thought. Words exert pressure that the Kleinian analyst construes as projective identification and the analyst puts his or her subjective affective experience of the pressure into thoughtful symbolic language. Meltzer describes the process as follows:

> Our approach to the analysis of dreams is bound to be very different from Freud's "jigsaw puzzle" or "translation from Latin to German" method. He was approaching the dream as a piece of mystification that needed decoding. . . . We are approaching the dream as a sample of a continuous process that is the very heart of the matter of the patient's mental life; a glimpse par excellence into the theater where meaning is being constantly generated.
>
> (1976, p. 429)

The conceptual language Klein chose to describe phantasy, which is described as a state both different from and antecedent to conceptual thought, is what the thoughtful analyst, extrapolating from observations of infants and of small children at play, imagines (fantasizes) to be the subjective mental state of the infant. Intentionally or not this suggests that infants are capable of thinking or imagining in terms involving self, other, impulses, feeling states, complex motives, body parts and functions, and executing defense mechanisms of splitting and projective identification against unwanted intrapsychic content. Such concepts and assumptions would seem more descriptive of achievements of the system of representational abstract thought that Klein called the depressive position. The defense mechanisms of splitting and projective identification are described as though intended to rid the child of unwanted parts and put them inside another person, or to incorporate specific aspects of the other person into the self, yet we know from other of Klein's writings that the mental process she is describing is not one where self, other, and aspects of self and other are differentiated. For example, in summarizing Susan Isaacs' account of a man who believes that "breasts bite, penetrate and soil," Segal remarks: "Underlying this projection there is the phantasy of his having actually projected his biting mouth, his piercing penis, his soiling feces, into them" (1979, p. 119). Elsewhere she says: "The infant overcomes his fear of disintegration by the introjection of and identification with the ideal breast" (ibid., p. 122) and: "The aims of projective identification can be manifold: getting rid of an unwanted part of oneself. . . control of the object. . . . The good parts may be projected in order to avoid separation, in order to idealize the object, and also in order to avoid internal conflict. . . (or) given to the object for safe-keeping" (ibid., p. 120). And envy, a sophisticated mental operation, is said to play a central role in the phantasies that characterize the paranoid-schizoid position. These mental operations require complex thinking for an infant whose mind has been described as undifferentiated and somatopsychic; thinking that is more characteristic of fantasy than of phantasy.

Klein does not acknowledge that there is any connection between her model of positions and Freud's model of processes, although once she wrote in passing that:

> If we want rightly to comprehend children's play in connection with their whole behaviour during the analytic hour we must take into account not only the symbolism which often appears so clearly in their games but also all the means of representation and the mechanisms employed in dreamwork.
>
> (1926, p. 134)

There is almost no evidence in subsequent discussions of her work, including the summary of the so-called controversial discussions in the British Psycho-Analytical Society (King and Steiner, 1991), that such a connection has been made by others. From their respective Kleinian and Freudian perspectives Susan Isaacs at the time of the discussions and Anna Freud years later noted similarities in their points of view but did not directly compare the models. Isaacs writes:

> Phantasies are the primary content of unconscious mental processes. . .
> [they] are primarily about bodies, and represent instinctual aims

towards objects. . . . Freud's postulated "hallucinatory wish fulfill-ment" and his "primary introjection" and "projection" are the basis of the phantasy life. . . . Phantasies are not dependent upon words, although they may under certain conditions be capable of expression in words.

(1948, p. 95)

Isaacs says: "Freud does not say that the infant has unconscious phan-tasies. But the capacity to hallucinate is, in my view, either identical with phantasy or the pre-condition for it" (King and Steiner, 1991, p. 277) and:

Klein has further shown, in her analytic work with children of two years and over, how the child's play exemplifies the dream mechanisms – symbolization, condensation, dramatization, displacement, and the rest. We know that the dream shows these mechanisms to be funda-mental processes – the "primary process" – of the mental life, under-lying all our relational thinking and apprehension of external reality.

(King and Steiner, 1991, p. 282)

Anna Freud remarks in her dialogue with Joseph Sandler (Sandler and Freud, 1983) that the primary process "mechanisms" of condensation and displacement are related to introjection and projection and to the undiffer-entiated mental state she describes as having "insecure boundaries."

Klein did, however, incorporate into her positions model concepts from Freud's subsequent structural and dynamic models, and borrow his 1920 amplification of instinct theory to include a death instinct, as well as one of his uses of the concept of unconscious *phantasy*. Freud used the concept of phantasy in his description of the mental operation characteristic of the primary process: "With the introduction of the reality principle one species of thought-activity was split off; it was kept free from reality-testing and remained subordinated to the pleasure principle alone. This activity is phantasying, which begins already in children's play" (1911a, p. 220f). However, elsewhere (for example, 1900), Freud described phantasy more like the commonly accepted definition of the term *fantasy*, implying representational symbolic thought characteristic of the secondary process and Klein's depressive position.

I can but speculate about the reasons that Klein did not acknowledge she was following in Freud's footsteps, despite the remarkable similarities between the phenomenology of the process and position models. Freud's background was in neurology and medicine, and his earliest efforts to formulate psychoanalytic theory were derived from studying what at that time were believed to be medical conditions, such as aphasia and hysteria. He wanted his new discipline to be a "scientific psychology" (1895) and hoped at least in the first half or so of his career that one day his formulations would be reduced to those of neuroscience. His English translator and pupil Strachey respected his wishes, and went to great lengths to choose names for concepts that sound "scientific," often at the cost of distancing the reader from common sense and simplicity. Melanie Klein was one of many "lay analysts" to study with Freud. In fact she never obtained a university degree and her studies were in art and literature, not science. The language in which Freud's early discoveries are couched must in consequence have been uncongenial to her as it is so experience-distant. The clinical context in which she operated was different from Freud's consulting room, where verbally sophisticated adult subjects with his help gradually understood themselves better. Hers involved, for the most part, play therapy with children in which the patient could not be expected to formulate the meaning of the experience in adult terms. They were much less likely than Freud's adult patients to distinguish dream from reality, to talk about their dreams, and more likely to be "closer" to issues of bodily function regulation. In her efforts to empathically comprehend how the mind of the child worked Klein made a rich literary narrative-like theory with her imagination or fantasy.

Klein's contribution to understanding primordial mind

Klein's major contribution to understanding primordial mind is para-doxically a significant weakness as well. She demonstrated the truth of what Freud had but speculated about, namely that it is the substrate of psychosis. However, she amplified Freud's belief that primordial mind is inherently psychotic. She also perpetuated the confusion in Freud's model about whether or not primordial mind is qualitatively distinctive from representational symbolic thought or is simply an arcane variant. Like Freud's primary process the paranoid-schizoid position is a biological theory of innate affect. Freud formulated the primary process from the vantage point of a single instinct theory – wishes related to pleasure and avoidance of the experience of the build up of unpleasurable tension. By the time – two decades later – he postulated a second (death) instinct and what has come to be called the dual instinct theory he had more or less abandoned the primary process model. Klein believed that phantasy commences as a consequence of primal rage, apparently a birth trauma related to disruption of continuous intrauterine need satisfaction. At birth a virtual ego splits in defense in order to restore a *feeling* of satisfaction in the absence of *actual* satisfaction, projectively identifying (as external to the pleasure self) the rage and also the experience of satisfaction. Like Freud she believed that primordial mind is psychotic, that "normal" infancy is a psychotic state and that normal development is a kind of ameliorative therapeutic progress. Klein emphasized the importance of integration of the psyche; the progression from splitting of the ego and projective identification in the paranoid-schizoid position to development of the capacity for ambivalence, intrapsychic conflict and self-reflection (guilt and the wish to make reparation) that is characteristic of the mature depressive position.

In summary: Freud and Klein

Freud and Klein appear to have been unaware of one another's important contributions to the nature of primordial mind, and the radical difference in conceptual language chosen by each one has tended to make mutual recognition even more difficult, yet there is a remarkable similarity in their ideas, both their strengths and their confusions and limitations. To begin with, they seem to have been mapping similar phenomenological terrain: a concrete body-based mind that is: sensory-perceptual, auditory-visual and somatic-motor; undifferentiated in the sense of not observing ordinary distinctions between self and other or world; immediate, discontinuous and stimulus-bound; and neither symbolic nor reflective. Both are basically biological theories based on innate affect or instinct. The role of environment is secondary – ameliorating or exacerbating. In both theories infants and small children are looked upon as essentially pathological or psychotic, at war with their own innate affects and with reality and civilization. Development is a kind of therapeutic process. These assumptions are not surprising considering the pathological clinical data on which both their theories are based. The person is born into the world basically at odds with and defending him or herself against innate biological instincts and the limitations of extra-uterine reality, and uses psychotic mechanisms to distort experiences that are felt to be unsupportable, creating in their stead a more palatable delusional sense of satisfaction. Freud called this hallucinatory wish-fulfillment and Klein described creation of an all-good ego or self by mechanisms she called paranoid, schizoid and manic.

Confusion between symbolic thought and primordial mental activity

Both Freud and Klein chose conceptual languages that unconsciously bias the reader to believe that primordial mental activity is a thoughtful symbolic process. Both Freud and Klein describe mental activity that is concrete, somatically and perceptually based, undifferentiated and unintegrated, and that creates a subjectively believable "reality" in which internal elements are confused with external perception and experience in a way that is delusional and hallucinatory. But at times both use language that suggests that the mind possesses capabilities to make distinctions and to process experience more characteristic of a mature thoughtful self. Freud talks about wishes, which sound more like fantasies or thoughts than the biological processes he claims them to be, and about defense mechanisms, which suggest sophisticated processing of discrete mental material. But the primary process lacks the capacity for thought, and the mechanisms of displacement and condensation are defined much like synonyms for lack of psychic differentiation and mental representation. In many places Freud describes primordial mind as having symbolic capability. Klein's model is even more confusing in this regard. The conceptual language she uses to describe phantasy, the expression of a mind that is undifferentiated and unintegrated, is that of an adult's effort to empathize by using fantasy about what is going on in the mind of a thoughtful person whose behavior he or she is observing, conceiving of distinct body parts of self and other, feelings and motivations. Both Freud and Klein suggest that a mind that is supposedly discontinuous and unintegrated is capable of experiencing conflict and initiating defensive operations. Both report clinical interpretations that couch presumably concrete enactments in terms implying that they are symbolically meaningful to the analysand.

Confusion of infancy and early childhood with psychosis

It is not surprising that both Freud and Klein, whose ideas about infancy and development were extrapolated from therapeutic encounters with pathological subjects, confused normal infancy with psychosis and normal development with the psychoanalytic therapeutic process. Both Freud and Klein look upon infancy and childhood as a psychotic state or an auto-immune disease in which the person is basically at odds with and defending its being against its own innate biological instincts and the limitations of extra-uterine reality, and uses psychotic mechanisms – phantasy, hallucination, delusion, splitting and projective identification. The infant is characterized as repudiating reality and its frustrations, defensively distorting experiences it finds unsupportable, and creating in their stead a more palatable, delusional sense of satisfaction. Freud calls this initial process avoidance of unpleasure hallucinatory wish-fulfillment whereas Klein describes defensive distortion by splitting and projective identification in order to create an all-good illusion of self relating to bad objects. She uses the terms paranoid, schizoid and manic defense to describe "normal" infancy.

By contrast, Daniel Stern (1985), who has studied infants extensively, has been one of the most vocal proponents of the belief that infantile mind is an adaptive organ that is initially inherently realistic and sophisticated in its capacities to make sensory-perceptual discriminations and process the data – in other words, that rudiments of thought are present from birth. He states that "there is a non-psychodynamic beginning of life in the sense that the infant's experience is not the product of reality-altering conflict resolution" (1985, p. 255).

A mind in conflict and defense versus a mind that is different

Both Freud and Klein view primordial mind as a defensive conflict-solving apparatus and articulate conflict between unpleasurable and overwhelming instinctual tension or unpleasure (Freud) or innate rage (Klein) on the one hand, and the most primitive impulses toward self-preservation in the form of a wishful state of satisfaction (Freud) and an intact good-self (Klein) on the other. This primordial conflict is believed by Freud and Klein to mobilize primitive defense mechanisms, in the case of Freud a primal repression or aversion, as well as displacement and condensation, leading to a sensory-perceptual experience of gratification (hallucinatory wish fulfillment). In the case of Klein the primitive defenses are splitting of the ego in order to sequester a good-feeling self, and projective identification of unwanted feelings and attitudes. Each also has a model for more mature conflict. In the case of Freud it involves thoughts, feelings, impulses and memories that are unwanted because of unpleasant experiences associated with them and because of their incompatibility with the dictates of reality (ego) or conscience (superego), and are therefore repressed. In the case of Klein, the ego of the depressive position has relinquished splitting and projective identification in favor of integration in the form of bearing ambivalence and conflict, and utilizes instead the new defense of repression. There is limited evidence that primordial mind possesses such capabilities of integration and differentiation, and indeed that it is a basically defensive rather than expressive system to begin with.

Problems of conceptual language

Freud and Klein devised idiosyncratic conceptual languages for their models that are not readily shared and built upon. Klein's theory is couched in the language of adult imagination or fantasy about children's bodily and instinctual preoccupations. Freud tried to create neuroscience-like terminology in order to make his ideas credible to the medical-scientific establishment, even at the cost of avoiding simpler common-sense terms for some of what he was describing. For example, *das es* is translated as *the id* rather than the more common sense *it*, and *ego* is left in its Latin form rather than being translated as "I" or self. Both were conceptually biased in their descriptions of "normal" phenomena by the fact that their data were derived from pathological subjects.

Chapter 3

Western models of primordial mind II: Jung, Bion, Matte-Blanco

Freud and Klein were the pioneers and theoretical giants of the exploration of primordial mind. Jung was a contemporary of Freud and his contributions provide an interesting perspective. Because they tend to be more impressionistic than theoretically complex, and because he drifted outside the orbit of Freud's psychoanalytic movement, they have not received as much attention as they deserve. Bion's work expands upon a Kleinian base and Matte-Blanco was influenced by Freud.

Jung

In a rich paper Carl Jung (1959a) proposed that there are two qualitatively distinctive forms of mental activity in dialectic relationship throughout life, without employing such prejudicial dichotomies as maturity/immaturity, normality/psychosis or rationality/irrationality: "The unconscious bases of dreams and fantasies. . . are not in themselves infantile, much less pathological" (1959a, p. 32). In a way that resembles Matte-Blanco and to a lesser extent Bion he distinguishes between two kinds of "thinking", which he calls "directed thinking" toward "reality" and, after William James, "irresponsible thinking" – what Freud called free association. He describes this other kind of thinking with such terms as fantasy, day-dreaming or myth-making. He relates fantasy to the collective unconscious, ancient cultures, mythology, the mind of children, dreaming and creativity:

> We move in a world of fantasies which, untroubled by the outward course of things, well up from inner phantasmal forms. This activity of the early classical mind was, in the highest degree, artistic; the goal of its interest does not seem to have been how to understand the real world as objectively and accurately as possible. . . Thus there arose a picture of the universe which was completely removed from reality, but which corresponded exactly to man's subjective fantasies. . . children

think in much the same way. . . We also know that the same kind of thinking is exhibited in dreams. . . a world of impossibilities takes the place of reality.

(ibid., pp. 24–25)

He writes:

In childhood we go through a phase when archaic thinking and feeling once more rise up in us, and that all through our lives we possess, side by side with our newly acquired directed and adapted thinking, a fantasy thinking which corresponds to the antique state of mind.

(ibid., p. 31)

He also writes about cultural difference: "There was a time, however, in the ancient world, when the fantasy was a legitimate truth that enjoyed universal recognition. . . the fantasy of our adolescent is simply a re-echo of an ancient folk belief which was once very widespread" (ibid., p. 30).

Elsewhere (1959) Jung proposed the concept of synchronicity, a kind of relationship that is analogical and hierarchical rather than linear-causal. He believed there is a deep order in the universe that reflects itself in parallelism of meaning at many levels, from unconscious mental archetypes to the organization of culture. As Stein describes it: "The psyche is not something that plays itself out in human beings only and in isolation from the cosmos. There is a dimension in which psyche and world intimately interact with and reflect one another" (1998, p. 202). In the posthumous (2009) publication of *The Red Book: Liber Novus*, Jung chronicles his personal dialectical struggle between the archetypal and the directed thinking aspects of his own mind and their relationship to health and psychosis. This struggle is described in Chapter 9.

In his writing about synchronicity and the hierarchical layering of world and mind Jung anticipated developments in systems theory and complexity theory that I remark on in Chapter 17 in relation to my own concept of hierarchical systems theory. What I find important in his highly impressionistic accounts is the equal status he assigns to thoughtful and primordial mind, the importance of understanding the dialectical relationship between the two, and the way he relates primordial mind to the richness of inner life, to cultural differences, and to dreaming, creativity and psychosis.

Bion

Wilfred Bion's (1962, 1967, 1992; Grotstein, 2009) ideas about mind were influenced by Freud and Klein. Like Freud he believed that dreaming is a fundamental manifestation of unconscious primordial mind, and from Klein he borrowed ideas about what happens when the normal function of dreaming goes awry and mind becomes psychotic. He proposed a conceptual language devoid of what he called the "penumbra" of commonly accepted meanings that accompany the terms used by theorists like Freud and Klein. It is highly abstract, with functions and factors, English and Greek alphabetic designations and a logical-mathematical grid. His much-misunderstood and now clichéd phrase "without memory or desire" is his way of saying that learning and knowing in waking life, including the apperception of the analysand by the analyst, requires a suspended state of reverie. His actual words are: "The suspension of memory, desire, understanding, and sense impressions may seem to be impossible without a complete denial of reality; but the psycho-analyst is seeking something that differs from what is normally known as reality" (1970, p. 42). The combination of his impressionistic way of knowing and the seemingly precise yet abstract nature of his concepts has led to much debate about what he actually intended. Indeed, he believed tolerance for ambiguity is an essential aspect of learning and knowing. As with Klein, many analysts have been profoundly touched by his work and have attempted to explicate it, including Grotstein (2009), Symington and Symington (1996), Ogden (2004), Muller (2005), O'Shaughnessy (1995) and Ferro (1995).

Bion was an epistemologist who believed that the process of thinking and knowing (K; seeking O, or ultimate reality) occurs through the mediation of the dream state, and that dreaming is an important precursor element in the thinking process. Dreaming, he believed, occurs not only while sleeping. It is a background activity in waking life in the form of reverie, a contemplative state that transforms affectively saturated experience into thought. Dreaming serves what he called the alpha function, which creates a differentiation gradient between conscious thought and unconscious content by transforming the raw chaotic sensory-perceptual-affective data he called beta elements into an alpha screen with narrative sequence that can be represented and symbolized. This enables the person to reflect, to multitask, to be aware of having a mind and thoughts, and to conceive that there are multiple points of view. Bion writes: "To learn from experience, alpha-function must operate on the awareness of the emotional experience" (1962, p. 8), and adds:

The "dream," together with the alpha function, which makes dream possible, is central to the operation of consciousness and unconsciousness, on which ordered thought depends. Alpha-function theory of the "dream" includes such elements of classical psycho-analytic dream theory as censorship and resistance but these serve the function not of resistance but of differentiation of conscious and unconscious and help to maintain the discrimination between the two. . . the alpha elements. . . cohere as they proliferate to form the contact barrier.

(ibid., pp. 15–16)

Bion was concerned with the nature of normal development as well as the development of psychosis. In the normal course of development mother acts as the container of infant projections. She performs the alpha function of reverie, metabolizes the experience, and gives back to the infant the beta elements along with some of her capacity for performing alpha process. The capacity for dreaming develops out of a successful container/contained interaction between the two. When containment, dreaming and the alpha function are disturbed because of excessive hostility, lack of attunement and distortion in the caregiver–child relationship, beta elements cannot be alpha-betized into mental representations and narrative structures and as a consequence thought, and the capacity for repression, which differentiate conscious thought from a dynamic unconscious, do not develop.

Bion's theory reflects Freud's inconsistency about the relationship between dreaming and thought. Bion believed that there are two qualitatively different dream or dream-like processes, corresponding to what he described (1957) as the psychotic and non-psychotic parts of the personality. His theory is grounded in Freud's conservative version of his primary process model, which describes dreams as an aspect of symbolic thought. However, he also subscribed to Freud's idea that dreams are hallucinatory avoidances of the experience of frustration (1992). "Normal" dreaming is proto-thinking. The model for the other process is derived from Kleinian understanding of phantasy, the qualitatively different activity that underlies psychosis. In his theoretical framework the dreaming associated with psychotic phantasy is the manifestation of destruction of thought. In the absence of alpha function, beta elements of raw experience remain concrete fragments that cannot be metabolized but are somatically evacuated or expelled along with bits of ego by projective identification, creating a beta screen – delusion and hallucination. He writes: "If the patient cannot transform his emotional experiences into alpha-elements, he cannot dream. . . the patient who cannot dream cannot go to sleep and cannot wake up" (1992, p. 7). This statement is not to be taken concretely, for he also writes that the dream

can be employed for two dissimilar purposes. One is concerned with the transformation of stimuli received from the world of external reality and internal psychic reality so that they can be stored (memory) in a form making them accessible to recall (attention) and synthesis with each other. The other. . . is the use of the visual images of the dream for purposes of control and ejection of unwanted. . . emotional experience. . . a vehicle for the evacuatory process. The dream itself is then felt to be an act of evacuation in much the same way as the visual hallucination is felt to be a positive act of expulsion through the eyes. . . . The fact that the dream is being employed in an excretory function contributes to the patient's feeling that he is unable to dream.

(1992, p. 67)

In such a situation it is not possible to distinguish conscious from unconscious or to think, remember, repress or dream. Muller writes: "Patients with disturbed alpha-function have an unmediated relation to their experience: their contact with the world is marked by immediacy, lack of differentiation, and absence of stable markers" (2005, p. 34). In other words, the result is a different description of primordial mind – more like Freud's radical description of the primary process as qualitatively different from thought and Klein's paranoid-schizoid position.

Evaluating Bion's contribution to the understanding of primordial mind

Bion followed in Freud's footsteps insofar as he emphasized that the process underlying dreaming is of central importance in mental functioning. He places more emphasis on the importance of that process in waking life than does Freud, because he believes that it is a precursory step in learning and in thinking. In that regard he has developed the aspect of Freud and Klein's models that holds that primordial mind is related to or is a variant of symbolic thought rather than a qualitatively different operation entirely. In contrast to Freud, Bion believes that the process underlying ordinary dreaming is not intrinsically abnormal or psychotic. It is not a defense against one's own affects and against acceptance of consensual reality. However, his conception of primordial mind includes dreaming that is part of thought as well as the psychotic process of hallucination and delusion that results when alpha function fails and fragments of mind are expelled. In my experience schizophrenic persons do report dreams if questioned, and their structure and significance is no different from those of non-psychotic persons. What distinguishes them from non-psychotic persons is not an inability to dream, but the absence of a thoughtful reflective mind to differentiate the the dream from waking experience and hence to think about it.

I agree with Bion that the process underlying dreaming is a normal modality of learning, not one of defense against intolerable affect and reality. Moreover, I believe it underlies other normal phenomena of adult life. However, I believe the learning that takes place is not related to thought but to a different primordial process, which I describe in Chapter 5. I concur with Freud and Klein that the dreaming function is concrete and actualizing, undifferentiated and unintegrated, quite unlike thought.

Matte-Blanco

Ignacio Matte-Blanco (1975, 1988; Rayner, 1981; Rayner and Tuckett, 1988) proposed a theory of mind that combines mathematics and logic. His theory, like that of Bion, is couched in highly abstract terms but his books are liberally interspersed with illustrative clinical vignettes. Specifically he is concerned with differentiation – the role in mental activity of the interplay of sameness or identity and difference. He points out the inherent limitation and bias of psychoanalysis, a thoughtful Aristotelian logic-based activity, in trying to know about primordial mental activity that is qualitatively different. This is illustrated by Freud's belief that he had discovered an irrational unconscious when according to Matte-Blanco he was exploring another system of logic with which to view the world. Matte-Blanco proposed instead a bi-logic, consisting of symmetrical and asymmetrical logics, the asymmetrical activity that we ordinarily think of as logic being bi-valent, a logic of differences. Some characteristics of symmetrical logic include absence of contradiction and negation, displacement and condensation, timelessness, undifferentiation of external and psychical reality, replacement of logical connection and causal-temporal logic with event sequences and contiguity, and replacement of similarity with identity. This, it will be evident to the reader, could be a description of Freud's primary process. This mono-valent logic that he calls symmetrical stands in contrast to what we ordinarily think of as logic, namely the bi-valent process that articulates differences and he calls asymmetrical. He writes that "there are things in nature that cannot be understood in terms of only two-valued logic" (1986, p. 251). In this view there are two aspects of unconscious function: one that is repressed or dynamic and hence an aspect of Aristotelian logic and another aspect of unconscious mind that cannot correctly be termed "irrational" as that involves seeing it through a rational lens.

Where Matte-Blanco differs from Freud and from most who have tried to model primordial mind is in his belief that this unconscious process that he called symmetrical logic cannot be made conscious and truly understood with logical thought because it is qualitatively different. It can only be understood in relation to the effects it has on bi-valent or asymmetric logic – the distortions it creates in the rational thought process. Awareness of difference and of similarity is a part of conscious thought. "Every time we are in front of a bi-logical structure we are in front of the fact that the same reality is simultaneously treated, on the one hand, as if it were divisible or heterogeneous, formed of parts, and, on the other, as if it were one and indivisible" (1988, p. 72). Such bi-logical structures combine symmetric and asymmetric logic. Matte-Blanco "coined the term bi-logic to refer to a system which is submitted to two sets of rules: those of two-valued logic (it could also be another, for instance three-valued logic) and those of symmetrical logic" (1986, p. 251). When there is no longer a thoughtful relationship between the two logics the result is a set of total symmetrization and unconsciousness.

Bi-logical structures are stratified according to the amount of symmetrical or asymmetrical logic employed. The number of strata is potentially infinite, but Matte-Blanco has described five and some of their implications. Three of these binary structures – Alassi, Simassi and Tridim – are the best known. In an Alassi structure there is dissociated *al*ternation between symmetric and *asy*mmetric logic. At one moment the mind seems governed by the asymmetric logic of thought and at another moment by the symmetric logic that resembles Freud's primary process. In a Tridim (three dimensional) structure symmetrical logic is concealed by an asymmetrical (dimensional) form. Mind works in numerous dimensions but can only conceptualize four – three spatial dimensions plus time. As Matte-Blanco says: "The three-dimensional image of the internal world, however much it may have helped in a first approach to the problem, soon reveals itself as utterly insufficient to reflect the enormous complexity of psychical reality" (1988, p. 239). In Chapter 6 I describe how dreaming is such a Tridim structure insofar as multiple meanings must be fit into three dimensions, some symmetric and others asymmetric:

Simassi, the last of the common structures Matte-Blanco describes, is "a simultaneous co-presence or intertwining of as-symmetrical logic and symmetrical logic" (1986, p. 252). The mathematical concept of infinity is such a structure. A line is also an infinite number of points. This appears to be what the mathematician Mandelbrot (1967) was referring to in his classic article *How Long is the Coast of Britain?* in which he concluded based on measurement with magnifications ranging from outer space to molecular that it is infinite in length. Matte-Blanco writes of the

> striking incompatibility between the perceptual aspects of the dream, clearly submitted to classical logic, and the multiple meanings of each of the dream images and actions. . . fundamental antinomy between the indivisible and the heterogenic modes of being. And this amounts to saying that the indivisible mode permeates dream.
>
> (1988, p. 268)

Affects, as diffuse global states, are experienced symmetrically whereas emotions, particularized and thought about, are asymmetric. Emotions can intensify and generalize when the element of asymmetry or differentiation is lost so that they become symmetrical and all things become suffused with them. Matte-Blanco describes a phenomenon called frenzy, which involves extreme symmetrization of affect: "In bi-logical frenzy we see various simultaneous appearances of the sexual relations between the parents. For the indivisible mode they are the same thing. For the thinking (heterogenic) mode they are different things, and are not the parents" (1988, p. 268).

Symmetrical frenzy, the extreme of insertion of symmetric into asymmetric logic, is what is known as schizophrenia. "In symmetrical frenzy we see the 'invasion' of the indivisible mode which results in a diminution of consciousness which leads to confusion and eventually to loss of consciousness. No consciousness can exist in the absence of the heterogenic mode" (1988, p. 268).

Matte-Blanco's contribution to understanding primordial mind

One of Matte-Blanco's most significant contributions is to place "the other" mental activity that I call primordial on an equal footing with thought in terms of its importance and influence in human affairs. He makes us aware of our western cultural bias, the limitations in knowing that are inherent in psychoanalysis as a thoughtful, asymmetric, logical, difference-articulating language. He has outlined how mind works and knowledge is accrued in two different, equally valid ways that stand in various dialectical relationships with one another, a concept that is central to this book. Such an idea is the basis of my delineation of equally valid cross-cultural differences in ways of being and knowing between spiritual cultures whose bi-logical functioning is skewed toward symmetrical logic and western cultures that privilege bi-valent or asymmetric logic, as well as the basis for pathological conditions such as schizophrenia in which symmetrization is carried to the extreme of frenzy. Matte-Blanco emphasizes the dimensions of differentiation-undifferentiation and integration-continuity in distinguishing among his two logics, as well as the question of whether the relationship between them is controlled or dissociated – ideas that I will elaborate in later chapters.

The significance of Matte-Blanco's contribution

Bi-logic is a neutral, non-judgmental way to conceive of how mind ordinarily works in two qualitatively different ways in a variety of permutations and combinations. Matte-Blanco's ideas about bi-logical structures and about the bias inherent in using logical thought to conceptualize unconscious mind shed light on why Freud and Klein, and to some extent other theorists as well, have been inconsistent and confused about whether primordial mind is a variant of symbolic thought or is a qualitatively distinctive, concrete, undifferentiated and unintegrated process. It may also help to understand why Freud and Klein conceive of the aspect of mind that is not rational as inherently psychotic rather than normal but different. In Matte-Blanco's terms both Freud and Klein seem at times to be describing the primary process as a bi-valent asymmetrical structure and at other times as a mono-valent symmetrical process. Similarly Klein may be seen to use the language of asymmetry or difference to describe a process that is symmetrical in which such distinctions do not exist. Matte-Blanco's conception of dreaming as a Tridim structure, a combination of symmetric and asymmetric logic and an effort to fit the result into a three dimensional mental apparatus, might also be seen as a way to integrate Freud's seemingly disparate views of the dream as an example of symbolic thinking and as an illustration of an entirely different concrete, undifferentiated process. Matte-Blanco's terminology, like Bion's, is idiosyncratic and not intuitively comprehensible. One of the strengths of his writing is his capacity to identify the inherent bias against primordial mind (symmetrical logic) that results from our having to view it through the eyes of thought. However, when Matte-Blanco uses the concept of logic, which in common usage is almost isomorphic with thought, to describe primordial mind ("The unconscious, therefore, is a set of different bi-logical structures" [1988, p. 60]) he is engaging in the same kind of bias.

Perhaps a reason why both Bion and Matte-Blanco believe that dreaming is related to thought and is not the product of a qualitatively different mental activity is that both dreaming and thought utilize common language elements and imagery. But that does not mean these are used in the same way. Bion's description of stratified bi-logical structures might also be looked upon as the result of degrees of regulation/dissociation between thoughtful mind and primordial mind.

The models of primordial mind outlined in Chapters 2 and 3 have all for the most part been based on psychoanalytic data from work with seriously disturbed persons, mostly adults. In Chapter 4 I review theories constructed from a more normal database.

Western models of primordial mind III: Piaget, Werner, attachment theory and implicit knowledge

One of the conclusions that might be reached from the preceding chapters is that the context from which psychoanalytic theories of primordial mind are derived exerts a powerful but often invisible or unconscious influence on the theoretical models that result. A theory is an epistemology, and theories that are conceived from the western objectifying perspective of logical thought tend to marginalize primordial mind by considering it unconscious, irrational and potentially disruptive, even psychotic. Theories that have evolved in the context of a clinical consulting room with seriously disturbed persons tend to confuse what is normal with what is pathological, especially with regard to the nature of infantile mind and the process of development. Theories derived from settings outside Freud's particular consulting room methodology have had a difficult time gaining credibility within the psychoanalytic establishment for the same reason that psychoanalytic theories are pathomorphically biased. That is, they have little to say about disturbed persons. Psychoanalysis has been late to embrace experimental methodology, neuroscience methodology and, of particular importance to this chapter, the methodology of infant and child observation. In this chapter I explore the contributions of two of the most influential developmental psychologists, Jean Piaget and Heinz Werner, the burgeoning field of infant observation studies, and related neuroscience findings generated by the work of John Bowlby on attachment and by the relational psychoanalysis movement.

Cognitive-developmental psychology: Piaget and Werner

Heinz Werner and Jean Piaget approached primordial mind from an entirely different perspective – cognitive developmental psychology – although both were cognizant of psychoanalysis and were influenced by Freud's work.

Piaget

Jean Piaget and Heinz Werner made their major contributions around the same time and place in Europe as did Melanie Klein. Jean Piaget (1936) abstracted his theory from infant observation. He modeled stages in the development of mature thinking or logical operations. In his schema the primordial stage of mental activity is the sensorimotor phase of infant development, a phase of undifferentiated egocentric concrete mental activity and global undifferentiated sensory-perceptual-motor-affective tropism toward an environment perceived as aliment, initially oral ("the breast") in form. The concept seems similar both to Freud's primary process, with which he was familiar, and to Klein's model of phantasy. Piaget believed that development occurs in a linear sequence in which the sensorimotor phase is replaced by transformation into more mature mental systems. So far as I know, he did not consider the possibility that it is a distinctive form of mental activity that continues to be an option throughout life, assimilating into its substance learned forms such as formal vocabulary and information about the culture in which one lives.

Werner

Heinz Werner (1948, 1957) acknowledges that his thinking was influenced by Freud and Piaget. He describes primordial mind from the perspective of an objective observer in contrast to Freud who was attempting to create a model based on the neuroscience of his time and Klein whose terminology reflected her subjective fantasy-imagination about infant mind. He describes primordial mind as holistic or "syncretic." He writes of undifferentiation, an initial "unity of world and ego. The world is separated only slightly from the ego; it is predominantly configured in terms of the emotional needs of the self (egomorphism)" (1948, p. 361). He says:

> In different types of primitive mentality psychological functions are more intimately fused, that is, more syncretic, than in the advanced mentality. . . . In advanced forms of mental activity we observe thought processes which are quite detached from the concrete sensori-motor perceptual and affective sphere. In the primitive mentality, however, thought processes always appear as more or less perfectly fused with functions of a sensori-motor and affective type. *It is this absence of a strict separation of thought proper from perception, emotion and motor action which determines the significance of so-called concrete and affective thinking. . . characteristic examples of syncretic activity.*
>
> (ibid., p. 213, italics mine)

Werner adds that in the syncretic state "the object is represented not explicitly, but implicitly by means of motor-affective behavior" (ibid., 1948,

p. 250). He writes: "In the young child, however, there is a relatively close connection between perception and imagery" (ibid., p. 389) and again: "For the child the reality of the dream and of the waking world are relatively undifferentiated. At this stage waking reality often exhibits some of the characteristics of the dream" (ibid., p. 391). The major operating system of mind is one in which the kinds of operations and distinctions characteristic of thought have yet to develop.

Werner was interested in primordial mind in adults as well as children. He quotes a sophisticated adult subject who has taken a drug (mescaline) that seems to induce syncretic thinking: "Seeing comes to the fore, so that I value 'seeing' and 'thinking' equally. . . . The operations of reason are identical with the sequence of visual perceptions" (ibid., p. 331). A chronically ill schizophrenic patient of mine who oscillated in and out of florid psychotic states once described to me the sequence in which his auditory hallucinations developed, saying that they often began with a phenomenon that I have noted in myself and venture to say is normal, namely preoccupation with a rhythmic sound such as the ticking of a clock which becomes associated in the mind with a repetitive word or word sequence so that one almost "hears" the word or words as part of the sound. The mind of my patient as he abandoned mature thought in favor of primary mental activity, by contrast with that of Werner's subject who ingested mescaline, came to be dominated by an autonomous hallucination rather than by reflective thought. The minimalist composer Steve Reich (1992) wrote a composition called "Come Out" based on the recording of some autobiographical remarks by a passenger in a New York City taxi he drove at one time that illustrates a similar transformational process.

In other words, what Freud described as hallucination – the experiential sensory-perceptual actualization product of condensation and displacement – and Klein called phantasy – the product of sensory-perceptual-somatic mind that identifies the world by splitting and projection – is in Werner's schema the magical mental process characteristic of the syncretic stage of development. He remarks: "There is no fundamental difference between the sphere of subjective phenomena and that of (intersubjective) objective phenomena. . . . It is, in fact, out of this very fusion that magical. . . modes of thought are evolved. . . . In the realm of magic. . . dream and vision are magically effective realities" (1948, p. 339, italics mine). He writes that primary mental activity is sensorimotor: "objects emerge in terms of 'things-of-action', where perceptual qualities of things are determined by the specific way these things are handled" (ibid., p. 129).

Like Piaget, Werner believes that development consists of the replacing of more immature by more mature forms. The developmental dynamic of Werner's model is called the orthogenetic principle: "The development of biological forms is expressed in an *increasing differentiation* of parts and an *increasing subordination, or hierarchicalization*. Such a process. . . means. . .

the organization of the differentiated parts for a closed totality. . . in terms of the whole organism" (ibid., p. 41). He describes "the fundamental law of development – increase of *differentiation* and hierarchic *integration*" (ibid., p. 44, italics mine). This statement seems to express a fundamental truth about primordial mind – that it functions in a manner that is neither differentiated nor integrated. Hans Loewald states this quite clearly in his 1980 description of the primary process: "The process is primary in a deeper sense insofar as it is unitary, non-differentiating, non-discriminating between various elements of a global event or experience. . . . In secondary-process mentation duality and multiplicity are dominant, i.e. differentiation, division, a splitting of what was unitary" (1980, p. 196). Werner believes that the activity of the syncretic mind is "thought" in its original archaic incarnation whereas I believe it is a different form of mental activity that happens to be fully formed and adaptive at the beginning of life, and continues throughout life, while thought, from its archaic beginnings, develops separately. Werner's example of the person who ingested mescaline notwithstanding, he seems to believe that what he calls "advanced" thought evolves from and eventually replaces "primitive" thought, not that two mental processes develop separately and co-exist throughout life. His model is also weighted toward cognition rather than motivation and affect.

David Rappaport (1951) is one of the few psychoanalysts who realized the importance of Werner and Piaget's work and its relevance to Freud's model of the primary process. He writes:

> Where the primary process. . . hold(s) sway, ideas belong with a drive. . . everything belongs with everything that shares an attribute of it. . . ideas merge with each other and with percepts. . . (conceptualized as "syncretism"); reasoning does not move inductively. . . or deductively. . . but from part to part. . . (conceptualized as "transduction"). Conception in this phase is "physiognomic," and correspondingly the world is animated and ideas have omnipotence (H. Werner).
>
> (Rappaport, 1951, pp. 708–709)

Piaget and Werner tried to conceptualize the same elephant in the room as did Freud, Klein, and Matte-Blanco. Their models have particular strengths. The major one is their choice of terminology. Because they are based on normal infant and child observation their conceptual terminology is not derived from psychopathology and they do not tend to confuse normal development with psychopathology. The downside is that what they have to say about psychopathology is limited as a consequence. Because their conceptual language does not imply a scale of better–worse, mature–immature, superior–inferior or rational–irrational it is also more suitable for describing mental activity in non-western cultures in a non-prejudicial way, although they did not attempt to do this. Their descriptions go beyond subjective fantasy and strive for objectivity, but without inventing a new and idiosyncratic abstract language. They have the potential of a foundation that can be built upon.

The interpersonal matrix of primordial mind and its development

Explorations of the interpersonal matrix of primordial mind have taken place from several different directions. Some have originated from within the classical psychoanalytic consulting room, some from psychoanalytically informed infant observation, and some from neuroscience. Some of the neuroscience findings are presented in this chapter; others are summarized in Chapter 16.

Freud wrote: "It is a very remarkable thing that the unconscious of one human can react upon the other without passing through consciousness" (1915b, p. 194). The subject of communication is incidental and peripheral in Freud's work, mostly related to discussions of the transference. Klein wrote about defensive processes of projective identification (and introjection) and while her contribution is generally considered to be about individual intrapsychic life, the idea of projective identification and its effects on the introjecting analyst-recipient is groundwork for a theory of primordial mind operating within an undifferentiated relational matrix. Elsewhere I have written (1981a, 1981b) about possession configurations in relation to normal development and primitive personality organization – the undifferentiated symbiotic bonding created by introjection and projection – without properly crediting her contribution. Winnicott's oft-quoted remark that "there is no such thing as an infant" (1965, p. 586) aptly captures the idea that psychologically as well as physically an infant is not a separate person so much as part of a dyad with its caregiver.

Margaret Mahler (Mahler, Pine and Bergman, 1975) and Heinz Kohut (1971, 1977) made important contributions to understanding of primordial mind. Their influence is now mostly in the background as their particular theories are no longer widely embraced. The work of Margaret Mahler on the symbiotic phase (Mahler, Pine and Bergman, 1975; Fonagy, 1999b; Blum, 2004) broadened understanding of the undifferentiated nature of infantile mental life. Earlier in my own career (1981a, 1981b) I published two papers on primordial mind influenced by Mahler's symbiosis concept and Klein's ideas about splitting and projective identification. Like Freud and Klein, Mahler modeled primordial mind after adult psychopathology. She believed that undifferentiated and unintegrated mental activity and the kind of relationships that develop from it (symbiosis) is inherently immature, even pathological, and is to be outgrown in the course of normal development. In conceiving the idea of normal development and maturation as achievement of personal separation and individuation she was confusing a western cultural norm with a "scientific" fact about human nature. So she did not consider the possibility that there might be a normal mental process qualitatively different from thought that might be the foundation for activities and relationships that are normal and adaptive within appropriate contexts.

Kohut's theory of the selfobject transference and the mirroring phase of development is another way of emphasizing the importance of integration and differentiation in development. However, like Mahler he conceived of development as a process of linear transformation in which immature and pathological forms are gradually transformed into more mature ones. This does not take into account that thought may develop separately and that there may be a different primordial mental process that predominates in infancy but continues throughout life in significant and normal ways depending on whether and how it is controlled and regulated by thought. Instead he believed that infantile mental activity is chaotic and meaningless until formation of the first selfobject configurations around the second year of life (Robbins, 1980), and that this way of being and relating is gradually outgrown in the course of development.

The strands of investigation of primordial mind that persist and continue to grow and have become intertwined involve interpersonal or relational theory and attachment theory of implicit or procedural learning and knowledge. Relational theory arises from the premise that mind is never fully differentiated and integrated and that the western emphasis on separation and individuation is to some extent a myth. The concepts of implicit or procedural learning and knowledge derived from attachment theory are the basis for a model of core learning and relating that is very different from thought and co-exists with it throughout life.

Harry Sullivan (1953b) was one of the first to define psychoanalysis as the study of the person in relation to other persons rather than the study of individual psyche, founding what has come to be known as the relational school of psychoanalysis. John Bowlby (1969) formulated what is called attachment theory. While it has been the object of considerable controversy and criticism among psychoanalysts (Fonagy, 1999b; Blum, 2004), the study of infant attachment has gradually gained independence from Bowlby's specific theory (see Ainsworth, 1982; Ainsworth et al., 1978; Bretherton, 1987, 1995; Bretherton et al., 1979) and through articulation of the concepts of implicit or procedural knowledge and learning has become an important lens through which to understand primordial mind.

The primordial mental activity involved in infant attachment that is qualitatively different from rational thought has variously been referred to as unformulated experience (Stern, 1989); subsymbolic process (Bucci, 2000); primary affective memory or primary affective unconscious (Panksepp, 1998); and the unthought known (Bollas, 1987) but the term that is now most frequently used is implicit or procedural learning or knowledge or memory (Watt, 1990; Clyman, 1991; Emde *et al.*, 1991; Grigsby and Hartlaub, 1994; Beebe and Lachman, 2003; Stern, 1985; Stern *et al.*, 1998; Squire, 1986). There is considerable cross reference between the conception of unconscious process related to implicit or procedural memory and knowledge and the conception of unconscious process developed by the relational school of psychoanalysis, for example in the work of Mitchell (1995), Emde (1983, 1990), Stern (1989), and Beebe & Lachmann (2003). Both refer to the irreducibly subjective element of relationships, or to put it differently the aspect of the person that is neither objectively differentiated from the other nor thoughtfully and reflectively integrated as part of the self system. The difference may be that relational theories conceive of this primordial aspect of mind as unconscious in the sense of irreducible subjectivity whereas those who utilize concepts like implicit knowledge and learning are trying to formulate a qualitatively different primordial mental process that co-exists alongside thought. Emde states that: "There is a major amount of nonconscious mental activity that is neither preconscious (i.e. readily accessible to consciousness using recent or working memory) nor defensively excluded (i.e. involving repressed memories or isolated affects). . . a variety of organized automatically functioning procedures and rules for guiding behavior in particular contexts (1993, p. 415). Schore writes that:

> Both psychoanalytic theory and cognitive science agree that meaning systems include both conscious (e.g. verbalizable or attended to) aspects of experience and unconscious or implicitly processed aspects of experience. Implicit processing in modern cognitive science is applied to mental activity that is repetitive, automatic, provides quick categorization and decision-making, and operates outside the realm of focal attention and verbalized experience.
>
> (1997, p. 832)

As Lyons-Ruth puts it, "implicit processing may be particularly relevant to the quick and automatic handling of nonverbal affective cues, which are recognized and represented early in infancy in complex 'proto-dialogues' [Trevarthen, 1980] and so have their origins prior to the availability of symbolic communication" (1999, pp. 586–587).

Bowlby wrote that attachment communication includes "facial expression, posture, and tone of voice" (1969, p. 120). Inspired by the suggestion of a primordial mental activity that drives infant–caregiver relationships and that is different from thought, Robertson (1971) made a now classical film showing the nuanced subtle interactions of gesture, facial expression and sound between infants and their mothers. Neuroscience findings are beginning to document the basis of this choreography and hence the primordial mental activity that underlies it in the synchronous activity of similar brain areas of mother and infant. Trevarthen (1980) describes coordinated visual eye-to-eye messages, tactile and body gestures, and auditory prosodic vocalizations serving as a channel of communicative signals that induce instant emotional effects. Manning *et al.* (1997), Sieratzki and Woll (1996), and Bourne and Todd (2004) note that most women hold their infant on the left side of their body. Schore (2003, 2005) notes that this position allows the mother's left eye and ear to contact the infant's left eye and ear and the results are processed by the respective right or non-verbal hemispheres of each partner. Lorberbaum *et al.* (2002) found that the infant's cry activates the mother's right brain, and her vocal responses tend to be encoded in the infant's right hemisphere. Tzourio-Mazoyer *et al.* (2002) have demonstrated that infants process maternal face recognition in the right hemisphere and Ranote *et al.* (2004) have shown that mothers who look at the faces of their infants show complementary activation of right hemisphere structures.

Another strand of research related to infant–caregiver synchronicity in the attachment phase has led to the discovery of so-called "mirror neurons," located on the outer surface of frontal and parietal lobes (Gallese *et al.*, 1996; Tomasello, 1999; Molnar-Szaracs *et al.*, 2005; Pally, 2007), and speculation about their developmental significance. Dimberg *et al.* report that electromyographic studies of the facial responses of subjects to the facial expressions of others show unconscious (somatic) mimicry, that "both positive and negative emotional reactions can be unconsciously evoked, and that important aspects of emotional face-to-face communication can occur at an unconscious level" (2000, p. 86). The mirror neuron system does not appear to differentiate subject from object, and hence is an important contribution to understanding the undifferentiated and unintegrated quality of primordial mental activity. The subject responds behaviorally to perceived cues from another as though they were coming from the self, as expressed in the saying "monkey see, monkey do." This function of the mirror neuron system would appear to describe the mutual forceful inductive process that, as I will elaborate in Chapter 5, distinguishes primordial mental activity from thoughtful communication of meaning, and suggests it is not an innate defense against attachment as Klein maintained, but rather part of a normal learning and attachment process.

What is transmitted and learned in the mutual primordial mental activity (PMA) interactions of earliest life is complex and as yet poorly understood. Basic internal rhythm, however, is an important aspect. We live in a world of circadian rhythm and finding an internal rhythm or homeostasis is an essential aspect of self-regulation, leading to a balance of security, internal cohesion and self-regulation over disruption, anxiety and fragmentation throughout life. Adults whose PMA is dissociated from thoughtful regulation are usually not good parents. Their behavior is usually driven by "negative" affects – hostility, anxiety, depression and despair – and is not under mature thoughtful control, thereby leading to behaviors that distort the affective relational substrate of infant mind in the process of early bonding. This aspect is explored in Chapter 13 on psychosis.

Attachment theory and the concept of implicit or procedural learning and knowledge are very important contributions to understanding basic affective-relational patterns, both ordinary and disordered. However, this is a necessary but not a sufficient characterization of primordial mind. There is an active mental process that exists from birth that assimilates (learns) and enacts the affective-relational pattern of response to caregivers that has been called implicit or procedural knowledge. The infant is not the *tabula rasa* of some definitions of implicit or procedural knowledge on which the force of the caregiver passively impinges. Infant mind operates according to an active cognitive-affective relational process both of learning and of expression, not simply a pathological reflex response to other human beings. This primordial mental activity builds upon the attachment configuration or implicit knowledge that has been assimilated at the beginning of life, but it is an active mental process that incorporates the disturbed attachment or implicit procedural substrate.

This ends the review of the numerous contributions to understanding primordial mental activity and brings us to the proposals I make in Chapter 5.

Primordial mental activity

My purpose in reviewing the major theories of primordial mind in the preceding three chapters has been to describe the phenomenology from as many vantage points as possible, and in so doing to underscore the common elements in the theories as well as the differences. Some of the common elements direct attention to the core characteristics of PMA and others reflect limitations and problems. From this analysis I have abstracted the core constituents and assumptions of a satisfactory model of primordial mind:

Elements and assumptions of a model of primordial mind

1   Primordial mental activity is a qualitatively distinctive function of mind that is not directly related to thought.
2   Primordial mental processes persist throughout life and are not transformed into thought in the course of development.
3   Primordial mental activity has as much influence in human experience as does thought.
4   PMA can only be rationally understood and conceptualized within the limiting framework of western thought. Nonetheless, insofar as possible the description of PMA should not reflect the inherent western cultural bias against mental processes other than thought – that they are irrational, immature, primitive, and somehow inferior.
5   Primordial mind is inherently normal. It should not be conceptualized using terminology that is derived from and based upon pathology and hence presumed to be immature, irrational, defective or psychotic. Judgments about normality and pathology depend upon the socio-cultural context in which the phenomenology of PMA is manifest.
6   PMA is not inherently defensive though under some circumstances it may be used in preference to thought as a defensive adaptation.
7   The phenomenological manifestations of PMA are dependent on the particular relationship between it and thought.

8   Primordial mental activity plays a significant role in learning, in expression, and in communication.

Describing primordial mental activity

At the outset I acknowledge my debt to Freud for his seminal work on the primary process. My personal dialectical relationship with his ideas has enabled me to crystallize the central elements of the primary process that can be built upon. I have chosen the term *primordial* rather than *primary* in order to emphasize that there are important differences as well. The term *mental* signifies "of the mind," or psychological, as contrasted with "of the brain." "Mental" is a broad concept that embraces thought but is not synonymous with it, for thought is but one system or function of mind. The term *primordial* is not intended to imply that the system is a precursor or early stage in the development of thought, but rather to indicate that this mental capacity is fully functional at birth and continues throughout life as a core process, gradually incorporating elements of experience that have been learned, albeit in order to use them in a manner different from thought. Although rudimentary capacity for thought is also present at the beginning of life, components of the brain responsible for thought mature slowly over the first decade or so of life so that the capacity for thought cannot be relied upon extensively until around puberty. "Primordial," then, signifies that the system is an entity unto itself present from the very start and is not a developmental precursor of thought, an arcane aspect of thought, or a regressive transformation product from an antecedent stage of mature thinking. *Activity* (expression or impression) signifies both the subjective experience of an actual happening rather than a mental event, and the concrete sensory-perceptual-somatic-motor expressive quality of mind that distinguishes it from the reflective subjective experience that is an aspect of representational thought.

Comparing primordial mental activity and thought

There are major and possibly insurmountable problems in creating a conceptual language that is not idiosyncratic and that is free of terminology that expresses subtle bias or evokes other contaminating associations. Finding terminology that does not suggest primordial mental activity is of itself immature or pathological is difficult enough. The work of Werner and Piaget has served as my guide in this regard. Having to create a model of a way of experiencing and knowing that is qualitatively different from thought from within an epistemological perspective confined by thought is much more challenging. Among the western thinkers whose work I am aware of Jung comes closest because he is aware of cultural difference. He introduced the concept of synchronicity (1959) to denote meaning expressed in qualitatively different ways. Matte-Blanco was also aware of the inherent bias imposed by rational thought as the term is commonly understood, and although he proposed an ingenious solution (two kinds of logic) it is difficult to grasp a novel definition of such a well-known term. The problem I have struggled with in this chapter and throughout the remainder of the book, not entirely successfully, is to create a conceptual language to describe primordial mental activity, like those that Werner and Piaget formulated, based on the kind of intention expressed by Jung and Matte-Blanco, that is as free as possible of the prejudices created by using western culture as the norm and psychopathological mind as the base. To illustrate the pitfall I have tried to avoid I have prepared Table 5.1 (overleaf) to distinguish PMA from thought in a way that does not take into account these biases. There are evident similarities to aspects of the theories I have described in Chapters 2–4.

Thought

Thought involves self-reference and recursion, i.e. integration of experience with a continuous organizing self or psyche that differentiates inner personal mind from outer reality and self from other separate centres or universes of being and action. Thought involves self-observation and objectification of experience, and the capacity to make comparisons and contrasts. What one thinks can be distinguished from what one believes or is certain about. Thought is motivated and guided by identifiable emotions as well as the desire to adapt to one's environment. Body sensations and perceptual experiences are recognized and distinguished from feeling states. Experience has meaning that is derived not only from its immediacy but also from reflection, objectification and evaluation on a timeline by contrast with other experiences held in memory, and with contemplated future experiences. Narrative sequence and causality take into account the concept of an external world differentiated from oneself and one's beliefs that is governed by logic and causality of its own. Conflict is experienced as an internal event, not just in relation to an external world. Choices and decisions are related to these internally experienced processes. Interpersonal communication is by exchange of ideas; the use of force, pressure or action is optional. Imagination spins possible scenarios, wishes, goals and ambitions. Language can be used either expressively in its literal or formal sense or communicatively in its metaphorical symbolic sense to exchange meanings and ideas.

On page 54 I present Table 5.2. It represents my effort to describe PMA in a way that is relatively free of cultural and psychopathological bias.

Table 5.1 Primordial mental activity in relation to thought from a
perspective biased by culture and psychopathology

	PMA	Thought
What motivates mind	Somatic sensation and affect; inability to bear feelings and accept reality	Identified emotion and adaptation to reality
How meaning is experienced and expressed	Psychosomatic: sensation and perception. Wishful beliefs, myths, superstition. Hallucination and delusion	Reflective, recursive, referential. "I think that. . ."
Nature of personal narrative	Fragmented, unintegrated snapshots. Inability to perceive time, logic and causality	Integrated thoughts, emotions and adaptation. Acceptance of logic, causality, passage of time
The center of experience and expression	Absence of separate cohesive sense of self. Not separated and differentiated psychically from others	Separated and individuated. Self-referenced, intrapsychic, reflective
Mental activity	Phantasy. Sensory-perceptual, somatic, undifferentiated	Thought including imagination or fantasy
Is the world perceived in relative or absolute terms?	Anthropomorphic confusion of self and world leading to absolutism in belief, hallucination and delusion	Differentiation of self from other. Intrapsychic self that compares, contrasts, understands passage of time and can be objective
The nature of expression, communication and learning	Concrete. Lack of mental representation. Inability to symbolize, reflect and communicate meaningfully	Meaning exchanged in form of ideas and symbols
Language	Concrete. Words treated as things	Entire range of linguistic complexity; words carry meaning
Development	Maturation involves separately learning to think	Thought matures and PMA is repressed and relegated to dreaming

Primordial mental activity

Primordial mental activity (PMA) is psychosomatic, i.e. body-based mind.
It is driven by affect and somatic sensation. Meaning is related to sensation,
perception and action. The subjective quality of experience is that of
immediacy, actuality, belief, a happening, rather than something to contemplate. Experience is holistic or syncretic, combining elements of mind
and world into isomorphic entities. Self and cosmos are not differentiated,

Table 5.2 Primordial mental activity in relation to thought from an unbiased
perspective

	PMA	Thought
What motivates mind	Somatic sensation and affect	Identified emotion and adaptation
How meaning is experienced and expressed	Psychosomatic: sensation, perception, motor, belief, "it is"	Reflective, recursive, referential. "I think that. . ."
Nature of personal narrative	Chaining or linking of sensation and perception by idiosyncratic affect	Integrates emotion and adaptation and hence is logical, causal, recursive, time-sensitive
The center of experience and expression	De-centered, existential, collectively referenced in cosmos	Self-referenced, intrapsychic, reflective
Relativity or context?	Absolute. Actuality of experience. Belief. Holistic syncretic perception	Relative to others, external world, passage of time. Mind compares, contrasts, can be subjective or objective
The nature of expression, communication and learning	Concrete, literal, forceful, peremptory	Exchange of ideas and meanings
Language	Full vocabulary, grammar and syntax. Words used concretely as things	Entire range of linguistic complexity; words carry meaning
Development	Utilizes learned material but process itself does not develop	Developmental transformation in systemic complexity

so experience is holistic. Laws of contradiction, contrast and difference do
not apply so that entire identities shift and one person or thing can be
isomorphic with another.

The narrative quality of experience depends on somatic sensation and
affect, and the immediate snapshot quality of experience is chained together
with a series of "and thens." PMA calls upon the same sensory-perceptual
acuity as thought. It uses the same learned vocabulary, grammar and
syntax as thought, but words are used in a way that is formal or concrete
rather than symbolic.

PMA is a deep or fundamental modality of expression, communication
and learning. It is immediate, peremptory or forceful, concrete and enactive;
it expresses belief, apprehension and certainty. In its expressive mode PMA
exerts pressure to actualize beliefs, and in its receptive or learning mode it is
the way the world is affectively apprehended and assimilated. It is

responsible for the deep somatopsychic learning process known as introjection and as implicit or procedural learning, a process that is most characteristic of early life before the development of a thoughtful alternative.

PMA is inherently neither realistic nor unrealistic, normal nor abnormal. Those phenomenological evaluations depend upon several factors: 1) The shape or nature of the primordial affect configuration or implicit learning from the original affective-relational pattern with caregivers during the attachment phase. Is there synchrony between caregiver and infant, and is the expectation that emerges reasonably consistent with what most people in the community experience? 2) The socio-cultural context in which it is phenomenologically manifest. Is it adaptive (realistic) or maladaptive (unrealistic) within the community? 3) The relationship between PMA and thought. Are they integrated or dissociated and in what way?

The relationship between PMA and thought is a complex one that is explored from various perspectives throughout the book. Arieti (1966, 1967) suggested the term "tertiary processes" for those particular combinations of primary and secondary processes seen in art and creativity. Noy (1969, p. 174) expresses the relationship in situations that are not pathological as follows:

> This hand-in-hand functioning necessitates the concomitant function of two systems: one equipped to deal with reality, and another equipped to deal with the self. These two "sets" of programs have to operate together, meaning that every input processed according to reality-orientated programs has to be "translated" by passing through a second process of self-centred programs – and, vice versa, any activity originated by self-centred motivation has to be "translated" from its self-centred organization through reality-orientated programs in order to be expressed as behavior.
>
> (p. 174)

As noted in Chapter 3, Matte-Blanco describes various structures that reflect the interaction of symmetric and asymmetric logics. Some of my own conclusions, which I elaborate in subsequent chapters, are: The two involve different neural circuits. PMA is present from the start of life whereas the capacity for thought develops slowly over the first decade. During the process of maturation PMA and thought acquire a relationship of relative dissociation or integration. The outcome depends upon innate or constitutional aspects, the childhood interpersonal environment, and the socio-cultural context and expectations. Integration involves thoughtful control over the times, places and purposes for which PMA is used. It is related to mental health and to uses of PMA that are constructive in the community. With the exception of nocturnal dreaming, dissociation is related to serious mental illness.

Chapter 6

Dreaming

The phenomenon of dreaming is a central data source for Freud, Jung and Bion's western cultural models of intrapsychic unconscious mind. Dreaming is important in non-western cultures as well. In spiritual cultures dreams, both sleeping and waking, are viewed as part of the existential spirit world.

To begin I review major theories of dreaming and highlight their strengths and limitations. These can be evaluated in two categories. The first has to do with the relationship of the underlying mental activity to thought. The second has to do with the epistemological perspective of the theorist. Psychoanalytic models tend to view the mental process underlying dreaming as pathological. And most of them are biased by the perspective of western culture that recognizes and values conscious rational thought and views what is not thought as deficient in the sense of being primitive, immature and unconscious, rather than simply being different.

The relationship of dreaming to thought

Hypotheses about the relationship of dreaming to thought can be grouped into several categories. The work of some theorists falls into more than one.

The dreaming process as an aspect of thought

As I described in Chapter 2, Freud composed two theories to account for dreaming, a conservative one that depicts it as the product of a thought-related symbolic activity, and a radical one that describes it as a unique manifestation of mind. Klein hardly mentioned dreaming in her work. However, some who followed her have related dreaming and phantasy, which was described in Chapter 2, as both having characteristics of thought and as being qualitatively different from thought. In some neo-Kleinian writings, including those of Bion (see Chapter 3) and Meltzer, dreaming is described as a thought-related process. Bion (1962, 1992; Grotstein, 2009) describes dreaming as a continuous process manifest as states like reverie during wakefulness and dreaming proper at night. It is the alpha process by which the beta elements of sensation, perception and raw affect are transformed into representational narrative symbolic elements of thought and knowledge. This alpha-betization process creates a screen, contact barrier or gradient that separates thoughtful reflective consciousness from unconscious elements including repressed thoughts and memories. Meltzer (1984) has expanded on Bion's conception of dreaming as proto-thinking, and in 1976 he writes about dream interpretation as follows: "The patient learns to modify his dream-language to accommodate our limited comprehension, as one may talk pidgin English to a foreigner for his greater understanding" (1976, p. 429). This suggests persons communicating in thought but speaking foreign languages.

Dreaming reflects a mental process qualitatively different from thought

Freud (primary process), Jung and many Kleinians describe dreaming as a process qualitatively different from thought. Freud's radical description of the primary process, which I described in Chapter 2, includes absence of contradiction, displacement and condensation, timelessness, undifferentiation of external from psychical reality, replacement of logical connection and causal-temporal logic with event sequences and contiguity, and replacement of similarity with identity. Dreams are concrete enactments rather than symbolic representational vehicles. Werner and Kaplan (1963) cite two of Freud's dreams. In one the concept of superfluity becomes something overflowing, while in another the concept of being manipulated literally becomes having one's hand shaken. Bert States writes: "The dream is the instantiation of a felt meaning" (1992, pp. 10–11).

As noted in Chapter 3, Jung (1956) asserted that mind has two qualitatively different "normal" manifestations that are in continuous dialectical relationship throughout life; a rational, realistic aspect and a creative, fantastic, mythopoetic one that is related to dreaming. He called these "directed thinking" toward "reality" and "irresponsible thinking" respectively.

Meltzer makes an entirely different statement than the one quoted earlier when he writes that "phantasy goes on all the time and when asleep it is called dreaming" (1984, p. 38). Referring to himself as a Kleinian he implies that dreaming and thought are not examples of two languages as the term is usually understood:

> Our approach to the analysis of dreams is bound to be very different from Freud's "jig-saw puzzle" or "translation from Latin to German" method. . . We are approaching the dream as a sample of a continuous process that is the very heart of the matter of the patient's mental life; a

glimpse par excellence into the theater where meaning is being constantly generated.

(1976, p. 429)

As for Bion, while he described dreaming as thought-related he also agreed with Freud that dreams are wish-fulfillments, ways of avoiding the experience of frustration rather than thoughtfully coping with it (1992, pp. 47–48).

Simultaneous conceptions of dreaming as thought and as a qualitatively different activity

In Freud's writing and that of some Kleinians and of Bion two different conceptions of dreaming emerge not only in juxtaposition or vacillation but also more or less simultaneously. Freud's descriptions of condensation and displacement include such adjectives as "plastic" and "ambiguous," and his synonyms for them include *compression, replacement, exchange, transformation* and *reduction*. They describe a state of undifferentiation, in which things are not thought *about* but experienced as actual happenings. However, the "mechanisms" are simultaneously described as thought-related defensive processes. Kleinians describe *phantasy* using a conceptual language of thoughtful *fantasy* – a mental process involving complex thinking and conceptual differentiation of body parts, feeling states and intrapsychic defensive processes. Klein asserted that phantasy is simultaneously concrete and symbolic: "Symbolism is the foundation of all phantasy, sublimation, and of every talent, since it is by way of symbolic equation that the things, activities, and interests become the subject of libidinal phantasies" (1930, p. 220). Segal (1957, 1978) popularized the term "symbolic equation." Interpretations of dreams from a Freudian perspective and of psychotic manifestations from a Kleinian perspective are often couched in symbolic language, as though the analysand is capable of understanding them as such, in the face of theoretical models that indicate otherwise. While Meltzer interprets dreams from a Kleinian perspective based on the assumption they are different from symbolic thought, in his 1984 book he elaborates Bion's idea that dreaming is part of the process of thinking.

One reason dreaming is considered symbolic may be that the actual dream experience is readily confused with the waking thoughtful state in which it is captured, re-cast into narrative thought, and then thoughtfully processed. Dreams are *experienced* as real happenings. With the single exception of lucid dreaming (see Chapter 11), no thoughtful mind co-exists with which to contemplate the experience. It requires conscious effort on awakening to capture fleeting traces before the images vanish in order to be able to say, "I have had a dream." Subsequently what is dealt with is the experience as rendered into representational thought and language which is the only way to think and talk about it. The symbolic verbal product is not the dream. States notes that the dream "is difficult to talk about precisely because it consists of having such experiences, and talking about them in almost any manner tends to draw one into a conceptual mode of thought" (1992, p. 5).

Bion: Two dream processes?

Two theorists – Bion and Matte-Blanco – are in camps more or less by themselves. Bion believes that there are two qualitatively different dream or dream-like processes, corresponding to what he has described (1957) as the psychotic and non-psychotic parts of the personality. The "normal" dream is a process of proto-thinking. The other kind of dreaming arises from the qualitatively different process that arises when proto-thinking and the metabolism of beta elements of experience into alpha elements suitable for thought fails – the process that underlies psychosis. The dreaming associated with psychotic phantasy is the manifestation of destruction of thought. Elements of raw experience remain concrete fragments that cannot be metabolized but are somatically evacuated or expelled by projective identification creating a beta screen that consists of delusion and hallucination. Bion writes: "If the patient cannot transform his emotional experiences into alpha-elements, he cannot dream. . . the patient who cannot dream cannot go to sleep and cannot wake up" (1992, p. 7). This statement is not to be taken concretely, for he also writes that the dream:

> Can be employed for two dissimilar purposes. One is concerned with the transformation of stimuli received from the world of external reality and internal psychic reality so that they can be stored (memory) in a form making them accessible to recall (attention) and synthesis with each other. The other. . . is the use of the visual images of the dream for purposes of control and ejection of unwanted. . . emotional experience. . . a vehicle for the evacuatory process. The dream itself is then felt to be an act of evacuation in much the same way as the visual hallucination is felt to be a positive act of expulsion through the eyes. [In this case] the fact that the dream is being employed in an excretory function contributes to the patient's feeling that he is unable to dream.
>
> (1992, p. 67)

Matte-Blanco: Dreaming combines two processes

Matte-Blanco's theory of bi-logic is outlined in Chapter 3. He believed that there are two qualitatively different mental processes or "logics," symmetrical and asymmetrical. Symmetrical logic, which is considered illogical in everyday discourse, has the qualities Freud described as primary process.

Asymmetric or bi-valent logic is based on recognition of difference and contrast (differentiation). Matte-Blanco avoids some of the confusion between the two kinds of mental activity that has beset others by observing that symmetrical logic cannot be made conscious and truly understood with logical thought because it is qualitatively different, but that does not make it any less "real" and powerful. It must be understood in relation to the effects it has on asymmetric logic, that is to say the distortions it creates in the rational thought process.

Most mental activity is bi-logical, the consequence of structures that combine symmetric and asymmetric logic. Dreaming is one of these, a *tridiem* structure arising from fitting multiple meanings, some symmetric (undifferentiated) and others asymmetric, into a differentiated, three-dimensional way of thinking. Matte-Blanco describes the result as follows:

> a) One can see in it the presence of symmetrical logic in that two [or more] different persons are implicitly treated as only one; i.e. the original person and the person on to whom displacement takes place are really the same person in different "incarnations", just as happens in a symmetrized class or set. (b) Classical logic is present in the fact that one sees the appearances of two [or more] quite different and separated persons: no identification. It is only by means of the analysis of the associations that one can discover the (secret) identity of the two [or more]. It is, therefore, a dissimulated bi-logical structure. . . In the Tridim structure one can, at first sight, detect only the heterogenic-dividing mode, while the indivisible mode is dissimulated, precisely by means of splitting-displacement, which makes one appear as two.
>
> (1988, pp. 48–49)

The role of cultural and pathological bias

In Chapter 1, I described how derivation of theories about the basis of mind from a western cultural perspective and from data derived from pathological subjects makes it difficult to appreciate the presence and importance of the dream state as a normal and omnipresent mental activity that is different from thought. As Matte-Blanco points out, we cannot actually experience the world through "eyes" qualitatively different from our own. Phenomena of the other kind tend to pass unnoticed or to be misinterpreted as immature, abnormal, primitive or otherwise inferior in relation to thought. In Chapter 3 I've already quoted that Jung wrote:

> We move in a world of fantasies which, untroubled by the outward course of things, well up from inner phantasmal forms. This activity of the early classical mind was, in the highest degree, artistic; the goal of its interest does not seem to have been how to understand the real

world as objectively and accurately as possible. Thus there arose a picture of the universe which was completely removed from reality, but which corresponded exactly to man's subjective fantasies. . . children think in much the same way. . . We also know that the same kind of thinking is exhibited in dreams. . . a world of impossibilities takes the place of reality.

(1959b, pp. 24–25)

In spiritual cultures the dream state is not viewed as an unconscious aspect of the psyche but as the vehicle of cosmic journeys and struggles and as a mode of relating to others and to the community. Such journeys involve shape-changing (western undifferentiation) and transformations between human, animal and natural worlds. The dream state is not distinguished in terms of waking and sleeping, rationality and irrationality, but is a place to go (trance or ecstasy) in waking life and an essential source of information about individual and community. The disciplined awareness and use of these primordial mental processes is considered the highest form of development which enriches community life in spiritually based cultures – much the same way that we view rationality, logic and science in the west.

The following description comes from personal communication with Egan Bidois, a Maori shaman (*Matakite*):

Moemoea or dreams are another important source of knowledge. "They are not limited to a sleeping state at all. For *Matakite* they occur independent of sleep. It depends on one's interpretation of what sleep is. One translation of the word *moemoea* is vision. The person might be wide awake and functioning as usual, and yet in a spiritual sense exist in a completely different place and time. Dreams can just be dreams, but for Maori and *Matakite* they can also be doorways in and out of various realms of existence where we may venture outward, or others may venture in. Within those states we are removed from the physical self, removed from the physical inputs and discoloring interpretation and interaction that physical existence creates. Instead we are more what I believe is our true selves, our true forms, which are first and foremost spirit. Through *moemoea* we cast off those physical bonds and boundaries and are able to more readily engage and interact with spirit.

Pathological bias

The primary source of data for psychoanalytic theories of dreaming has been treatment of mentally disturbed persons. The theories of Freud and Klein (1975a, 1975b) in particular imply that the underlying mental activity is immature, defensive against intense affective experiences and aversive to consensual social reality; in short, pathological in comparison with thought.

Freud looked upon dreaming as regressive (Litowitz, 2007). He wrote that "a dream, then, is a psychosis with all the absurdities, delusions and illusions of a psychosis" (1940, p. 172) and in several places in *The Interpretation of Dreams* specifically used the expression hallucinatory wish fulfillment to describe it. Kleinian phantasy involves schizoid splitting of mind in defense against innate rage, and creation by defenses that are called paranoid and manic of a delusional, all-good self. Psychotic mechanisms are used to distort insupportable experiences and create in their stead a more palatable delusional sense of satisfaction.

Meltzer's derivation of a model of dreaming illustrates the issue. His ideas are based on work with psychotic children he calls autistic. He states clearly that his ideas about dreaming are derived from understanding manifestations of phantasy in the consulting room. The result can be expressed as a syllogism: the mental activity of autistic children is phantasy, dreams are phantasy, therefore the mental activity of autistic children informs us about dreaming.

The models of Jung and Matte-Blanco are free of pathological bias. Jung writes that "the unconscious bases of dreams and fantasies. . . are not in themselves infantile, much less pathological" (1959b, p. 32). Pathological bias works synergistically with western cultural bias to create the assumption that dreams display a netherworld within the mind that is primitive, deficient, immature and unrealistic, driven by untamed and dangerous passions, and to obscure our appreciation of a qualitatively different form of mental activity from thought.

Dreaming as an expression of primordial mental activity

The dream is an affect-driven sensory-perceptual actualization; a narrative without a thoughtful narrator or a logical script. The expression is global, holistic or syncretic; absolute insofar as there is no "realistic" differentiation of internal from external, no respect for real time, no reflection, comparison or contrast. The experience is of a concrete happening rather than something symbolic to be reflected upon. The affect-driven narrative takes the form of sequential happenings and transformations of time, place and person that have no personal narrative continuity and do not make logically integrated realistic "sense."

The relationship between dreaming and waking

In waking life the relative preponderance of PMA and thought differs according to the stage of development, the particular person, and sociocultural context. The relationship between PMA and thought may be one of dissociation (psychosis) or of integration, and the integration can take many forms ranging from suppression, which is the norm in western culture, to a variety of controlled expressions. The phenomenon of lucid dreaming that is described in Chapter 11, where some persons dreaming during REM sleep are simultaneously thoughtfully aware and able to control the content of the dream, supports the hypothesis of two qualitatively different forms of mental activity. It is an instance of the relationship between these two aspects of mind while sleeping. The place of dreaming in spiritual cultures is explored further in Chapter 8, and there is an example at the end of this chapter.

The interpretation of dreams

The fact that primordial mental activity is not symbolic and is not related to thought is not tantamount to saying that dreams are without meaning. The recognition that there has been a dream and the subsequent steps necessary to understand it are waking thoughtful activities. The first stage is recollection of the evanescent traces of dream experience and casting it into the form of a thoughtful narrative or script, *as if* the dream itself were a drama, which was not the case because there was no thoughtful script to begin with. In the second stage of thought, focal attention is directed to experiential sequences in the dream. The third stage utilizes analogical, metaphorical and gestalt processes to construct a thoughtful meaning. *The metaphorical process is not in the dream as such but in the interpretive thought process.* In fact, Freud often conceived of dreams not as symbolic but as gestalt enactments of a person's intrapsychic *weltanschauung*. For example, in describing his interpretation of one of his patient's dreams he remarks, "And after reflecting a little I was able to give her the correct interpretation of the dream, which she afterwards confirmed. I was able to do so because I was familiar with the whole of the dreamer's previous history" (1900, p. 152).

Illustrations

A group of experts on Middle Eastern cultures believe that Arab women dream of falling significantly more often than their western counterparts. Whether they are correct is not the point I wish to make. They further speculate that this relates to unconscious fear of being looked upon as "fallen women" in a culture that places emphasis on female chastity. Such dreams concretely actualize a mental state. No matter how universal a symbol in waking thought *fallen woman* might be, in such dreams it is not a symbolic but a concrete actualization of a mental state. In order to understand the meaning of such a dream it is necessary to subject the experiential images to a process of analogical reasoning. In order to understand the meaning of dreams it is necessary to find the often idiosyncratic actualization of the dreamer's mental state that expresses the relevant analogy and translate it into the realm of thought.

A patient who was often confused and unable to think clearly about herself and have a dependable mind of her own with which to process experience had the following dream: *A woman on whom she was dependent kept ignoring her when she asked important questions. After this happened several times the woman suggested they go out to lunch, and the patient immediately agreed.* In our discussion of the dream my patient realized the woman represented an undifferentiated amalgam of her mother and herself. As we discussed how she colluded with her mother to avoid facing and clarifying problems in their relationship we realized that the cogent element in the dream was that she was "out to lunch."

During the period of time I was puzzling about what examples of primordial mental activity I might include in the book I had an interesting dream. It was two days before my birthday, which was of particular personal significance to me in my struggle to come to terms with the reality of aging. I awoke in the morning from a restful sleep in a gradual and natural manner and for some moments believed that the experience of the dream I am about to report had actually happened, and that I had actually been the observer of a vignette that illustrated primary mental activity, that I might use in this very chapter. I had a sense of urgency to get to my computer and write it down before I forgot it. Gradually, with a growing sense of disappointment, I realized that it had only been a dream, and I had no "real" vignette to report.

Soon I realized that the dream was interesting in itself. In it I was taken by a host whom I did not actually see to a home to interview an older couple about their life, as part of a study I was conducting on the aging process. We opened the door and I was greeted by the man of the house who was obviously old and somewhat infirm. There was a rather ripe odor suggestive of a combination of dirt and decay. The furnishings of the room were conventional, in poor taste, out of style and well-worn. I asked the man about his and his wife's situation in life and how they looked upon the aging process, but in my dream-state I quickly realized he could not tell me because his mind was working in primordial mode and his subjective sense was that the time in which he was living was the only time there was. He experienced no sense of history and no sense of perspective or ability to reflect, for he was living out a belief that there was no such thing as passage of time or aging. On reflection I realized that the belief that I had acquired a real, everyday life example of primary mental activity was in fact only a wish, and "all" I had was a concrete expression of some of the features of primary mental activity such as timelessness and absence of reflective capacity (nothing to think about), concreteness and narrative linkage of images by affective valence.

I sustained a painful chest injury and was having considerable difficulty sleeping. During a brief period of sleep I dreamed that I was looking at my computer screen and seeing a numbered sequence of boxes indicating levels of pain. I discovered that I could delete pain level by level, by clicking the mouse. I awoke in considerable pain. This transparently wish-fulfilling dream involved a literal enactment of deleting pain; it was not symbolic.

In another dream I was trying to find the social security number of an important person in my life about whose state of mind I was at that time puzzling. On reflection I realized that I had actualized the metaphor about "getting someone's number," that is, establishing a sense of who that person is.

A friend shared that she had dream in which she was going into a field. As she reflected that the overall theme of the dream, the other details of which I will not recount, was her concern about her choice of career, she realized that the dream had actualized what if thought about would be a metaphor, the *field* of work.

A patient who was an artist dreamed he was painting another person's torso vivid green. As he contemplated the dream, he realized that he had actualized the metaphor "green with envy," and he realized he had envious feelings about the person whose torso he had dreamed of painting.

I dreamed I was buying chairs. I bought more and more, but somehow they looked cheaper and less useful, and when I tried to get rid of them no one seemed to want them. On waking reflection I realized that the theme of the dream resembled my waking concerns about the stock market, which was then crashing, as well as some doubts about the wisdom of some major life decisions I had made. Like so many of us, I had been investing money with ambitions that became ever more grandiose as the market boomed. As it began to crash I realized that ambition had won out over good judgment and I had ignored some good advice to sell while I was ahead and be satisfied with more than reasonable profits. Then, as the market began to crash, I was in conflict between selling and accepting the reality of a big loss in order to avoid the risk of an even bigger one, and denying the reality of loss and buying more shares at a lower price in the hope of working financial alchemy to turn disaster into profit. In a similar vein I had recently made a significant life change that had not worked out as I had hoped, and I was struggling over whether to make the best of this unsatisfactory situation or make another equally major change that would involve accepting the disappointment and moving on. Two personal symbols of security in my waking life – "shares" of stock and "chairs" (my own special chair has always symbolized feeling at home) – had become undiffer- entiated concrete elements in a happening. On reflection I was able to re- cast the "events" in thoughtful symbolic form.

Another friend was experiencing the ravages of serious physical illness. After a day of significant and disquieting symptoms he dreamed that he was around or with a flock of birds over the Pacific ocean, which he could see like a map below him, heading toward the south pole. In what seemed to him simultaneity he was also outside a kind of large, round, cage-like enclosure, surrounded with ornate wrought iron fencing. There was an entrance and he knew it was dangerous to go in because there was no way out and it spiraled and dropped downward. The dramatization of colloquialisms such as "going south," or "going down the tubes," or "the bottom is falling out" was apparent to him on waking, but these things only became symbolic after the analogy between the action and thought was recognized and put into words. This dream is also of interest because of the undifferentiation or simultaneous conjunction of two different images and ideas.

Many dreams enact aphorisms and colloquialisms (missed the boat, carrying a lot of baggage, going into a field, green with envy, getting someone's number, being out to lunch). Unless one is familiar with the general culture and the particular idiom of the dreamer it can be difficult to make sense of these or even to know what segment of the dream contains the "punchline." The interpretive process involves taking the "event" and reasoning by analogy.

I do not want to make the blanket assertion that all dreaming is non-symbolic. As Freud noted, a representational process is involved: chairs for shares; delete key for pain removal; falling for fallen woman. I had a curious dream that seemed to be about representing. It involved trying to find a kind of template – "A4" – that would help me to understand what I took to be the structure of headphones with a microphone that had two pads on each earpiece and the mouthpiece. "A4" was conceived of in the dream as a kind of wheelbarrow or tricycle structure with the apex of the A containing two pads and the ends of each of the legs each containing two more. I was making a symbol or a model. The key for me seems to be that the representation is in the form of an idiosyncratic, subjectively experienced enactment. Waking understanding involves thought: differentiating the dream state from the sleeping experience, reflecting upon and searching for meaning by analogy, and then perhaps translating meaning into symbolic thought.

Dreaming in spiritual cultures

Dreaming in spiritual cultures has been studied by a number of cultural anthropologists. Kracke (1999) has written about the Parantintin of the Amazon basin; Vitebsky (2001) about the Siberian Yakut; Nakashima Degarrod (1989) about the Chilean Mapuche and, along with Price-Williams (1982), about other Amerindian cultures; and Fabrega and Silver (1970) about the Zinacanteco of Southern Mexico. The work of others is summarized by Walter and Fridman (2004). Among the world's tribal and spiritually based cultures, still numerous despite the destructive conquests of "civilizing" western colonization, dreaming is not viewed according to distinctions such as waking/sleeping, internal/external/ reality/unreality, rational/irrational, self and other, past and present. In such cultures the dream itself has the same underlying primordial structure as dreaming in western culture. However, dream sharing and interactions based upon such sharing is also part of a community process that has a similar primordial structure. Both experiences have a concretely actualized, person–world undifferentiated, somatic (sensory-perceptual-motor) quality. And the nocturnal dream is not qualitatively or existentially distinguished from similar phenomena of waking "real" life. However, as we will see in the example to follow, persons in such cultures do not mindlessly enact their dreams; rather a thoughtful process that is integrated, often under the guidance of a shaman, regulates such interactions. Dreams are looked upon as time and space journeys in a unitary cosmic reality consisting of natural and supernatural realms and good and evil, stratified in the natural world between underworld, earth, sea and sky rather than conscious and unconscious mind. On such a journey the person might be transformed into another person or a significant animal. An important distinction between the sleeping and waking dream state, however, is that in waking life the primordial aspect of the interaction is also regulated and directed by thought in order to maintain harmony according to the values of the community.

In these cultures, as I describe in Chapters 11–14, shamans are the guides or mediums who transit between the worlds of thought and of dreaming and are sanctioned by the community to interpret meaning and direct action. The shaman thinks about the experience analogically, but the analogy is to real events, past, present and future, rather than to intrapsychic concerns, and he or she derives meaning, omen and portent from the process. In other words, the model of PMA accounts for much of the waking experience and interaction of persons in spiritual cultures just as well as it accounts for the experience of the sleeping dreamer in western culture, but in the waking state that meaning and interaction is interpreted and directed by thoughtful mind.

Before elaborating these ideas, however, I take note of the fact that the distinction between the dream as an irrational, intrapsychic, unrealistic experience and as an alternate form of personal expression, learning and engagement in the waking community is not always entirely clear-cut in western culture. Charles Dickens' *A Christmas Carol* is an example. Ebeneezer Scrooge vents his mean-spirited miserliness on his clerk, his nephew Bob Cratchit, before closing shop for the holiday on Christmas Eve. Bob and his family are living in poverty because of his meager salary, and they have a seriously ill child, Tiny Tim, who is not receiving the medical care he needs. Scrooge falls asleep on Christmas Eve and has dream visitations from the spirit world by his equally avaricious and now deceased former business partner. He is taken on a journey back to his deprived and tormented childhood, which he had forgotten about, is warned by his deceased avaricious former business partner about what will happen to him if he does not change, and is taken on a prophetic journey to the future in which he sees that Tiny Tim will die if he does not mend his ways. He awakens informed by these nocturnal journeys, changes his behavior and hence his life, and harmony in the little community of which he is a part is re-established. The nature and function of the dream in *A Christmas Carol* is similar to that in spiritual cultures, as we will see in Chapter 8. Dreaming and waking experience are integrally related, time is not rationally differentiated, ancestors are alive, the dream expresses belief, and thoughtful understanding of it as portentous guides action in the community.

Dreaming as an aspect of community interaction: The Asian tattoo and the stolen child

In Chapters 8–10, I present material on culture, shamanism, and the relationship between shamanism and psychosis, obtained from personal experience in Maori culture. The two dreams, related events and community interactions I summarize next were told to me by a Maori acquaintance. They illustrate the undifferentiation between the worlds of the dream, the spirits and the everyday world of interpersonal events, and the way these elements interact with one another in a socio-centric spiritual culture with consequences in community life that seem remarkable to westerners immersed in self-centric thinking.

The characters I shall designate as M, the Maori acquaintance who experienced and reported the events to me; C, a female co-worker of M's who had a casual acquaintance with M and his wife, W; and D, their infant daughter. C told M of a dream she had in which M's wife W was lying prone with her back exposed. Asian characters were tattooed down her vertebral column and at the sacrum they diverged to the left. C reported the dream to M because it was highly out of the ordinary to have a dream about a work colleague, and she found the dream both strange and possibly portentous of community meaning. Some months later W had a very upsetting dream in which D, her infant daughter, had been kidnapped by an Asian couple. In the dream W followed the couple to a house where they were holding the child captive and tore off the wallpaper, revealing the names, written in an Asian language, of many children, one of whom she knew was her daughter. In the same dream W sensed "something" in a tree outside the house. It was an invisible ominous watching presence. M asked his wife W what she thought it might be, and after repeating she had only sensed something she added it might be "a mischevious monkey of some kind." The day following this dream M experienced a sharp pain in his back in the exact distribution of the Asian characters tattooed on his wife's spine in his colleague C's dream, deviating at the base of his own spine. He experienced the pain as spiritual rather than physical.

M spent some time thoughtfully reflecting on what all this meant, and it occurred to him that he and his wife were godparents of the first child of an Asian couple, and that there had been some friction between the couple and members of their extended family members over their decision to go outside their culture to find godparents to their child, which was construed as severing ties with the child's ancestors. Thinking about his wife's dream M decided the Asian family had "*viewed* it [Maoris becoming godparents] as an alien abduction. We had stolen away their next link in their family chain." In Maori culture, as in the Asian culture, children are the continuing link with the past and with the ancestors and, as M stated when he told me the dream, that "is a very *grave* thing indeed." He realized this couple had recently had another child and wondered if they were considering asking M and W to be godparents again, whether the dream represented the deviation of the ancestral line which is the spine of the culture, and whether W's complementary dream and M's pain in the spine might be an omen or prophecy about the significance of such an action. M believed that the pain he had experienced "was an indication that I was on the right track and basically if I did the right thing the pain would cease." He reasoned that the house in which the names were written under the wallpaper was the family house and that his wife's dream and his pain had been a way of bringing to their attention how they might feel if such a thing were to happen to them. At this point he decided to ask his Asian friends if they were considering asking him and his wife to be godparents to their new child and they said yes, they had been meaning to ask for some time but had not had the opportunity. M told them that he and his wife were honored but explained why it might be better if they looked within their own culture. The pain at the base of his spine, which had been intermittent since the day following his wife's dream, then ceased. His friends decided to do as he suggested.

M concluded that the elders of the Asian community had used this means of conveying a message, and he decided to speak with the elder in the Asian community whom he believed might be responsible. He apologized to her for the hurt she and the community might have experienced. Then he sought out the grandmother of the child for whom he was godfather, a woman he sensed had a deep spiritual understanding, and he told her the entire story, how he had interpreted the dreams and what he had done to make restitution. She nodded knowingly. He asked her about the ominous presence in the tree in his wife's dream, without mentioning what she had sensed it might be, and she said, "Ahhh, the monkey!" and told him that a monkey was the family guardian figure whose role it is to protect their ancestral line and to torment and punish those who might bring harm to it.

I have described dreams by two casually related persons, one of whom is Maori, the thoughtful interpretation that they conveyed messages of community significance, the interactions he initiated as a result, and the sharing of PMA within the group. Each dream conforms to the principles of primordial mental activity, as does their interweaving in the waking life of members of the community through the initiative of a thoughtful interpreter. The result is primordial mental states in thoughtfully controlled interaction. The dream world is undifferentiated from the spirit world, the world of ancestors, and the present journeys and interactions of the participants and the result, guided by thought, regulates and maintains harmony in the community.

Chapter 7

The primordial mind in everyday life

I began the discussion of phenomenological manifestations of PMA with what might be its most striking manifestation – dreaming. There are more extraordinary manifestations to come – creativity, minds in interaction in spiritual cultures, shamanism and psychosis. Primordial mental activity is not of itself an extraordinary thing, however; it is as much the fabric of "ordinary" everyday life as thought. These other manifestations are more difficult to detect, especially in western culture, because they do not stand out and demand attention, and because their use of the same formal information and language, and of the same innate abilities to make sensory-perceptual distinctions as does thought, tends to mask their presence. In this chapter I make reference to less obvious phenomena, including examples of more or less simultaneous and dissociated expressions of similar material in thought and in PMA, and of heated interchanges from a recent American presidential campaign.

Attachment

In Chapter 4 I described one of the less obvious manifestations of PMA, the finely choreographed and seemingly reflexive interaction between attuned parents and their infants. Primordial mental activity has significant adaptive value at a time when thinking is rudimentary and communicative language has yet to develop, because the peremptory, affect-inducing power of infantile crying and thrashing about conveys states of need and distress and influences caregivers immediately and deeply. Reciprocally, some of life's deepest learning on the part of the infant occurs at this phase of undifferentiated psychosomatic identity (not identification).

Social phenomena involving trance and ecstasy

There are many culturally unremarkable ways in which people deliberately shift the balance from thought toward an altered supernatural or spiritual state of mind that is characterized by passionate beliefs, holistic responses to others and to the environment, and at times hallucinatory and delusional experience. Fasting or starvation, isolation and sensory deprivation, sleep deprivation and mind-altering substances tend to induce trance states whereas sensory-motor overstimulation during group ritualistic behavior including rhythmic responsive chanting and dancing tend to produce ecstasy. There are numerous social sanctions for such behavior. Most religions have important practices and observances of this kind, though in many instances they have become attenuated symbolic observances for the average person and are mind-altering only for the serious practitioner. The fasting of Islamic Ramadan, Jewish Yom Kippur and Christian Lent; rigorous Buddhist-inspired meditation sittings; Catholic experiences of seeing visions at shrines; practices of monastic isolation, food and sleep deprivation, and sometimes self-flagellation or scourging; and fundamentalist Protestant practices of ecstatic responsive singing and dancing are a few examples. All these psycho-somatic-sensory-perceptual-motor practices tend to induce undifferentiated hallucinatory and delusional belief states and, as is characteristic of the force or pressure of PMA as a learning modality, they can become socially contagious. The mass hysteria that results may in some instances have the quality of group rapture, a "love in," but in other instances, when driven by rageful affects, can have a darker side and impel people into a frenzy of action associated with undifferentiation of their own negative affects (unrepresented rage) from the feeling states of perceived enemies. The result is such things as cultism, persecution, demagoguery, war, genocide, and destruction of one culture, nation or people by another. Such expressions cross the border into the psychotic spectrum, which is the subject of Chapter 13.

Primordial mental activity rarely manifests itself in pure culture without some evidence of thought. Dreaming and extreme instances of schizophrenia are two examples of PMA in the absence of thought. Mostly, however, thought is present to some degree and the behavioral result depends on the relationship between the two, ranging from regulation of primordial mind so that its expressions are constructive in the life of the personality and the community, to extremes of dissociation so that PMA dominates mental life in ways that are not so constructive. I suspect that in the course of ordinary daily life we all go in and out of primary mental states, generally without awareness that any transition is occurring. Sometimes this phenomenon is random and the states are not integrated with thoughts while at other times it occurs in a more disciplined and controlled way.

One interesting phenomenon I speculate about is habit formation in adults, acquisition of complex and more or less automatic patterns of expressing and responding through a thoughtful learning process that eventuates in letting go of much of the thoughtful part under certain selective circumstances. Examples that come to mind include the more or less automatic ways I have come to respond to my patients with my own personality, learned through decades of training, while simultaneously in parallel process "thinking" theoretically about what is going on and fine tuning the automatic part as a consequence. This may be similar to the state of reverie Bion describes, and its relationship to the thoughtful, highly theoretical part of his mind that obviously played a major role in his clinical work. A friend of mine who teaches yoga describes the results of a lengthy, arduous, thoughtfully conducted learning process in much the same way. Another experience common to most of us is learning to drive a car. It is possible that the learning process occurs on two levels more or less simultaneously, and that over time the thoughtful mind gradually and in a controlled way relinquishes control to primordial mind.

Examples of simultaneous dissociated expression of PMA and thought

The particular examples I have chosen from my clinical practice illustrate a phenomenon in which similar mental content is expressed in more or less simultaneous dissociation by primordial mind and by thought. I believe this is the structure that Matte-Blanco intended with the concept of "Simassi." For illustration I turn to examples involving patients in psychoanalytically informed treatments who were not manifesting severe psychotic pathology at the time of the vignettes.

A married woman I will call Dorothy, whose therapy gradually revealed the significant emotional distance she maintained but more or less effectively disguised from others with her friendly and compliant attitude, was nearing the end of her reproductive years without having faced and resolved the question of having children. At the time of the vignette she informed me that her husband, who would like children, had begun to point out that she never discussed the issue with him and to insist that they talk about it and try to resolve it. This led her to realize how little she had thought about it herself, and how much she tended to withhold what thoughts she did have from others.

Dorothy began the hour I am about to describe in a familiar manner, avoiding eye contact. She told me that as she was driving to her session she found herself having what for her are unusual thoughts, wondering what it would be like to be a mother. She described a fantasy of walking along a beach holding her baby with her husband nearby, and then remarked that she could not recall the remainder of the fantasy. A lengthy silence ensued in which I began to feel distant, as though I did not exist. Eventually I made myself interrupt the silence by reviewing in a sympathetic manner what she had told me at various times about the striking absence of fantasy and imagination in her life in general, as well as her lifelong reluctance to share personal thoughts of any kind with anyone else. She was grateful for my comment and we began to talk of the relationship between the dearth of fantasy and her reluctance to entertain hope and then be disappointed, and related the reluctance to her position in her family, where her emotional needs were generally overlooked and subtly labeled as weakness or "badness" and she was given much praise for seeming not to need anyone or anything.

After about half an hour she suddenly recalled the remainder of the beach fantasy. It involved looking directly at both the baby and her husband as a way of sharing the emotional experience of mothering and conveying a sense of dependency and need for help. She realized the reflexive nature of her tendency to isolate herself and became frightened about its implications both for her marriage and for motherhood. I inquired whether she could recall what had transpired around forgetting the fantasy earlier in the hour. She described having images in her head and having a struggle over what they meant and what to do about them. I remarked that this seemed to be the very issue she was talking about, isolating herself and convincing herself that she did not need anyone. On hearing this she exclaimed, with obvious excitement, that she had just remembered that I was in the original fantasy; not *really*, she reassured me, but in the sense that I was a caring presence within her as she was holding the baby and being with her husband.

During this hour, as Dorothy talked thoughtfully about rejection and alienation in her life past and present, and about withholding and presenting herself as self-sufficient because to need something from someone was equivalent to being bad, she was simultaneously, in primary mental expression, isolating herself. She did not differentiate past from present or me from her own psyche. I felt the pressure of her silent dismissal of me as though I didn't exist. When she became more able to think about what she had been dramatizing in PMA she reassured me that I was not "really" there with her on the beach, experiencing in an undifferentiated manner her remaining confusion between thought and delusional belief.

From a diagnostic perspective, a patient I will call John might be said to have manifested a narcissistic personality disorder of mild to moderate severity. In his early thirties he had not yet achieved an autonomous identity with regard to the basic elements of career and close relationships. He remained somewhat adrift in his life and for the most part depended financially on his wealthy and accomplished father, working sporadically at jobs beneath his abilities and spending leisure time with friends, engaging in game playing that, from my perhaps generationally biased perspective, seemed adolescent in nature. The session that follows is intended to illustrate the simultaneous or near simultaneous expression of analogical mental content both in thought and in primordial expression.

John was a few minutes late to his appointment, which was not an unusual occurrence. As was also commonplace, he did not seem aware of his lateness, and proceeded to tell me that he had been thinking about how he functions according to a system learned in his family where members say all the "right" things, such as how much they care about one another, but are complicit in avoiding responsibility for one another's well-being. That is, "I won't notice and reproach you for your irresponsibility toward me if you don't notice mine toward you." He gave examples from family life and then voiced the fear that if I knew about this part of his personality I would reject him. He interrupted his narrative as he suddenly remembered that for several weeks he had been intending to tell me that he would have to cancel an hour less than a week hence. In a casual tone of voice he asked me to reschedule the appointment. I realized that I felt annoyed that he had given me such short notice, at his mindless pressuring of me and apparent lack of thoughtful awareness that this might inconvenience me. As I continued to listen without commenting I realized that he had involved me in an enactment of the very issue he was thinking and talking about. I suggested to him that we think about his "forgetfulness" and the meaning of his request. After an uncomfortable silence he acknowledged he had not been respectful of my needs and had assumed that I would make special accommodations for him so that he need not feel guilty or regretful about what he had done.

Suddenly he realized that his request to reschedule related to the issue about which he was talking, and associated what was transpiring between us to his role in his family. As he began to think and to learn about what he was actualizing with me, I felt more able to listen and think objectively and dispassionately. He told me that he was the designated family "flake," and that from an early age his parents sent him to a succession of therapists for his "illness," in addition to providing most of his financial support, so that he felt no obligation to choose a career and implicitly settled for the role of disturbed person who did not have to grow up and be responsible. He gave examples of his parents' self-preoccupation when he was growing up, and of his sense that they did not want to know about his needs and distress and about the inconsiderate way they were treating him because they were so absorbed in their own issues. He said that in return for absolving them of this responsibility, suppressing his anger and not blowing the family cover, he felt license not to have to become a caring, responsible adult. He admitted that in some respects he had not taken his treatment seriously or been considerate of me; it was his role to be the disturbed patient and mine to be his caretaker. He apologized for his thoughtless behavior, and began to look and act more enthusiastic as he resumed work on his internalized relationship with his parents.

John had a reasonably well-developed thinking capacity to begin with, so that the therapeutic task of reflecting on primordial mental expression presented the kind of challenge posed by being asked to think about one's dreams. Because at the level of thought he was already aware of some of the dimensions of the problems in question, it is difficult to construe this interchange from the perspective of a dynamic unconscious and repression of thoughts and feelings. At the same time it is apparent that his knowledge of himself was ultimately expanded and even corroborated by making conscious the fact that he was articulating the same issue analogously in conscious thought and in primary expression.

Another kind of relationship between thought and primordial mental activity that is especially common during the course of successful therapy of persons whose functioning has for the most part been primordial is alternation between thought, which takes psychological work, and primordial mental activity, which does not. I believe this is what Matte-Blanco was referring to when he named a bi-logical mental structure "Alassi." In the context of therapy such an abandonment of thought can have a defensive significance. The following vignette about Lisabeth, the course of whose therapy I describe in Chapter 14 along with her own first-person account, illustrates the struggle between thinking about her painful conflicts related to her mother and brother and having to make difficult decisions about action, and primordial mental activity. Thinking takes work, conceptualization and bearing of painful feelings, and being aware of conflicts and difficult decisions that must be made, whereas primordial mental activity based on wishful solutions is somatic-psychic and characterized by belief and enactment.

Lisabeth began the hour by telling me: "I feel like something is the matter with me today. I've been all over the place, distracted, I can't focus or settle down. I feel lethargic, no energy. I have no sense today of who I am or what's important to me. I don't know what's the matter." After a pause she added: "I was upset by yesterday." I repeated what she had said as a question: "You were upset by yesterday?" She responded concretely: "Yes." I asked what she meant. She said: "It was what we talked about." I countered: "Yesterday didn't upset you." I experienced her as being and acting, rather than thinking. I was not sure what to say to her so I remained silent. After a silence she began to recall something of what we had talked about in the previous hour and she remarked: "It's how I felt like my mother is alive and I'm part of her. How I told you after she died and I looked in her wallet and found the photo of X [a man mother had claimed to be involved with after her divorce from Lisabeth's father, but Lisabeth rarely ever saw]. I had to keep it because she had kept it. I don't know what to do about all this and it bothered me." I responded: "Something is bothering you *now*" and she said: "I guess I haven't felt like doing any work on my problems." At this juncture she recalled times earlier in the day when she started to think more specifically about writing her older brother a letter expressing her anger at his lifelong demeaning treatment of her and repeated attacks on her for any expression of individuality and autonomy, and her related almost literal belief she was excrement. Early in our work Lisabeth was literally and somatically convinced I believed she was "shit." She regularly had near-disabling cramps and diarrhea in the office bathroom prior to appointments. As she talked about this she used the phrase: "The thought passed through my mind." I responded: "You mean that you eliminated it from your mind." After concretely reiterating what she had said as though I had not heard her correctly she began to think, and agreed.

During the day she had recalled a specific incident from childhood where her brother had recruited her to help him catch minnows for fishing bait and was demeaning of her behavior. She remarked: "I wrote 'minnows' on the paper and put it in the drawer so I would remember it." I commented: "You excreted it into the drawer so you could eliminate it from your mind." Again, after some thought, she agreed. Then she said she thought briefly about including in the imagined letter a suggestion that they meet face to face in order to have a mature discussion about the state of their relationship, but she concluded: "It would probably end the relationship." She realized she hadn't thought more about that, either. I was aware that she and her brother had had virtually no communication for several years other than some discussion about handling practical matters related to their mother's death, and prior to that several instances where he had exploded with rage at her, the last involving telling her and her husband to leave his house. I commented: "But there is no relationship, only an illusion. If you were to meet it would have to be to determine whether there could be one."

Suddenly she remembered she had probably forgotten to take her medication this morning. She had been taking a small dose of an SSRI for a long time and on a number of occasions when she tried to stop she had become more distressed and mentally disorganized. I reminded her of a recent conversation, typical of many in the past, when she voiced the belief that the solution to her problems would be to stop taking the medication or stop seeing me, in order to see if she could manage without. I remarked that this was yet another example of elimination rather than thinking and feeling. Then she remembered a conversation she had had earlier in the day with the wife of a tenant couple who were renting a condominium she owned. She had taken a personal interest in the woman, who was apparently mistreated by her husband. The woman tended to deny the abuse and to rationalize that her husband was special and "idiosyncratic." Lisabeth told the woman that she needed to confront her husband. She said to me: "I told her, 'you don't have all the time in the world;' I played the older mother figure to her. But I realize now that her excuses were exactly how my mother excused my brother's bad behavior [he lived with their mother all his life and often had violent tantrums] and I saw him the same way, as special, unusual, idiosyncratic, and made excuses for him." "You continue to," I responded. She realized she had behaved with this woman like her mother tended to act with others, freely pontificating to them about how they should live their lives, while denying that her own emotional and relational life was very limited. Next she recalled another thought from earlier in the day, a wish to be back at her old job. She realized this was really a wish to escape, as she had used the idolization of her former colleagues as a way to deny and dissociate herself from her problems and pretend everything was fine.

By this time in the hour she had become much more active and thoughtful. She returned to the issue of initiating a mature conversation with her brother and told me that she knew when she wanted to schedule it, but realized she was afraid of him and commented that the time she had in mind felt as though it would be too soon, like it was right now. "When would that be?" I asked. "About a month from now," she said. I remarked: "You feel that time does not exist; then is now, there is no remembering and no future, and also that you have all the time in the world." She responded that her brother's rage at her had always been in the open, but he had no idea how angry she was, and she was frightened about what might happen should she tell him. I knew both from the transference and from various vignettes she had shared that although she had never exploded with rage at him as she said he had toward her, there were many ways in which she had more or less subtly attacked and devalued him. In her therapy it had taken much work for her to be able to identify, conceptualize and accept her own rage. So I remarked: "He probably doesn't know he's angry at you, either; you didn't know about your anger. There has never been a direct, mature discussion between you; it's all been enacted thoughtlessly." "That's true," she said. "It's been the family style. If someone had told me I was angry I would have acted condescending like mother while believing that there was something wrong with them." She continued: "I'm afraid he'll get in a rage at me and tell me I'm bad and I'll crumple again and apologize and beg and agree I've been a shit."

She was now able to remember that she had been thinking more seriously than before of resolving her pathological dependencies on mother and brother, and having a direct, mature discussion with her brother. But because the thought had frightened her she had psychologically reverted to a lifelong undifferentiated identity with mother that involved not having to think for herself and do psychological work (her mother had infantilized her in some respects and never expected her or her brother to act maturely), and led to the related feeling that mother knew everything, whereas she, Lisabeth, was just a shit. The hour was drawing to a close, and it was apparent that, as was often the case, she felt much better than at the start. I remarked that the issues of separation she was talking about were very important but perhaps even more important was the question of why she could not remain more consistently self-aware, be able to stop and think rather than evacuate her mind and spring into unconscious action. After some discussion I concluded: "You choose to be a mindless nothing and let me/mother define what's going on because if you had a mind and a thoughtful self you might have to separate from mother and from me and lead your own life, and the prospect frightens you."

An example from politics

Finally, I turn to an example from the rhetoric of politics taken from news releases about the 2008 American presidential campaign between the Democratic candidate and ultimate victor, Barack Obama, and the Republican John McCain. McCain had been attempting to differentiate his views from those of the incumbent Republican president, despite a significant past record of agreement and support, by claiming that he represented change. Obama responded to that comment with a metaphor actually taken from remarks McCain had made about Hillary Clinton during the Democratic presidential primary race – "You can put lipstick on a pig but it is still a pig." Obama's remark was a thoughtful metaphorical attempt to pressure his opponent. McCain heard the remark concretely as an assault, as perhaps he himself had originally intended it in his comment about Clinton, and responded indignantly with the belief that Obama had concretely called his female running mate, who was then a figure of contention in the campaign, a pig. Not only was his interpretation literal and enactive, but its objects or predicates, lipstick and pig, had been disconnected from the subject – which was whether McCain represented change – and reconnected in an undifferentiated wishful way (the wish being to find something in his opponent to attack) with his running mate (lipstick= female=running mate=pig). The words are no longer elements of metaphor but epithets or stones, and the result is a kind of name-calling. McCain also seemed not to remember that it had been he who first used the phrase "putting lipstick on a pig," during the preceding Democratic primary election campaign.

In another instance McCain did not differentiate his negative feelings about Obama from what Obama had clearly and thoughtfully said and did not distinguish who was attacking whom or what. He responded to a thoughtful position of Obama's that children should be educated to identify inappropriate advances from adults concretely as though Obama were a pedophile. He asserted that Obama was an advocate of sex education for kindergartners.

Subsequently, in an apparent effort to deny the reality of a major economic downturn that most people were blaming on the Republican administration then in power, McCain asserted that the economy was in fine shape. When challenged with data he claimed that what he really meant is that American workers are the best in the world. In so doing he fused or failed to differentiate two ideas (being American and the economy), eliminated contradiction (bad economic news/the economy is in fine shape) and created a forceful assertion of belief (not communication) that he was right and his opponent un-American.

McCain's rhetoric can be understood in terms of primordial mental activity in which there is no contradiction or conflict between ideas – black=white=black – so that they become joined together to make a wish seem real and presented as a belief with force. Time does not exist, and there is no history to confirm or contradict the current statement. As there is no causality or logical sequencing there can be no testing of ideas against an objective or external reality. The words themselves are not used to represent or symbolize ideas and thereby to communicate meaning with the intent of stimulating thought, but rather in a formal or literal or epithetic sense to express beliefs or call names and hence pressure others. Obama's responses are thoughtful, but he consciously uses metaphor to throw something back at his opponent.

Many political battles are because PMA is "chosen" as a more forceful form of rhetoric than communicating thoughts about substantive issues and allowing them to stand or fall on their merits in the minds of equally thoughtful listeners. Those who operate more from thought tend to dismiss their rivals as lacking intelligence, not valuing facts or logic, and even as outright liars. Those using primordial mental activity believe that opponents lack faith, and in an instance such as this election are Godless, unpatriotic and un-American. From each perspective there is "truth" but from a broader perspective that takes into account the misunderstanding that occurs when a thoughtful expression comes up against one of PMA, both are mistaken.

Chapter 8

The relationship between mental processes in spiritual cultures

There is a reciprocal relationship between mind and culture. Within neurobiologically limited parameters the cultural context in which we live and develop our minds determines our cosmology, the way we look at ourselves in relation to the world around us. Our minds, in the process of social interaction, in turn produce and reproduce the culture. I have divided cultures into two broad categories for heuristic purposes – spiritual and western – in order to highlight the particular mental operation that is most highly valued – PMA or thought – as well as the particular relationship between the two that characterizes each. I recognize that there is almost no such thing as a "pure" culture type due mostly to western colonization of most of the world, so that such a division is an oversimplification. The term "spiritual" is not synonymous with "religious," but connotes a life that is oriented to and guided by the world of the spirit and the dream.

The self-centric perspective of western industrial civilization, which makes dualistic distinctions between the separate self and external reality and between aspects of personal mind that are considered rational and others that are irrational thought and irrationality, is the inescapable perspective from which I write. It is very different from the collective or socio-centric perspective of spiritual cultures, which include numerous ethnically homogenous tribal cultures and subcultures within western cultures.

Table 8.1 summarizes salient characteristics of mental activity in spiritual cultures dominated by PMA in contrast to western culture, which is dominated by rational thought. Each culture type employs a unique spatial metaphor. The western self-centric perspective defines growth and maturation as a process of separation and individuation of the person from a "real" world that is looked upon as external, and development of a complex inner "mind of one's own." The individual mind is structured vertically within this horizontal self–world duality. There is a thoughtful, rational, conscious part and a mysterious, irrational unconscious part. There are other mental distinctions as well, for example between a remembered or historical past and a present that is very different, between the state of sleep

Table 8.1 Mental activity in western and spiritual cultures

	Western culture	Spiritual culture
What motivates mind	Identified emotions	Affect-based premonitions, intuitions, beliefs
Nature of experience and narrative	Self-centric and dualistic. The separate mind objectifies the "real" outside world and the inner self and uses rational logic to comprehend the personal journey through life demarcated by time, events and memories, and ended by death	Socio-centric and holistic. The spirit journeys through a timeless, existential, dream-like cosmos interpreted in terms of spiritual and ancestral presences and their significance to the community
Dimensions of time and space	Divisions include self and world or other, intrapsychic and external reality, reality/unreality, rationality and irrationality, past (memory), present and future	Existential timeless cosmos in which the soul journeys and encounters good and evil, and natural and ancestral forces
Development involves	Separation and individuation into a self with an inner life in relation to an external world	Understanding one's special place in a collective community and cosmos
Expression, learning and communication	Meaning exchanged through ideas and symbols	Meaning informed by dreaming and PMA; interactions guided by thought
Relationship between PMA and thought	Thought predominates and PMA is devalued and suppressed, except in select situations	PMA predominates and there is a lively dialectic between thought and PMA, each informing the other

and its unique phenomenon of dreaming and the state of wakefulness and "reality," and between individual life and death.

There remain an astounding number of tribal cultures in the world (Bourguignon, 1973) to say nothing of larger eastern cultures based on Hinduism and Buddhism. There is an impressive similarity among their views of person and cosmos (Eliade, 1964; Nicholson, 1987; Robbins, 1996), especially considering that the smaller cultures are likely to be separated in terms of geography and communication, and over the millennia as well. Spiritual cultures are socio-centric. My personal experience with such cultures comes from contact with New Zealand Maori who do cultural healing in a western-sponsored mental health clinic. Such cultures are based on the idea of a unitary collective consciousness, consisting of persons and elements of the natural world, which is timeless, never ending. Members of such cultures appear self-effacing to western eyes but they are not. They do not aggrandize themselves or stand out in relation to others because they know that it is the timeless eternal collective of which they are a part that is important. The cosmos is stratified existentially, as forces operating in the world within which the person is journeying and acting, not intrapsychically within a separate self that is differentiated from the external world. Within this cosmos they also make dualistic and tripartite distinctions, but not on such dimensions as reality/unreality, rationality/irrationality, or past/present. All experience is considered to be equivalently "real" and valuable.

Significant distinctions relate to such matters as belief (good and evil); the ancestral world and the day-to-day world; the soul or spirit and the body; the underworld, the earth and the sky. The underworld, the demonic emotional struggles of the spirit between good and evil, and the dream state, are not viewed as unconscious elements within the psyche, but are perceived as cosmic forces amongst which the person journeys or travels, interacts with others and struggles, both waking and sleeping, alive and "dead" (but not gone). There are stories of creation and extinction, but while death of the body is accepted there is not the kind of distinction between past (the dead) and present (the living) as in western culture. In these cultures the ancestral world continues to exist in spirit as audible and visible presences, voices and visions that are just as real and present as any other interpersonal experience. Maori, for example, derive meaning by sharing dreams and other spiritual experiences and interacting based upon them, as the example in Chapter 6 illustrated. They are commonly in visual and auditory contact with their ancestors who guide and admonish them. In these cultures the soul or spirit is not believed to be isomorphic with the body, but rather an essence that can travel in time and space. What westerners call death or termination of individual life is for spiritual cultures the permanent severance of the relationship between the soul and body but not loss of a separate self.

The spiritual world view is of a golden age, a once unified and harmonious cosmos not entirely unlike the Biblical Garden of Eden, that split apart, fractured or disintegrated due to a global cataclysm, with the result that the person lost vital connection. The task of person and culture is to re-establish these primary connections, and the guide in many of them is the shaman (Nicholson, 1987; see also Chapter 10), who has developed the special ability to transit back and forth between this fragmented, dismembered, cataclysmic state and thought, between the equivalent realities of the spirit world of ancestors and the more mundane day-to-day world, through a process of trance and ecstasy, or, as I would put it, to make controlled thoughtful transits between thought and PMA. Shamans utilize the information they gain in the service of the community and of healing. Their function is roughly analogous to the role of the psychoanalyst in western culture, except that the latter is not so generally respected and valued within the culture.

We are all constrained by our cultural context and westerners can only "know" about such cultures through the perspective and language of logic and "reality," hence there is an inevitable tendency to label such a world view as lesser, immature, primitive, superstitious and irrational. The western concept of anthropomorphism, for example, refers to a mental process that transforms and distorts "reality." In spiritual cultures shape-changing is a reality, a part of the way the cosmos works, making transformations between human, animal and natural worlds part of a spiritual journey through the cosmos. Even the concept of mythology has such an evaluative connotation. After all, what would we think if an Amazonian tribesperson referred to western science as mythology? In contrast, I believe that the variables that distinguish one culture type from another have to do with relative preferences for thought or for primordial mental activity, and with the nature of the relationship between the two in a given culture.

While most spiritual cultures seem to value the regulatory function of thought, albeit not so much as western culture, at least one culture has been discovered that has successfully resisted westernization and remained a closed society that appears neither to understand nor to value thought and instead functions totally in a way that seems consistent with the model of primordial mental activity. Daniel Everett, a missionary turned linguist and cultural anthropologist (2005, 2008; see also Colapinto, 2007) lived for many years among a Brazilian tribe known as Piraha. He is a linguist and has used his findings to contest the assertion of his former mentor Noam Chomsky that all languages have a "universal grammar," the test for which is the presence of recursion. While his reports have aroused curiosity and controversy in the linguistic community their significance for cultural anthropology has not been explored.

The Piraha are a hunter-gatherer tribe of perhaps 350 living in a series of small villages on the banks of the Maici River in the Amazon basin. Though small in number, the population is stable and the culture and language are remarkably resistant to outside influence, which has primarily consisted of Portuguese traders and Christian missionaries. The Piraha disdain to learn any language other than their own, which has a prosodic, bird-like singing and whistling quality with extraordinarily subtle nuances. Everett lived among them intermittently for several decades, first as a missionary and then as an anthropologically oriented linguist, and he and his former wife and children may be the only outsiders to have mastered their difficult language. His accounts have kindled a major nature/nurture controversy among linguists about whether there are universal invariant principles of grammar that are hard-wired or whether language is mostly indigenous and contextually determined. The linguistic aspect of Piraha and its relationship to primordial mental activity are examined in Chapter 15 on language. I believe that the linguistic phenomena are artifacts or aspects of a broader cultural difference that is best accounted for by the hypothesis that this tribe demonstrates an almost exclusive preference for primordial mental expression over thought.

Everett's general conclusion is that "Piraha culture constrains communication to non-abstract subjects which fall within the immediate experience of interlocutors" (2005, p. 621). He calls this the *immediacy of experience principle* (2008). The Piraha live entirely in the present moment in which reality is synonymous with immediate sensory-perceptual-motor experience. They make frequent use of a particular adjective/adverb to express something entering or leaving immediate perception, and what is out of sight is absent from discourse until again concretely present. Piraha language expresses what *is* and not what *was* or *will be* or what might be food for thought, so to speak. It is not used symbolically to represent other things or abstract ideas.

Piraha have no trouble navigating through life; places are identified not by an "internal" mental map or symbolic names but by concrete associations to things like the personal activity that is or was done there, or an identifying geographical feature or a connection with particular wildlife. Directions are given not in abstract concepts (right, left, etc.) but in relation to similarly immediately palpable concrete aspects of the environment and physical being.

In this world of immediacy there is no concept of time or words to express past, future or duration; no verbalized sense of logical sequence, causality or consequences. It follows that there is no memory in the sense of something that happened at another time and no collective history. They do recount experiences within the sensory-perceptual lifetime of the person, but these are told as though they are happening currently. They do not anticipate or plan for the future, either. For example, they do not stockpile goods for a future time when they might be needed.

As their experience is immediate so their discourse contains no fantasy and no shared cultural fiction or mythology. Piraha mental activity seems devoid of the qualities of abstraction, symbolization and logic that characterize thought. They do not make art, tell stories that involve imagination or fantasy, or create myths. Everett's visits to the Piraha have been by float plane, landing on the Maici river. Since the first of his visits the natives have taken to making airplane models out of balsa wood, but the activity is immediate and stimulus-bound, generated by airplane arrival. Not long thereafter the activity ceases and the models are discarded for they have no abstract or memorial significance; nothing remains to be thought about. This literal quality, lacking symbolism or analogy, was illustrated when a visitor attempted to communicate why he was spraying himself with bug repellent by imitating with gesture and sound the sound and flight of the insects and the activity of killing them, hoping that his pantomime would elicit thought and a representational name. He concluded with a gesture that linguistics calls recursive by slapping an imaginary mosquito. The

Piraha who were observing the show turned to Everett in puzzlement and asked why the man was hitting himself.

In this light it is not surprising that the Piraha have no written language, which requires a degree of abstraction and mental representation. And their spoken language lacks abstract qualitative descriptors. For example, while the natives are sensitive and responsive to color cues they do not have abstract words for colors. Instead they substitute likeness or identity. The object is not "red," it is like blood. They do not remember the name of a visitor; instead he or she is dubbed by the name of a native Piraha whose features bear some resemblance. Their language has few pronouns; instead they refer to concrete and specific names.

Piraha language also lacks numbers and sequential counting or quantifying concepts, another instance of absence of logic and abstraction. Even after months of classes Everett and his family conducted with the natives none were able to count to ten or add 1+1. This was not for lack of motivation, for it had been demonstrated to them that such learning might have value in helping them to negotiate more effectively with Portuguese traders with whom they have considerable commerce.

What westerners might think about as ideas, to the Piraha are things placed adjacent to one another, sequenced by contiguity or linearity rather than by temporal or causal logic. There are no subordinate clauses in Piraha speech, no recursive combining of one idea within another in a sentence.

Piraha language contains few kinship terms, and kinship bonds such as marriage are loosely maintained and very much of the moment. The most likely explanation is that they do not have abstract ideas of connection or bonding or an enduring representation of the relevant emotions. Someone who is gone from immediate sight or hearing is no longer a subject of discourse, although he or she is readily recognized on return. While the Piraha show affect and are generally a playful people who help one another out in practical matters, they do not seem to be aware of feelings about one another in the sense of enduring representations or emotional states that are necessary for more abstract notions of attachment. Where feelings of anger might be expectable there is instead action or enactment, usually in the form of distance or disengagement, and distraction with other aspects of immediate experience than the relationship.

Everett recounts vivid experiences about how Piraha deal with death and child rearing that are also consistent with a hypothesis of primordial mental activity, absence of emotional representation, of a sense of time past and future, and of consequences. A woman died a protracted death in breech childbirth while observers seemed indifferent. Everett recorded subsequent dialogue with her husband who repeated over and over words like "she is not here now" accompanied by tone and behavior that conveyed his obvious distress, but devoid of any articulation of emotion or attachment.

Infants and small children are given what to western eyes is an unusual degree of "freedom" to do whatever they want. Everett notes the absence of punishment for forbidden behavior or protection from harm, both of which involve a sense of time and ability to think logically about consequences. He observed a scene where an infant played with a sharp knife, risking self-mutilation, in the presence of seemingly unconcerned adults. Infants are nursed until the arrival of another child, often around four years, and then weaned abruptly and entirely, often screaming for nights on end while parents, nursing the new baby, seem oblivious. Ordinary western conclusions about such behaviors, for example that the Piraha do not care about one another, are belied by their close community, and affectionate and helping attitudes toward one another. Everett's interpretation is that they have a high degree of respect for one another's individuality and autonomy, and he points to the degree of self-sufficiency adults manifest, but this seems an equally implausible hypothesis because it involves abstract conceptualization of self-actualization and of goal-directed child-rearing. It seems more likely that they lack an abstract conception of causality and consequence, and that they are concrete and stimulus bound. In the instance of weaning, the idea of baby and need may be concretely expressed by the totally dependent nursing infant, much as Piaget and Klein recognized in their theories.

It may seem contradictory to my observation the the Piraha have no mythology, no myths about creation and destruction, to suggest that Piraha is a spiritual culture; but in fact its members are believed to become spirits, to change shape and identity, and they share belief in a spirit or dream world that they "see," believe, and collectively interact with. They share a sensory-perceptual-motor cosmology that for them is simply another aspect of reality. Their attitude toward dreams is that they are another kind of immediate real experience. Behavior that to the western observer seems to involve supernatural mythological beliefs and practices is not symbolic or fantastic to the Piraha. The spirit or dream world is equivalent in reality value to what we think of as the "real" world, and is contacted through spiritual transit into the land of the dead, often in enactments where persons are believed to change form and function. Everett (2008) recounts being present at what appeared to him and his family to be a mass hallucination by villagers of Xigagai, an evil spirit. A large group of natives could "see" Xigagai clearly and describe him in detail, and they were amazed that Everett could not. From a practical perspective their sleeping pattern might help to account for the absence of a boundary between primordial mental activity in dreaming and in waking life, and their readiness to resonate to one another's perception, for they have no clear demarcation between a time to sleep and a time to be awake, and generally sleep for an hour or two at a time throughout a 24-hour period.

Despite the absence of thought, of labeled and expressed emotions toward one another, of sharing by thoughtful linguistic communication, the

Piraha are not a solipsistic people whose use of primordial mental activity is maladaptive or psychotic. During the first three years of life there is a very close physical and emotional sharing bond between parents and infants. As adults they are a tightly bound social community of individuals who share similar experiences and similar basic affect states. This is strongly suggestive of positive primary bonding in the early attachment phase and a template of implicit or procedural knowledge that is caring and hence elaborated in a positive way by the primordial mental process.

The Piraha have been unable or unwilling to learn other languages even though they have been exposed to outsiders for several centuries, especially the Portuguese. Everett believes that their remarkable resistance to change relates to a qualitative disparity between their language and others, but perhaps it is because they "know" and value the fact that their minds work differently. They refer to themselves concretely as "straight heads," in contrast to those who speak other languages who are "crooked heads." Such behavior has an interesting resonance to western tendencies to view tribal cultures as immature, irrational, superstitious and even psychotic. The peculiarities Everett observed cannot be a matter of genetic inbreeding of neurological defect, for although the Piraha do not allow marriage outside the tribe it is accepted that their women are sexually active with outsiders, particularly the Portuguese traders. Hence their gene pool is always expanding and not entirely inbred.

Everett's work has stimulated both admiration and criticism, the latter mostly related to his challenge to the disciples of Chomsky and the principle of universal grammar. Some linguists have even conducted experiments with the Piraha to attempt to demonstrate that they are capable of recursive (self-referential) thinking even if they prefer not to use it, but the results have not been convincing. It is certainly possible that thought and the capacity for thought is present in the culture, for it is difficult to imagine human beings without some thought. However, those who believe that the Piraha are capable of thought and thought-based language must consider the possibility that the listener is unconsciously supplying the missing ingredients from his or her cultural context in order to "make sense" as, for example, when someone intent on communicating with a schizophrenic person "makes sense" of nonsensical utterances.

The Piraha are the only people I am aware of who seem to function almost exclusively in PMA. The hyperbolic example highlights some of the features of this mental process. Most cultures combine PMA and thought. Their mature members utilize thought to regulate the times and places where PMA is used and the uses to which it is put. The broad division between spiritual and western cultures, then, reflects the predominance of a particular mental activity, PMA or thought.

Chapter 9

The mind of a shaman

The term *shaman* comes from the language of Siberian hunter-gatherer tribes. Anthropologists use it as a generalization for community-designated authorities who act on behalf of the tribal community as mediums and interpreters between "this" world and the spiritual-ancestral world. Shamanism is almost as widespread as tribal cultures. A survey of 437 such cultures by Bourguignon (1973) found evidence of it in 89 per cent of cultures. Shamans provide important information not accessible to ordinary individuals and act as guides, finders, prophets and healers, helping to maintain harmony between the members of a community and the interpersonal, natural and supernatural worlds (Walsh, 1990). The shaman has mastered thoughtfully controlled entry into and exit from an altered state, trance or ecstasy. Viewed in light of the difference between spiritual cultures and western cultures noted in Chapter 8 the spiritual cosmology is represented existentially or spatially whereas western cosmology is represented in vertical strata within the individual psyche. The role of the shaman in spiritual cultures bears some resemblance to that of the psychoanalyst in the western world; that of guide on journeys to the "world" of PMA and of integrating interpreter of the phenomena encountered. Carl Jung, as we will see, appears to have been both psychoanalyst and shaman. He used the knowledge he obtained through painful journeys into his own mind to inform the way he worked with patients in his clinical practice. More about him in Chapter 10.

Contrary to western stereotypes shamans are unusually mature persons who have undergone rigorous and stressful training that enables them to negotiate in a controlled way between the mental worlds of thought and trance or ecstasy, to differentiate between the two states and to translate experiences from one context to another (Boyer *et al.*, 1964; Noll, 1983, 1985, 1989; Krippner, 2002; Walsh, 1990; Vitebsky, 2001; Eliade, 1964; Winkelman, 1990, 1992; Walter and Fridman, 2004). In the shamanic world the spirit is believed to be an essence that is not isomorphic with the body but can travel independently in time and space. If the soul and body are not periodically reunited, however, death is believed to ensue, hence transit into the spirit world is fraught with danger and requires special training and experience. Trance and ecstasy are the self-induced states that enable the shaman to travel to the world of the spirit, of dissolution, death and the dream, then reintegrate and be reborn. Trance or vision quest is a solitary, quiescent state induced by such things as sensory deprivation, physical hardship, isolation and ingestion of psychedelic substances, whereas ecstasy is induced by sensory and physical overstimulation, often in the presence of others, that reaches a crescendo of frenzy.

The altered state is one of belief or actual experience (Hoppal, 1987). The shaman enters the undifferentiated realm of experience where opposites and contradictions combine and merge, forms and shapes undergo metamorphosis, and experience is literal or concrete, taking the form of belief or happening. In this state the shaman "sees" and experiences things that do not fit into familiar categories, for example combinations of animal and human, one sex and the other. Achterberg notes "the distinction between body, mind and spirit is nil. Body is mind, and mind is spirit. Although the terminology might seem to indicate that the shamans are dealing with the mind, body and spirit as separate entities, in the literal sense they do not" (1987, p. 122). The experience is dream-like; in fact some cultures refer to it as dreamtime, indicating not only the gross similarity to dreaming but also suspension of the ordinary sense of time passing (Houston, 1987).

The shaman is an expert who has gained the perilous capacity for controlled travel to and exit from this world. Schmidt notes that: "The shaman takes power from the undifferentiated realm and brings it back" (1987, p. 67). Nicholson writes more specifically that "the shaman comes to know ultimate undifferentiated reality through his ecstatic experience and to know cultural differentiation through his analytic ability; further, he understands the need to arrange the world. Now he gathers this knowledge and goes to work" (1987, p. 69). According to Peters and Price-Williams (1980), who studied 42 societies from four different cultural areas, the relationship of the shaman to his or her altered state of consciousness has three characteristics: voluntary control of entry and exit, memory of the experience afterward, and ability to communicate with others during the altered state. Such capacity indicates that shamans are capable not only of functioning in PMA and in thought, but that they can integrate the two mental states and alternate between them in a controlled manner.

Shamans are chosen by the community in a variety of ways and for many reasons. One of them is demonstration of remarkable capacities as children. Some have an unusual richness and frequency of dreams, including ones that appear to contain important messages or prophecies. Many are capable of lucid dreaming or integration of the dream state and thought and it is possible that some experience synesthesia (Chapter 11). Some seem to have an uncanny ability to locate lost objects. Many have been voice-hearers since early childhood. A Maori elder who had attained the highest shamanic status in his community, that of *Tohunga*, and was widely known and respected for his accomplishments as healer, told me that when he was three years old his mother would find him in unusual places in the middle of the night, some of which he should not have been able to reach because they involved closed doors or other obstacles presumably insuperable to a child of that age. Often the "call" comes in the form of an adolescent disturbance that in western culture would be called a psychosis (Walsh, 1990) or a physical illness such as "epileptic" seizures accompanied by remarkable visions or dreams. The first-person account by Egan Bidois, a Maori *Matakite* or shaman, in Chapter 10, describes such an experience. Such phenomena are well documented for westerners in the Bible. Carl Jung experienced a pull toward madness at the apex of his career in mid-adulthood, and transformed the experience into one of enhanced ability and insight. More about Jung in particular and the complex interface between shamanism and psychosis will be found in Chapter 10.

Training to develop and harness these unusual traits is rigorous. It involves deliberate controlled exposure to and endurance of stress of the kind that is well known to induce what in the west would be called hallucinations, delusions and bizarre behavior. Such means as social isolation, physical and emotional stress to the point of torture, sleep deprivation, fasting and purging, and sometimes ingestion of mind-altering substances may be employed. These induce psychic experiences of torture, dismemberment, death or near-death, and under appropriate supervision and guidance lead to the experience of rebirth, reconstitution and identity transformation. The mastery of this kind of transit between mental states and the use of the journey to gain new information comprises the unique ability of a shaman. There is a resemblance, however attenuated, between such practices and those of the appointed seers of westernized religions including Christianity and Judaism, and perhaps the personal analysis that is required for certification as a psychoanalyst, which requires the trainee to engage with and come to terms with some of his or her own deeper unconscious mental processes as part of learning to help others navigate their personal journeys into emotionally difficult aspects of their psyches.

Whether shamans have unusual psychic powers, abilities to know and to influence what westerners think of as the real or external world, is difficult to research dispassionately from the deep-seated western perspective that tends to dismiss such ideas as foolish, superstitious, even psychotic. Western science, which is an aspect of thought, is one way of knowing, but it does not necessarily follow that it includes all of what can be termed knowledge. Joan Halifax (1979, 1982), a highly trained medical anthropologist, concluded that the scientific approach by definition precludes understanding of shamanic knowledge. In other words, while one can comment about the entire range of human experience from a single mental perspective, such a limited view is insufficient to understand the world through other perspectives. This is consistent with the thesis that thought and PMA are qualitatively distinct forms of mental activity. An analogy might be that although when we awaken we can re-cast the dream into thought, we have lost the essence of the experience; its inherent richness and meaning. This is much like the observation Matte-Blanco made that we can only know the realm of symmetric logic indirectly, by how it perturbs asymmetric logic.

Intriguing as the question of unusual shamanic powers is, it is incidental to a discussion of primary mental activity so I comment on it only in passing. Halifax concluded that the shaman has developed unusual sensitivity and compassion because he/she has confronted and struggled with the realm of human suffering in a way that those who dwell in rational thought and wittingly or otherwise suppress and relegate unconscious phenomena to sleep and dreaming do not. The shaman may heal by a voluntary identity merger (undifferentiation) with the sufferer and direct engagement with that person's suffering at a depth only attainable by someone who has grappled and continues to grapple with his or her own deepest suffering, fragmentation (dismemberment) and "death," followed by a process of re-integration, differentiation, and emergence as a cohesive, thoughtful person. It is a kind of psychological surgery, moving in a controlled, voluntary way from thought to PMA, and by that deep learning process into the "soul" of the other who is also in that state, doing the work and then returning.

There is much anecdotal evidence gathered by western observers and recorded in books including articles by interested observers that some shamans have uncanny abilities to heal and to find things hidden from the comprehension of others. Some of these accounts have been documented, though not in a way that would satisfy the canons of rigorous western science. For example, there are accounts of shamans who have healed persons with western-documented serious illness who have not responded to medical treatment, and of shamans who can identify and find hidden objects. Bosher (1974), an amateur anthropologist, writes of an experiment he conducted in a museum in Swaziland which involved hiding an unidentified object from a shaman who proceeded to go into trance, identify many of the characteristics of the object, and then find where it had been hidden. It is not only the western world that is skeptical whether shamans can perform paranormal feats. One of the tests or rites of passage of the apprentice shaman is to do such things and have them verified by members of his own community. Ingo Lambrecht (1998), a respected academic clinical psychologist in New Zealand, who wrote his doctoral thesis on the subject of shamanism, is also a *Sangoma* or South African shaman. His special abilities to find lost objects were recognized in childhood and developed through a rigorous and stressful initiation process involving apprenticeship to a teacher, known as *ukutwasa*. In the process of training he gained the ability to establish a controlled relationship with voices he had been hearing since childhood, using techniques including the capacity for lucid dreaming which he had discovered in himself in childhood. In the course of his training Lambrecht asked his teacher: "How would I know whether the voices I heard are the ancestors or just me simply going mad?" "Ah, that's easy," his teacher replied, "we *test* them." The "true ancestral voices" are those that in the eyes of the community offer accurate information, for example in finding valuable herbs and lost cattle, or in diagnosing and healing illnesses (Randall *et al.*, 2008, p. 337).

The discussion of shamanism has been culture-specific, as though it were a phenomenon of tribal spiritual cultures. Is there an equivalent of shamanic training and shamanism in western culture? If shamanism is defined as the consequence of an unusual degree of integration and dialogue between thought and PMA leading to phenomenology that is valued by the community, the answer might be a qualified "yes." Some members of monastic orders, some creative poets, novelists and artists (see Chapter 12), even some psychoanalysts might fit the description. Carl Jung's struggle with psychosis changed the nature of his therapeutic work with psychotic persons. Some of the methodology employed in the psychotherapy of psychosis involves enhancing dialogue and integration between thought and PMA. The very unusual psychoanalyst James McLaughlin (1993) might be another example. He was a dedicated student of his dreams. He kept elaborate records and used the dialogue between his waking thoughtful mind and his dreams to enrich his work. In subsequent chapters the complex relationship between shamanism, creativity and psychosis is explored further.

Chapter 10

Shamanism and psychosis

> Because I have fallen into the source of chaos, into the primordial beginning, I myself become smelted anew in the connection with the primordial beginning, which at the same time is what has been and what is becoming.
> (Carl Jung, October 1913, in *The Red Book: Liber Novus*, 2009, p. 247)

Shamanism as well as some forms of creativity and psychosis are generated from primordial mental activity. Yet they are very different from one another; shamanism and creativity utilize special abilities for the benefit of the community whereas psychosis is a state of disability that is a drain on community resources. The differences have to do with the extent of integration or dissociation of PMA from thought, and the adaptive or maladaptive relationship of the mental activity to the interpersonal and socio-cultural context. Creativity and psychosis are explored in chapters to come. This chapter is devoted to the complex relationship between shamanism and psychosis.

Until recently the centuries old western stereotype that equates tribal spiritual cultures with primitivism and immaturity prevailed, and many or most social scientists believed that shamanism is just another name for schizophrenia in such cultures (Noll, 1983; Kroeber, 1940; Linton, 1956; Devereaux, 1953, 1958; Silverman, 1967). Many cultural anthropologists have anecdotes about apparently psychotic persons who called themselves shamans. Just as some persons in western culture have messianic grandiose psychotic delusions, some persons in tribal cultures suffer from shamanic delusions. In this and the preceding chapter I make the case that most shamans are unusually mature individuals because of the trials they have had to master to reach their goal. However that does not mean there is no connection between shamanism and psychosis. The idea that some if not all shamans have had more emotional distress to struggle with than the average person, even incipient mental illness, is also commonplace among contemporary anthropologists. Joan Halifax (1982) calls the shaman a "wounded healer," capturing the relationship between disturbance, healing and growth, or as I would put it, the relationship between primordial mental activity and thought.

At least some instances of shamanism and psychosis seem to originate from a matrix common to both that has to do with the way future shamans are identified and chosen, either by others or by the personal experience of a "calling," a personal identity crisis of a kind that in western culture might be understood as an acute psychosis or at least the preamble to such a state (Walsh, 1990). An adolescent or young adult is forced to choose between struggling to master and control inner "demons" or succumbing to them. What is unique to spiritual cultures is that relatives or members of the community recognize a person with what are looked upon as special abilities in the realms of finding, prophesying and of dreaming, as well as a propensity to hear voices or have visions. In Chapter 11, I suggest that these characteristics represent an innate predilection for PMA and an unusual readiness to transit between PMA and thought. The outcome of such predispositions depends on whether the familial and cultural surround has been nurturing or invalidating and rejecting. In western culture such predispositions might either go unnoticed, leaving the individual in a state of alienation, or be defined and treated as pathological.

One clear difference between a shaman and a psychotic person is that the shaman is tested in a rite of passage by representatives of the community he or she is to serve for the presence of special abilities to gather useful information and to survive hardship. A common ritual of passage for the apprentice shaman is to find hidden objects while observed by others. In other instances special abilities to heal illness are noted. If we define psychosis as a state in which realistic adaptation and constructive self-care are severely limited, it seems unlikely that the judgment of an entire community could be deluded. However, as I note in Chapter 13, such group delusions have occurred many times in western culture, producing cults, gang leaders, and despots and their followers. Perhaps the relevant variable is frequency; virtually all spiritual cultures have shamans, whereas western cultures have leaders for the most part and cult leaders like Hitler only occasionally.

Voice hearers

In western culture increasing numbers of people are "coming out of the closet," identifying themselves as self-healed "voice hearers," persons who have had hallucinatory experiences all their lives and have learned to live constructively with the experience outside the mental health system (Tien, 1991; Coleman and Smith, 2006) and perhaps even come to believe it is a special gift. It is not clear where they fit on the spectrum from shamanism to schizophrenia and most likely there is no one size that fits all. Patti

Randall (Randall *et al.*, 2008) has written that she was mistakenly diagnosed as schizophrenic in early adulthood when she underwent what she believes was a cosmic crisis or spiritual emergency, and was subsequently harmed by administration of anti-psychotic medication. In support of her viewpoint she recounts her struggle to free herself from the mental health system, embarking on a program of self-healing, and finding her true calling in life as a psychiatrist dedicated to fighting against psychiatric stigmatization and misuse of medication. However, the detailed description of recurrent destructive and disruptive episodes throughout her life makes me wonder if her shamanic belief is a delusion and suspect she is a psychotic person who has had a dissociated or split relationship with the mental health system.

By contrast Debra Lampshire (2009; see also Lambrecht and Lampshire, 2009) heard alien persecutory voices from early in her childhood. She was isolated and withdrawn, and had few friends. Late in her adolescence she began a self-healing process that involved an acceptance of and active negotiation with her "voices," in the process of which she established a sense of power and control over parts of herself that had hitherto been frightening and threatening. A turning point was when she commanded "them" to wash her dishes and discovered that they could not. Subsequently, she recounts, she was able at least to detoxify their destructive impact on her life and sometimes to use them in a way she believes is helpful. Now she, too, lectures and writes about her experience in a way that might be viewed as being in the service of the community.

Carl Jung and *The Red Book*

At age 40, shortly before the outbreak of the First World War, Carl Jung, a man by whose own account had achieved everything one could want in life – a happy family, a successful clinical career and an international reputation as well as wealth – experienced a mid-life crisis. He felt he had lost his soul. He resigned his positions as President of the International Psycho-Analytical Association and as a medical faculty member at the University of Zurich. He became increasingly interested in the study of dreams and fantasies. He founded the International Association for Analytical Psychology and he lectured about mental unbalance, which he describes as a state of polarization or alienation resulting from suppression of one's unconscious mind. His subsequent "journey" of spiritual and psychological dissolution and rebirth is documented in diary form with beautiful calligraphy and illustrated with his own impressive art work in *The Red Book: Liber Novus* (2009). The original manuscript was hidden away until 2009 when it was photocopied and published with a translation and detailed biographical commentary by Sonu Shamdasani. In an epilogue written in 1959 Jung explains: "I worked on this book for 16 years. To the superficial observer it will appear like madness. I would also have developed into one had I not been able to absorb the overpowering force of the original experiences" (2009, p. 360). Despite his state of turmoil he continued to discharge all his personal, familial and professional responsibilities during this period, even serving in the army for a period of time during the war. His experience has characteristics of a shamanic calling and self-initiation. In the Jung quotes that follow I have italicized some words and phrases that seem especially illustrative of PMA.

Jung recounts that in October 1913:

> I was suddenly overcome in broad daylight by a vision. I *saw* a terrible flood that covered all the northern and low-lying lands between the North Sea and the Alps. It reached from England up to Russia. . . . I saw yellow waves, swimming rubble, and the death of countless thousands. This vision lasted for two hours. It confused me and made me ill. Two weeks passed then the vision returned, still more violent than before, and an inner voice spoke: "Look at it, it is completely real, and it will come to pass." I wrestled again for two hours. . . . It left me exhausted and confused and I thought my mind had gone crazy. . . . Once I also saw a sea of blood over the northern lands.
>
> (2009, p. 231)

These experiences continued, and Jung "swayed between fear, defiance and nausea. I wanted to throw everything away and return to the light of day, but the spirit stopped me and forced me back into myself" (ibid., p. 235). Gradually Jung decided to seek out rather than flee from these experiences, to see where his demons led him. He pursued this task, mostly at night, while continuing to work and to relate to his family. He struggled to keep his conscious thoughtful mind from suppressing the experiences and even found ways to induce the hallucinations and delusions in order to grapple with them. He describes the technique he developed for inducing fantasies, which sounds like trance induction:

> The training consists first of all in *systematic exercises for eliminating critical attention*, thus producing a vacuum in consciousness. One commenced by *concentrating on a particular mood*, and attempting to become as conscious as possible of all fantasies and associations that came up in connection with it. The aim was to allow fantasy free play, without departing from the initial affect. . . . *This led to a concrete or symbolic expression of the mood*, which had the result of bringing the affect nearer to consciousness.
>
> (ibid., p. 209)

Jung comments that when "visual types" do this they will see visions and when "audioverbal types" do it the result is words and sounds.

Shamdasani writes that Jung "experienced great fear and sometimes had to hold the table to keep himself together" (ibid., p. 204). Jung comments: "That I was able to endure at all was a case of brute force" (ibid., p. 205). Here is his description of one experience:

> In the following night, the air was filled with many voices. A loud voice called, 'I am falling.' Others cried out confused and excited during this: 'Where to? What do you want?' Should I entrust myself to this confusion? I shuddered. It is a dreadful deep. Do you want me to leave myself to chance, to the madness of my own darkness? Whither? Whither? You fall, and I want to fall with you, whoever you are. The spirit of the depths opened my eyes and I caught a glimpse of the inner things, the world of my soul, the many formed and changing.
>
> (ibid., p. 237)

He writes:

> The torment was great. . . . So the path of my life led beyond the rejected *opposites, united in smooth and – alas! – extremely painful sides* of the way. . . . I stepped on them but they burned and froze my soles. But the poison of the serpent, whose head you crush, enters through the wound in your heel. . . . *The outer opposition is an image of my inner opposition.*
>
> (ibid., p. 279)

In other passages in the book Jung seems to be describing characteristics of primordial mental activity. "Where are you leading me?" he writes: "Must I also learn to do without meaning?. . . What is there, where there is no meaning? Only nonsense or madness" (ibid., p. 235). His mind becomes animated, external and "real." "My thoughts are not myself, but exactly like the things of the world, alive and dead" (ibid., p. 250). Mind is concretely depicted as multiple human and animal characters, good and evil, engaged in a life and death struggle. Contradiction does not exist and opposites are merged – birth, life and death, male and female, animal and human. "If I plunge into the death encompassing the world then my buds break open" (ibid., p. 274). "The journey to Hell means to become Hell onself. I have become a monstrous animal form. I felt myself transformed into a rapacious beast" (ibid., p. 240).

I conclude that Jung was a shaman, one of the "wounded healers" who transformed his personal suffering into an unusual degree of integration and maturation and went on to use his special abilities to try to heal other suffering souls.

A Jungian analyst by the name of John Weir Perry (1974) wrote a phenomenological description of the schizophrenic experience as a death/rebirth identity transformation, and the cultural anthropologist Joan Halifax (1982) believes his account accurately describes the altered state of shamanic trance and journey. Some of the features of the death and rebirth experience seem accountable for by PMA in an increasingly controlled and disciplined interaction with thought. Perry describes that there is a kind of death involving dismemberment, torture, and descent into a terrifying spirit world. This might indicate lack of integration and concrete actualization of experience. A state of undifferentiation is suggested by the idea of cosmic conflict between good and evil and between other opposites or contradictions leading to a sacred marriage between them – the experience of being overwhelmed by the opposite sex, and the focus of psychic and cosmic geography on a single center. In such a state there is no conflict or contradiction. A mystical apotheosis and identification with a grandiose persona suggests some of the magical belief quality of a state where words have concrete power and there is no differentiation between self and world.

The concept of a life-transforming "journey" is not restricted to spiritual cultures; it has been a theme in western literature since the earliest days of the *Odyssey* and the *Iliad*. As with a dream, it is not clear whether the reader is to believe that Odysseus embarks on a "real" journey away from "home" and then returns to a world of love and security, or whether the story is to be taken as a concrete actualization of an inner journey. In Joyce's contemporized account, *Ulysses*, Stephen Dedalus is embarked on an inner journey. Other great literature including Dante's *Divine Comedy* and Bunyan's *Pilgrim's Progress* poses similar interpretive dilemmas. Christian belief, from the Old Testament to the story of Christ's crucifixion and rebirth, is replete with such stories. Just as with the outbreak of psychosis some of these identity-taxing "journeys" are associated with pivotal points in the life cycle: adolescent rites of passage, and mid-life "crises." In such journeys, as is characteristic of PMA, ordinary conceptions of time and space, reality and dream, internal and external, contradiction and conflict are suspended, and the experience of psychic death, torment, dismemberment and rebirth has the quality of a real happening.

First-person account by a Maori shaman

In Maori culture shamans are known as *Matakite*, the seers or hearers. Egan Bidois (2009) is such a person. Egan is also a respected mental health worker who works as part of a cultural therapy team within a western-medicine-oriented community psychiatric clinic predominantly devoted to the Maori population. Much of what follows is excerpted verbatim from personal communications he has given permission to share, and from an unpublished paper he has presented.

Egan introduces himself by saying:

> I am a voice-hearer, I am a seer, I am someone who has been pre-
> viously diagnosed with psychosis – and I am Maori. As such my
> culture influences my understandings of the experience." Within the
> Maori culture there is a shamanic hierarchy. *Matakite* are the seers,
> those that see, hear and know beyond the ordinary; those who are
> aware of and experience the spiritual realms. "*Matakite* literally means
> 'the face that sees and is all seeing' hence the term 'seer.' The *Matakite*
> are the links between the realms of what is seen and what is unseen;
> between the living and our ancestors, who breach the standard con-
> structs of time and through *moemoea* (dream) exist in and experience
> the past, present and future. *Matakite* are the receivers and the inter-
> mediaries between the realms. It is not uncommon for *Matakite* to talk
> to someone or about someone when the person is not present and
> perhaps has not even been met about events that person has not
> previously shared and to know of events happening in a completely
> different location. Time, space, form – all those seemingly irrefutable
> concepts and conditions that modern/normal man is bound by are not
> chains that *Matakite* wear.

Tohunga are a step beyond; they have also acquired the ability to heal.
"*Tohunga* are empowered by spiritual knowledge to act as healers to others.
Tohunga and *Matakite* have a close relationship; a *Matakite* could be seen
as a *Tohunga*-in-training. Not all *Matakite* are necessarily *Tohunga* or
destined to be such, yet all *Tohunga* are *Matakite*."

Egan tells us:

> I was born from a line of seers, of hearers and healers. It may be seen in
> "psychiatric-speak" as "genetic disposition;" we Maori simply call it
> *whakapapa* (ancestry). For us the non-physical, the spiritual elements of
> our *whakapapa* are also handed down. I have been seeing and hearing,
> feeling and knowing from as young as I can remember. As a child I was
> supported and enveloped within the safety of my family. I was nurtured
> and my experiences were seen as natural and were well utilized. My first
> memory of seeing "something" was probably around three years old. I
> remember waking one night and seeing this, well, the only way I could
> describe it was a pillar of light standing at the end of my bed. I say
> standing as this pillar of light was somewhat human-shaped. It to me
> felt like some form of person or "light-being." I felt it was facing me,
> though there was no discernable "face" or front or back to this shape. . .
> it just "felt" like it was facing me and watching over me. I remember I
> wasn't scared by it – apart from being somewhat mildly startled. [This
> turned out to be a recurrent experience.] One night I woke and it was

back – this time it had a companion. There was another pillar of brilliant white/golden light. This one felt female. This time they were both facing away from me, towards my bedroom window. It was then I felt something else – something quite ominous approaching from outside my bedroom window. I didn't see it, I just had this over-whelming feeling *something evil a coming*. At that point the two pillars of light came together, merged into a much larger sphere of light and flew out through my bedroom window towards this *something*. The *something* vanished and the ominous feeling ceased. I remember telling my mother about it and she wasn't at all concerned. I remember her simply saying, "That's good. It's not something to worry about." I spoke with my mother about how I was as a child. She said that I always had an awareness, looking at and interacting with "things" that other people were oblivious to. She said I always had this connection to others, to events, just "knowing" something had happened prior to being told about it. I was raised without fear of these experiences. They were accepted; they just "were" a basic part of who I was, within my immediate *whanau*/family anyway. As there are many within my *whanau* who also see/hear, those things flow through our *whanau* from generation to generation. I am just another thread in the rope, another link in the chain. The young person's ability to see/sense is turned into a game of sorts, and the child may be taken around with groups that may be doing spiritual work, ghost-busting, cleansing houses and so forth. The child is utilized as another set of eyes and ears, playing a game of hide and seek, running around being a "spotter" for these groups. The child sees it as fun, sees its experiences as having a purpose."

The community, however, was a bit different. Within the community were also people like me so I found acceptance with some people. However, in some sectors of society they are seen as "scary" or "abnormal" or "mental illness," so these experiences can be quite lonely ones. It can make you feel like a bit of a freak sometimes. Then when they know you and what you may do, they also wonder what "secrets" they may be keeping that aren't so "secret" to you. Some people feel that what they'd like to keep hidden may on some level be visible; sometimes that can cause people to avoid you.

Egan says: "I saw the male *Apa* [the ominous presence] again last year." Egan's first child, a son "born with my eyes, physically and spiritually" went through a period waking at night screaming in terror. Egan and his wife would rush to the bedroom and sense a dark ominous presence had been there. Egan talked with a *Tohunga* who told him he had to pray to the ancestors to deal with it and he did:

That evening my wife and I were drifting off to sleep, son next to us in his cot, when we both noticed a light in our hallway. . . a tall pillar of *ite*/gold light drifted down the hallway past our bedroom. 'What the. . .!' said the wife. Ahh, I thought. Haven't seen him for many years. Our boy has slept soundly since – well, apart from the teething, of course.

Egan goes on to talk about his illness and the more formal aspects of his becoming a *Matakite*:

In my late teens I was very self-centered, self-absorbed and quite angry about some things that had happened in my childhood. It was all about me.

I see now that my mindset at the time was simply not conducive to any training; I would have seen it as merely an attempt by others to tell me what to do, how to live my life; I simply wasn't in a space to listen.

When I was younger, teenager, I used to have these very vivid dreams in which I would be fighting different entities – demons etc. – in my dreams; literally fighting them. I used to wake with bruising, cuts and abrasions, scratches, skinned knuckles, sore bones, aching jaws and even slightly sprained wrists, etc. which you get when you're physically punching things or sustaining physical blows in fights. Of course the logical explanation for those physical marks would be that I was in some way harming myself while I slept, yet those in the house heard nothing, or I had bruising and scratches in places I couldn't reach anyway. Another explanation could well be that my mind itself merely physically manifested those marks due to such a firm belief that I had been in a fight. I guess those explanations are certainly more acceptable than perhaps I was actually fighting on a spiritual level.

At age 18 Egan left his family and community to study law at university.

It was when I moved away from the safety and support of my family to study that I became "unwell." When *Matakite* engage with someone they "see" (or sense, or hear, or feel, or combinations of all that) other people around that person, their attachments, their histories, their pains; we see that person in a greater context. I went from a small cluster of people and attachments to a large group of people and all those they carried with them. For me it was overwhelming; it over-loaded my senses. I was simply unable to deal with the huge increase in voices, visions, in what I saw and felt all around me. My rest was constantly being interrupted by "people" walking in and out of my dreams. The voices and visions, feelings and knowledge, were so forceful. I wasn't used to dealing with so much at one time. I did the usual things students do. I got involved in the student social scene, partying, drinking and all that. At one party I was offered marijuana by someone who said it would help me "chill out" and relax, but once that initial "chilled out" period ended the experiences came back even more amplified and intense. For *Matakite* it is like opening up floodgates.

Egan was committed to a psychiatric hospital suffering from auditory and visual hallucinations and disturbing thoughts.

The western clinical perception was that I was hearing and seeing things due to abuse of marijuana, when in reality I was abusing marijuana to cope with what I was seeing and hearing. So in some ways the psychiatric system was correct. I was indeed suffering from marijuana abuse; however, it wasn't the marijuana that started the ball rolling, it merely gave it a good solid kick along the way. What followed was many years of involvement with the mental health system. No amount of anti-psychotics or western intervention helped. Finally I was discharged as being "treatment resistant."

Egan returned home. He continues:

My healing came through Maori methods and my growth really took the path it was always destined to. I truly believe that my becoming "unwell," as traumatic and painful as it was at the time, was a blessing. I believe that I needed to self-destruct, to slam me so hard that I would drop my walls and be open to receive help. Like a phoenix sometimes some people need to burn to ashes before they can rise anew and take flight.

My healing was a process of self-discovery, of facing my own personal demons. It is through paying at cost that you gain a deeper appreciation for the experience and a deeper respect for it. That period of turmoil for me was cost. It was sacrifice of who I was; it was payment of pain and anguish. There was a more focused training and development that took place on my journey. It seemed that the right people I needed were at the right place at the right time. One person was very well versed in regards to different forms of meditation. She taught me methods of calming myself, of filtering experiences, of remaining still within the storms and turmoil that may sometimes bluster around you during these experiences. She taught me methods to regain and maintain focus. Her partner was also well versed in *Rongoa/* natural medicine. He put me on a cleansing regime of different concoctions to flush my system out of any residual medications or drugs but also of the poisons and toxins that we generate and hold within us throughout life. He was also someone well versed in *Wairua* ways of working. My first step was to cleanse me out – reset the clock, to learn to remain centered and connected, to remain open and to truly "listen" to whatever inputs were coming. The other step was to basically walk me through the experience; to re-expose me into that side of things progressively and to explain it to me. If at any point the experience became overwhelming then by way of *karakia*/prayer and other rituals and other items I wore and/or carried on my person those experiences were effectively closed off or turned down a notch until I was ready for the volume of them to be turned back up. Essentially it could be seen as spiritual desensitization and from there to be ready to receive whatever the experience had in store and wherever it led me.

For more than a decade Egan has been well and productive. He has had no contact with the western mental health system or with drugs, "Yet I see, hear and feel at levels beyond anything I ever have before; well beyond even those that pushed me into unwellness. The physical world and the spiritual world – to me – are constantly interwoven, intermingled, blended, one. I can still recognize the difference, still make that separation, but the veil that separates is as thin or thick as it is chosen to be." He married and fathered a child, and has studied to develop his abilities as a *Matakite* which he utilizes as part of a cultural treatment team in a mental health hospital/clinic setting for a primarily Maori population. Here is what he says in retrospect:

When one thinks about the concept of psychosis, of the definitions of such "symptoms" as hallucinations, delusions, then by all means what I experience could well fit within that perspective. . . . To see, to hear, to feel and to interact with "external stimuli" that for the most part most people are oblivious to; to hold beliefs in such. . . as one's own truth. . . I can see why I was tagged with that. . . label of psychosis. . . . Such experiences can be handed down from generation to generation just as much as eye color or other physical characteristics. . . what I have been born into. . . . I am not "unwell" because I hear or see or feel supposed non-apparent stimuli. Rather the non-apparent stimuli I hear, see and feel can effectively drive me into unwellness if not managed properly.

The process of knowing for *Matakite* is a complex, undifferentiated amalgam of sensory-perceptual, psychic or spiritual and somatic. Egan's senses and perceptual abilities seem more acute than those of ordinary people and he says this is generally true of *Matakite*. But he adds:

When I refer to "smelling" something on someone or about someone, yes it does "appear" like an olfactory experience, however I believe it is not an actual physical experience, with my olfactory sensors/receptors being triggered by an actual physical scent. Often the "smell" will be there without the person being present or even having met him or her. For instance if a case is being reviewed by the team, on occasion I'll "smell" the scent of something while the case is being discussed.

Egan speaks about his *Matakite* role in terms of being a cultural therapist as part of a collective.

Much like other clinicians we review what symptoms and presentations the person has and from that collective discussion and advice/experience of other clinicians an opinion can be formed around what the person may be experiencing. The difference is that for those who do cultural-spiritual assessments some of the contributing "clinicians" may not be physical in body but spiritual. At times we may be receiving information "live" from the supposedly non-living. I say "supposedly" because whether they exist in a physical embodiment or a spiritual one they are still "live" to me. There is an intuition – a "gut feeling." It just *smells* spiritual. Indeed in some cases I mean quite literally "smells" as well, as when someone's issues are related to abuse or "darker forces" there is a definite smell to it that I can most certainly identify. Sure, that would be termed "olfactory hallucinations" in the standard clinical sense, but I do relate specific smells to specific aspects. The other common aspect is auditory. I will quite literally hear the voices of my grandmother, or other ancestors, or other "helpers" or even the ancestors or "helpers" of the person being assessed, the same as there were another clinician in the room. However, the input from those voices is clear, concise and very specific. No "maybe." On follow up what those voices have imparted has been "bang on the money."

Moemoea or dreams are another important source of knowledge:

They are not limited to a sleeping state at all. For *Matakite* they occur independent of sleep. It depends on one's interpretation of what sleep is. One translation of the word *moemoea* is vision. The person might be wide awake and functioning as usual, and yet in a spiritual sense exist in a completely different place and time. Dreams can just be dreams, but for Maori and *Matakite* they can also be doorways in and out of various realms of existence where we may venture outward, or others may venture in. Within those states we are removed from the physical self, removed from the physical inputs and discoloring interpretation and interaction that physical existence creates. Instead we are more what I believe is our true selves, our true forms, which are first and foremost spirit. Through *moemoea* we cast off those physical bonds and boundaries and are able more readily to engage and interact with spirit.

It is not uncommon for *Matakite* to dream-hop into the dreams of loved ones when the loved one is facing something troubling in their own dreams. I do this with my wife. She finds it somewhat disconcerting to have me appear in her dreams and fight off something that is attacking her. In the morning she will comment on it and I will be able to tell her what she was dreaming about. For me the dreamscape can be a meeting place; a place to commune with my *tipuna*/ancestors; a place to discover things I need to know. It's a place/space/realm/ that can exist in between other realms. That state of being within those dream-states is neither here nor there, a crossover point between realms. Sometimes I seek answers to questions there; understanding and insight. It can also be a place of healing.

Egan speaks of the living presence of his ancestors:

The voices I predominately hear are those of my grandmother and my sister who have both passed on. My sister passed before I was born so I never got to physically hear her voice with physical ears, yet I know it is her voice. They keep me company, advise me, encourage me, and when necessary castigate me and keep me on the straight and narrow. I do hear other voices occasionally, and normally that is around whatever work I may be doing at the time. I have also heard the supposed auditory hallucinations that a client is experiencing which to me indicates that perhaps they are more "spiritual" in nature. There are times when cleansing houses or areas (I guess "blessing/ghost-busting" is a way of describing that type of work) I will also hear voices of those (spirits) still present. I also hear voices of "advisors" during specific work. To me they are just like any real living person who comes to assist with something one may be doing by providing expert advice and guidance. Sometimes I "overhear" conversations that may be happening elsewhere; I will approach the person and ask and my "knowledge" will be confirmed.

Just as in this physical world, the spiritual world consists of good and evil so *Matakite* need to ensure that they keep themselves (or are kept) safe during engagements within those realms. These experiences certainly have the potential to create a state of unwellness. The *Matakite* needs to also be able to receive inputs at levels he or she can cope with, which means "filtering" or prioritizing them. *Matakite* use prayers, specific objects and rituals to maintain coverage; blessed spells and enchantments.

I have selected a few personal examples of Egan using his gift in a healing role in his apprenticeship to become a *Tohunga*. He relates that:

A few years ago a good friend of mine was contemplating suicide. One day I was at work and I had this overwhelming feeling he needed me. I couldn't leave work, so I focused my energy towards him. In my *moemoea* I could clearly see my friend. He had just walked out of a shop and was opening up a fresh packet of cigarettes. I could see him standing on the pavement, the road ahead of him, shops and stores down the street. I could "feel" the level of sadness within him. I focused love and comfort and I "spoke" with him, saying over and over, "You'll be okay bro – it's all just whispers in the wind my brother." He seemed to stand there for a while, and then continued to walk up the street and my focus upon him ceased. We caught up again the following week. During our chat he mentioned he had been feeling really low in mood the previous week, to the point one day he was seriously thinking about ending it all. He had gone for a walk down to the shops to get some cigarettes, walked out of the shop and was unwrapping the packet when he just "felt" me there with him strongly. He couldn't explain it, and indeed he is someone who is logical and scientifically minded and has always been very skeptical of these things. He said he could feel me like I was standing right beside him, but also in front, above, all around. It was like I had completely enveloped him. He said he then "heard" my voice, plain as day. The look on his face when I then said, "Oh, saying you'll be okay, it's all just whispers in the wind by any chance?". He was stunned, well actually his exact words were [expletive deleted].

With regard to his healing powers Egan says:

There have been numerous times where I've been in conversation with non-Maori around experiences they may have of a spiritual nature, or picking out ailments within them, what they may be suffering, literally seeing growths in their bodies which they then confirm exist, pinpointing elements of dreams they may be having, so the "sight," the "knowledge" if you will, is certainly not relegated only to a set cultural group.

Events surrounding the hospitalization of Egan's sister for acute septicemia reflect both the healing and the personal element:

The day before she went into hospital I had a dream. It was about 5am when I awoke though for some reason I was within this semi-state of dreaming and waking. At that time I received a "visitation" from my grandmother. My grandmother is one of my *kaitiaki* (guardians). She is with me, I feel her presence and hear her encouragement and advice but I don't see her as such normally. She is just like a constant presence. So to see her in that semi-dream-semi-awake state somewhat startled me. I thought to myself, "hang on, what's up?" My Grandmother told me I had to go visit my sister [who lived in a distant city] and that I had to tell her not to go to work but go to the doctor. She had to get help and get help now or she'd die. Well I slipped back into sleep, and in my dream state I – for want of a better way of describing it – "dream-hopped" into my sister's dreams to deliver the message to her. In that dream-hop I saw myself outside my sister's house. I was running around outside it, banging on the windows and screaming at her to let me in. I went around to the front door and started to kick it down. She let me in looking all puzzled and I told her she had to go to the doctor, not to go to work, or she'd die. A weird thing (if that isn't weird enough) was that in this dream one of our cousins was with me.

My sister spent a few days in hospital. The day she was discharged I spoke with my sister over the phone and she said: "You know the night before I went into hospital you were in my dreams." "Oh yes," I said. She proceeded to tell me she had this dream in which I was running around banging on her windows and yelling at her to let me in, that I had started kicking down her door so she opened it and asked me what the heck I was doing. She said I had told her not to go to work, that she had to go to the doctor or she'd die. She also said for some reason that cousin was there as well. She couldn't figure out why on earth this cousin was there, he was just with me when she opened the door. I just laughed when she told me. She said she believes that dream was a warning, one that saved her life. The morning after that dream my sister had woken up and got herself ready for work. She wasn't too sure whether she should go to work or go to the doctor. She certainly wasn't feeling well at all. One of her workmates showed up to pick her up for work as usual and took one look at her and said: "Oh my, you don't look well at all, I think we need to get you to a doctor." My sister protested for while, though eventually thought, okay let's go get checked out. From the doctor she was rushed to hospital. The doctors told her that she was so sick with such toxicity if she went to work it is likely that the outcome for her would have been severe, quite likely even tragic. After that phone call I racked my brain again as to why this random cousin was in that dream. What role did he play, why he was there, what was the point of his presence? It then occurred to me that his being there wasn't the point of him being there at all, rather it was more a confirmation of the shared dream experience my sister and I had. If the content of the dream wasn't enough, then for both of us to also have had Mr. Random Cousin present confirmed that connection and communication had happened.

Finally, I offer an example of Egan's clinical work. His initial sensory-perceptual-somatic knowledge of the afflicted person was acquired several months prior to their first meeting:

> A young man was diagnosed with schizophrenia. He experienced what has been classified (by our doctor and other clinical professionals) as auditory, visual and tactile hallucinations. One day a nurse was talking to me about him, and I got a "sense" there was something more to it. I got a sharp pain in my upper abdomen, just below the chest, and had a vision of a *Ngarara*, which is an entity that often presents itself in the form of a very lizard-like creature. Its colors and scales can vary. This *Ngarara* I "saw" on the young man's back had its head over his left shoulder and was "whispering" into his left ear. The right leg was wrapped over his right shoulder and extended down to his upper abdomen – I could "see" its "claws" of its right arm/leg digging into this young man just below his chest. I suggested the nurse ask which ear heard the voices, where they were coming from, and what was their content, as well as whether he sensed other presences, and whether he experienced pain or injury in his upper left abdomen. I told her that he is hearing, predominantly in his left ear, low, almost unintelligible whispers, as well as two voices from the rear and off to the left degrading him and telling him to harm himself. I also suggested he had some extreme injury and pain in his upper left abdomen, and that there are other "presences" out in front of him, off to the right, that just stand there but don't speak. A week later the nurse told me that he hears muttering in his left ear, two negative voices from the left rear, and he feels some presences in the front to the right that don't speak. She added that he had stabbed himself in his left upper abdomen in a desperate effort to stop the voices.

Some months later the young man was referred to the service where Egan worked. Egan met with him for the first time, and:

> identified two beings (we might call them *Kehua*, which is more "spiritual entity") behind and off to his left. I also got the sense these two were actually portraying themselves to be something else. I got the sense they were masquerading and pretending to be a male and a female that this young man actually knew. I asked him to tell me a bit more about the two voices off to the left, the man and the woman. He was surprised that I had identified where the voices were, and that I knew there were two of them, male and female. He told me they were

living acquaintances who had once been very mean to him. Why were those *Kehua* masquerading as two living people? Well, as I said, just like in this physical world the spiritual one also has its tricksters. Within our culturally specific health systems there is almost a semi-acceptance of communication with the non-living. So for this young man to be hearing the voices of supposed "living people" the natural conclusion by most is that they aren't voices of ancestors or spiritual, but rather they are straight auditory hallucinations. That's exactly the opinion those working with him took. Those *Kehua*, I believe, took on the facade of the living to do exactly that, divert attention and essentially paint this young man as having a straight hallucinatory experience rather than a spiritual one. The young man and I also spoke about the others he could feel, but not hear, and again I was able to tell him there were three who were sitting there. My "feeling" is that they are related to him, most likely family; ancestors who have passed on who are there as support for him but for some reason are being prevented from helping.

The fact that these and other quite remarkable phenomena that Egan described to me cannot be experienced from a western perspective in a way that "makes sense," that is to say that fits western rational ways of knowing, does not mean that they can be dismissed as irrational superstition. While a western observer might understand the different way that Egan uses his mind as manifestations of primordial mental activity in a relationship regulated by thought, the observer cannot expect to be able to see things from that perspective so that they "make sense" the way they do to Egan. Perhaps the closest the western observer can expect to get in experiential terms might be to turn the tables and ask equivalent and probing questions about western culture. For example, might psychosis be thought of as personal disharmony with the cosmos requiring spiritual healing?

As we have begun to see, there are broad similarities between the superficially disparate phenomena of dreaming, psychosis and shamanism, as well as some differences. Shamanism and psychosis have a common basis in PMA but they differ with regard to the relationship of PMA and thought, and the place of the expression of that balance or relationship in the interpersonal and cultural context. In the waking state a preponderance of PMA does not necessarily indicate psychopathology if it is integrated with and controlled by thought. In western culture for the most part PMA is relegated to the murky depths known as the unconscious, and control consists of suppression, what might be thought of in dualistic terms as alienation of oneself from aspects of self that are experienced as potentially dangerous and disruptive. In spiritual cultures PMA is to be embraced as part of a unity of mind and an invaluable source of information about self and world, not something to be feared and shunned. Shamans have mastered transit between PMA and thought and act as guides and interpreters for those in the community who need the knowledge and guidance of the spiritual world but have not undergone the rigorous disciplined training necessary to make the journey to obtain information for themselves.

There are many ways that people shift the balance away from thought and attempt to induce altered states of consciousness dominated by PMA. The result might be labeled psychotic, hallucinatory and delusional, or supernatural or spiritual depending on the interpersonal and socio-cultural context. What is particular to the psychotic spectrum is not only that there is a predominance of PMA, but also that it is dissociated from comprehension and control by thought. Whether the result is adaptive, constructive and "normal" or maladaptive, destructive and "psychotic" depends on the interpersonal and social context, on whether entry into and exit from the PMA state is under the disciplined control of thought, and on whether the result is constructive and adaptive or disruptive and burdensome in the larger community. Changing focus from the individual to the community at large, induction of PMA in members of a group may benefit the community, as in organized religious ritual and practice, or it may spread out of control by mass hysteria and contagion and eventuate in violence and destruction.

Shamanism, psychosis and creativity may also share a common constitutional predisposition. In the next chapter I explore the phenomena of synesthesia and lucid dreaming.

Chapter 11

Special sensitivity: Synesthesia and lucid dreaming

Are there neurobiological underpinnings of primordial mental activity and constitutional predispositions toward it? In Chapter 16 I review research about the neural circuitry that underlies some of the phenomenology of PMA – attachment behavior, dreaming and schizophrenia. In this chapter I describe two phenomena most likely of constitutional origin – synesthesia and lucid dreaming – that may predispose a person to PMA and to ease of transitional connection or crossover between it and thought. Depending on the interpersonal, social and cultural context that provides positive or negative reinforcement for these in childhood, the outcome may be adaptive and constructive or maladaptive and pathological.

Speculation about possible constitutional origins of shamanism and psychosis highlights the important question of a research hypothesis. Do we look for a constitutional abnormality or impairment, or simply a difference – something like hair color – that distinguishes one person from another? When we seek to understand the constitutional predisposition to psychosis the implication is that what is being looked for is something abnormal or defective about the brain. Considerable research has been devoted to finding the lesion or deficiency. Studies of family members have attempted to demonstrate a hereditary schizotypical personality. There are subtle evidences of disturbances of the sensory-perceptual system of schizophrenic persons that include eye movement disorders and problems tracking stimuli (summarized in Robbins, 1993). Western bias notwithstanding, shamanism does not seem to be an abnormal phenomenon; indeed it may be a manifestation of an unusual degree of maturity in the sense of creative integration of thought and PMA. The implication is that constitutional factors might be looked upon not as vulnerabilities to psychopathology but as differences or sensitivities that may predispose some persons to develop psychoses and others shamanism or creativity depending on the socio-cultural and interpersonal context in which they develop. After all, there is no evidence that one hair color is normal and another pathological, but if we live in a society where "gentlemen prefer blondes" and kinky hair has more negative connotations the difference that starts out neutral can end up being a source of success for the former and difficulties for the latter.

Until full maturation of the brain and acquisition of the capacity for logical thought around the time of puberty, children at play are often able to be in the world of thought and reality and the world of dream and fantasy simultaneously, so there must be a period of neural plasticity early in life in which such crossover potential is normal. Synesthesia and lucid dreaming, the subjects of this chapter, are manifestations of two apparently inherited special predispositions or sensitivities to crossover between PMA and thought that may predispose a person toward PMA and enhance the potential for crossover or dialectical relationships between it and thought.

Synesthesia

The term synesthesia is derived from the Greek meaning *union of sensation* and denotes a condition in which experience in one sensory-perceptual modality triggers simultaneous experiences in one or more other modalities. For example, some people see visual images or colors when they hear music, or perceive letters and numbers in different colors, or hear music when they see landscapes or pictures, or experience particular tastes or smells when hearing or reading particular words. Research into this sensitivity began with Fechner (1871) and Galton (1880). It is an inherited sensitivity that may be found in as many as 5 per cent of the general population (Ward and Simner, 2005; Simner *et al.*, 2006), but it can also be drug-induced. Neuroimaging studies (Ward and Simner, 2005; Ramachandran and Hubbard, 2001, 2005) demonstrate linkages between the affected sensory-perceptual centers of the brain. There is some evidence that connections between sensory-perceptual modalities are ordinarily present in all children, and that a normal pruning process inhibits these connections as part of maturation (Maurer and Mondloch, 2006; Ward *et al.*, 2006). Whether environmental factors can inhibit this natural pruning process and contribute to adult synesthesia has not been experimentally documented. Synesthetic perceptions are related to affect and tend to be located in space (Cytowic, 2002). It has been personally verified in some instances and evidence strongly suggests in others that many creative people are synesthetes – for example, Van Gogh, O'Keefe, Messiaen, Sibelius, Kandinsky, Scriabin, Nabokov, Rimsky-Korsakov, Duke Ellington and Strindberg. Although Cytowic believes there is an association between synesthesia and psychosis the experimental evidence thus far is weak.

If the capacity for synesthesia is identified, validated and supported in childhood, and comes to have community value, then the person can develop special abilities to know and to heal and to create. If these experiences are not validated, are labeled as pathological, or if they occur under circumstances of overstimulation and failure of caring environmental support then they may become vulnerabilities to psychosis.

The process of knowing for *Matakite* in Maori culture is a complex, undifferentiated amalgam of the sensory-perceptual, psychic or spiritual and somatic. Egan Bidois' senses and perceptual abilities, like those of other *Matakite* and *Tohunga*, seem more acute than those of ordinary people and more interrelated as well. Let us consider some of Egan's comments in Chapter 10 from a sensory-perceptual perepective:

> When I refer to "smelling" something on someone or about someone, yes it does "appear" like an olfactory experience, however I believe it is not an actual physical experience, with my olfactory sensors/receptors being triggered by an actual physical scent. Often the "smell" will be there without the person being present or even having met him or her. For instance if a case is being reviewed by the team, on occasion I'll "smell" the scent of something while the case is being discussed. There is an intuition – a "gut feeling." It just *smells* spiritual. Indeed in some cases I mean quite literally "smells" as well, as when someone's issues are related to abuse or "darker forces" there is a definite smell to it that I can most certainly identify. Sure, that would be termed "olfactory hallucinations" in the standard clinical sense, but I do relate specific smells to specific aspects. The other common aspect is auditory. I will quite literally hear the voices of my grandmother, or other ancestors, or other "helpers" or even the ancestors or "helpers" of the person being assessed, the same as there were another clinician in the room. However, the input from those voices is clear, concise and very specific. No "maybe." On follow up what those voices have imparted has been "bang on the money."

An interesting dialogue between two persons who experienced hearing voices since childhood is reported by Lambrecht and Lampshire (2009) and elaborated by Lampshire (2009). Ingo Lambrecht (see Chapters 9 and 10) was raised in a South African family that became aware of his special sensitivities and his interest in paranormal phenomena early in his life and supported them. He undertook a rigorous training program and became a shaman (sangoma) and he became an accomplished clinical psychologist as well. Debra Lampshire grew up in a dysfunctional family and experienced isolation and alienation from an early age. She eventually became clinically psychotic. In early adulthood she began to wrestle with her demons, the threatening persecutory voices. She began to give them orders, and a watershed experience was when she discovered that they were unable to wash her dishes. One can entertain the hypothesis that both had a similar sensitivity in childhood; but the supportive environment Lambrecht grew up in predisposed him to become a shaman whereas the disturbed environment of Lampshire's childhood made the trait into a vulnerability to psychosis.

Lucid dreaming

Some persons discover early in life that they are capable of another crossover ability called lucid dreaming, the capacity to be thoughtful while dreaming and as a consequence able to regulate and direct the content of their dreams. The phenomenon of lucid dreaming has long been described but has only recently gained sufficient scientific credibility to justify experimentation and validation. The term "lucid dreaming" was coined by van Eeden (1913) but the phenomenon has been noted throughout recorded history as far back as St. Augustine, including reports by Thomas Browne in his *Religio Medici*, Samuel Pepys in his diary, and Tibetan Buddhist monks from the fourth century AD. "Legitimate" scientific study of the subject began with a book by Green (1968). In the late 1970s Alan Worsley was able to signal the onset of lucid dreaming to the parapsychologist Keith Hearne. Credible scientific verification is largely the result of the work of Stephen LaBerge in his sleep and dream laboratory at Stanford (1980, 1985, 1990, 2000). Since then the phenomenon has been verified and studied by notable dream researchers including Alan Hobson (Muzur *et al.*, 2002). It occurs during REM sleep like most but not all dreams. That conscious control of the dream is a reality and not another aspect of the "delusional" quality of dreams has been verified by reports from the dreamer using subtle pre-agreed signals such as a number of eye blinks or small muscle twitches that can be verified by independent observers in sleep and dream laboratories using simple observation, EEG and electromyography. Voss *et al.* (2009) report EEG studies demonstrating that lucid dreaming has features both of ordinary REM sleep and of consciousness (frontal activity).

The phenomenon of lucid dreaming sheds light on the relationship between PMA and thought as two distinct ways that mind can work, either in a state of dissociation or in an integrated, more or less disciplined and controlled relationship between PMA and thought. Ordinarily the states are integrated and thought is the controller. In western culture the integration mostly takes the form of suppression and sequestration of PMA during waking life, as it is looked upon as irrational and potentially destructive, except under particular circumstances such as dreaming, creativity, self-induced altered states and religious ritual. In pathogenic family environments (Chapter 13) the development of thought and integration of thoughtful control of PMA may be discouraged and if the boundary between them is constitutionally thin to begin with, the result may be a psychosis. Some persons become aware of special crossover ability in childhood but unless the interpersonal environment is attuned to such things the person may never become consciously aware that the phenomenon is notable. If such ability is detected early and responded to with familial-cultural support, as is often the case in spiritual cultures and especially in families of seers and shamans, the subject can train him or herself and develop it into a skill.

In spiritual cultures integration involves development of controlled entry and exit from PMA during waking life and utilization of the results for socially constructive purposes, and an inherent crossover sensitivity may be a strength. In this broad perspective lucid dreaming is neither an inherent capacity nor an inherent vulnerability. It might be better named "integrated dreaming" as it involves the capacity for dialogue between thought and PMA.

Ingo Lambrecht (personal communication, 2009) describes how he became aware as a child he had the capacity for lucid dreaming:

> I dealt with a repetitive nightmare during childhood, and in one of them I remembered in the dream itself how a person had talked about his lucid dream, and that made me turn and not run anymore. In other dreams I would choose to change the scenery, go elsewhere, or also decide to fly and sweep over the landscape like an eagle simply for fun.

Egan Bidois, the Maori *Matakite* whose story is chronicled in Chapter 10, also discovered this ability early in life:

> It's something I've always done. It's something I can also switch on and off whenever needed as well, as constantly lucid dreaming can also be damaging. The brain needs to rest. That's the point of dreaming, to shut off on a conscious level and rest.

Chapter 12

Creativity

Creativity, like shamanism and psychosis, is not an intrinsic attribute of the person but a matter of community judgment. It depends on the adaptation of the person within a particular culture, time and place. Why do people create and how do they create? Much has been written about these important questions. While inspiration/content and form/process are not entirely separable, in this chapter I focus on the latter question, the structure and dynamics of the creative process, from the perspective of primordial mental activity and its relation to thought. The consensus among persons who have studied the subject seems to be that two mental processes are involved in creativity. There are differences of opinion about their function and the nature of their relationship with one another.

Sterba (1940) described Freud's views about art as follows: "The fundamental dynamic force at the root of a work of art is an unfulfilled wish of the artist; just as in dreams and fantasies, the work of art represents this wish as fulfilled" (p. 258). In other words, a major element of the creative process is an unconscious primary process. Freud (1911a) believed that the artist is able to reconcile the pleasure and reality principles – the primary and secondary processes. He introduced the concept of sublimation, vaguely defined as de-sexualization or transformation of the aim and object of instinct.

Jung (1959a) proposed that there are two kinds of thinking, directed and irresponsible. Synonyms for irresponsible thinking include fantasy, daydreaming and myth-making. He relates this use of mind to the collective unconscious, to ancient cultures, to mythology, to the mind of children, and to dreaming and creativity. He writes:

> We move in a world of fantasies which, untroubled by the outward course of things, well up from inner phantasmal forms. This activity of the early classical mind was, in the highest degree, artistic; the goal of its interest does not seem to have been how to understand the real world as objectively and accurately as possible.
>
> (1959a, p. 24)

Klein wrote that "access to early infantile phantasy. . . contributes to the development of every talent or even genius" (1930, p. 22). Segal abstracted Klein's understanding of the creative process from the three papers she wrote on art as a struggle between the destructive rage of the paranoid-schizoid position and the reparative urges of the depressive position (1978, pp. 138–139). Segal adds that the artistic creation is "an unconscious demonstration of the fact that order can emerge out of chaos" (1952, p. 204). Winnicott (1971) formulated the concept of the transitional object to depict this achievement. Writing from a similar neo-Kleinian perspective Britton discusses the creative accomplishment as a depressive position resolution of the Oedipal situation which involves formation of a third position or triangular space that enables symbolization and thought:

> The closure of the oedipal triangle by the recognition of the link joining the parents provides a limiting boundary for the internal world. It creates what I call a "triangular space" – i.e. a space bounded by the three persons of the oedipal situation and all their potential relationships. It includes, therefore, the possibility of being a participant in a relationship and observed by a third person as well as being an observer of a relationship between two people.
>
> (1989, p. 86)

Britton makes a key distinction between a problem-solving imagination and a problem-avoiding imagination. He concludes that the artist is able to use the infantile phantasies of the primal scene in the problem-solving imagination. It is not clear whether these Kleinian and neo-Kleinian contributions relate specifically to creativity as an unusual human achievement or whether they are about the mature development of a thoughtful mind.

Turning to contributions from the realm of ego psychology, Kris (1952) conceived of creativity as the product of a dialectic between a mature aspect of the person (ego) and a primitive, immature, pathological aspect (primary process). He introduced the concept of regression in the service of the ego or controlled regression as a way to distinguish normality from psychosis. In creativity the ego gains access to primary process material, sublimates or neutralizes the instinctual component and transforms it into art. In psychotic regression the ego is overwhelmed by instinct and the primary process. In other words, Kris conceived of the primary process as primitive, immature and pathological in relation to the secondary process ego.

Noy has made some of the most important contributions to this discussion. He writes about

> the concomitant function of two systems: one equipped to deal with reality, and another equipped to deal with the self. These two "sets" of programs have to operate together, meaning that every input

processed according to reality-orientated programs has to be "translated" by passing through a second process of self-centred programs – and, vice versa, any activity originated by self-centred motivation has to be "translated" from its self-centred organization through reality-orientated programs in order to be expressed as behaviour.

(1969, p. 174)

Writing specifically about art he states that "the work of art should be viewed as one structure in which the integration of both these processes is accomplished" (1968, p. 642). Ehrenzweig (1953, 1967) believed that the primary and secondary processes function simultaneously in an artistic creation:

We found that there must be an unconscious perception which is not bound by the conscious gestalt (the surface gestalt) and which perceives competing form combinations such as background negatives or the minute forms of technique. Psychoanalysis shows that depth perception is not only free from the surface gestalt but follows a different form principle altogether.

(1953, p. 30)

Arieti (1974, 1976) made a proposal similar to Matte-Blanco's ideas about two kinds of logic and about structures that form when they interact. He calls the primary process "paleologic" and refers to artistic synthesis of the primary with the secondary process as formation of a "tertiary process."
Noy maintains that:

In prevailing theory, the primary processes are regarded as more primitive than the secondary ones. This seems like a very one-sided judgment. . . this is a "superiority" only if the function is evaluated from the viewpoint of reality. If the viewpoint is shifted to the self and its needs, then the contrary is true: the ability to represent a full experience, including all the feelings and ideas involved, is a higher achievement than merely operating with abstract concepts and words, and the ability to transcend time limits and organize past experiences with present ones is a higher ability than being confined to the limitations of time and space. Would it not be better to leave all this discussion of primitiveness or higher developmental rank and say simply that the difference between the primary and secondary processes is in their function and not in their degree of development?

(1969, p. 175)

Holt (2002) goes a step further and takes a position similar to that of Matte-Blanco:

The primary process cannot be chaotic, wholly unstructured, or random. It has properties different from those of its twin, and whether or not it actually constitutes a separate system of thought, it must be produced by enduring structural arrangements of some kind.

(p. 461)

Creativity, psychosis and shamanism all seem to be related, but there are significant differences, some of which I explored in Chapter 10 and others in Chapter 12. Many theorists, beginning with Freud and Klein, have related the primary process and phantasy not only to creativity but also to psychosis. Arieti's work (1964, 1967, 1976) is particularly notable in this regard. History is replete with associations of severe psychosis with unusual gifts to see beyond the ordinary, with special sensitivity and artistic creativity. Schizophrenese, the concrete language of schizophrenia that I describe in Chapter 15, seems to reflect a latent capacity to make literary metaphor. When Caroline, the chronic schizophrenic woman whose idiosyncratic language usage is used as illustration in Chapter 15, began to develop and to prefer the language of thought, it turned out that she had a hitherto unsuspected capacity to read and understand complex literature and even to make metaphor in the form of poetry. The number of young adults I have treated with the diagnosis of schizophrenia who showed some artistic promise prior to hospitalization and who went on to become successful artists after treatment seems significantly greater than can be accounted for by chance. Elsewhere (1969, 1993) I have written about two of them.

One type of creativity resembles psychosis in some respects but differs insofar as it is socially adaptive. Although the artist may function predominantly in primordial mental activity, may have a poorly developed and infrequently used capacity for thought, and may be considered by peers peculiar and even bizarre, his or her work is valued by the community. Another kind of creativity that is closer to shamanism is the product of a mature integration of PMA and thought, involving controlled induction of primary states of inspiration, and thought-disciplined development of technique and use of the information from such states to produce art work.

Carl Jung, whose personal journey and struggle (*The Red Book*, 2009) is summarized in Chapter 10, is an interesting example of the complex interface between psychosis, shamanism and art. *The Red Book* is without doubt a significant artistic achievement. From an artistic perspective it is a fantastic, beautifully illustrated journey through the underworld to the light; a tale of death and rebirth. From the perspective of this book it presents a struggle between PMA and thought that has a mature or integrated outcome. It resembles the journeys chronicled by Dante, Bunyan and Homer, and the art is reminiscent of some of the grotesquery of Bosch and Picasso. It is interesting to speculate about the interplay between thought and PMA in the minds of these creative persons, but I have insufficient knowledge of the subjects to do anything more than that.

Charles

I worked with Charles for many years, and his art changed dramatically both in form and in meaning during the course of his treatment. I present him as an illustration of the two types of creativity I mentioned and the interface between them. He became a successful artist in the eyes of the community during the early stages of his therapy, but then abandoned his art, his claim to fame, and even his belief that he was an artist when he realized the process involved a kind of repeated trance induction that reinforced the psychotic core of his personality. Still later he discovered that he was indeed an artist by temperament and he worked to find a different way of doing art that harnessed his primordial sources of inspiration to thought and disciplined action and that was meaningful and satisfying to his developing sense of self.

When I first met Charles he was barely able to function, withdrawn and isolated with almost no social contact. He had a sense of the world as a dangerous place and entertained serious urges to blow his head off with a gun as his father had done during Charles' adolescence. The only reason he was able to remain outside an institution was that he was supported by a large inheritance.

His earliest sense of identity in the course of therapy was around the beginnings of realization that his sour, dysphoric, withholding affective state and his somatic gastric pain and tendency to pant like a steam engine could be conceived of as an emotion – predominantly rage and to a lesser extent despair. He began to think of himself as an angry man, literally equating himself with rage. He started to build things and gradually began to create artistic installations involving manipulation of images taken from old films and film-clips, many from home movies or films of and taken by family members, to create hypnotically repetitive sequences of movement. It turned out he had considerable technical and building skills, and in order to make this as authentic as possible he sought out and refurbished "ancient" technology from the period the images themselves were first made. He did much of his work in a state of sensory deprivation, in the darkened studio, isolated from people, where he spent much of his time. The results gradually brought him a degree of attention and acclaim in the art world. It would seem accurate to say that he had found a way to induce a kind of narcotic trance in himself and in his viewers. The trance or dream-like state he evoked in himself left him in a state that seemed to combine withdrawal, helplessness, despair and rage, whereas the viewers of his work in galleries and museums seemed to have much more positive narcotic experiences. Despite the modest renown he experienced he remained socially isolated, and although he rationalized that others were unfriendly toward him and potentially dangerous I assumed others were responding to his unfriendly, withholding demeanor.

At the time he did this work Charles had no idea what its personal meaning might be, and he actively resisted inquiry with the belief, not uncommon among artistically creative persons – and it turned out to be correct in his case – that if he knew and thought about it his creativity would be lost. His belief posed a dilemma for me as a therapist devoted to uncovering meaning and committed to the belief that the truth shall set us free, and that knowledge is power. Perhaps it was inevitable that a therapy tilted toward development of thought and thoughtful understanding of and control over the primordial aspect of his mind would have such a result. Gradually he became aware that the subject of the work and the state of trance in which he did it was regressive insofar as it repetitively induced and reinforced the dream-like dysphoric state that amalgamated inchoate somatic distress, global feelings of helplessness, despair and rage, and an undifferentiated sense of living in a hostile inimical world, that had characterized much of his adult life. He became more interested in thinking and knowing, realizing full well that he might need to radically alter the direction of his life. As he developed an increasing capacity to think and reflect he concluded that the process of creation had involved thoughtlessly and repetitively immersing himself in, repeating and actualizing a childhood mental state of passive withdrawal, somatic distress, inchoate helplessness, terror, rage and self-induced narcosis. This had been his infantile method of coping with regular and repetitive nocturnal assaults on his person by his drunken psychotic mother. This repetitive "tape" had become both his creative inspiration and the manifestation of his psychosis.

After a struggle over whether he was losing something vitally important or gaining a new and positive sense of self in the world Charles gradually relinquished this kind of artistic work. Slowly, over a long period of time, he discovered he did indeed have a basic desire and ability to be an artist that was not isomorphic with the kind of creation he had abandoned. He realized that no matter how much recognition he received for his previous work it had not made him feel good as a person; he had never been able to have a positive sense of himself as an artist. His PMA began to draw less on dehumanizing, destructive subject matter and more on human and natural vitality and caring, and he used thought and identification of emotions more to regulate and control his primordial experiences. He began to express himself less mechanically and more fluidly and spontaneously in several different media, mostly painting, drawing and sculpture, and to work to develop better technique, to choose and develop themes, many having to do with color, light, depictions of nature, and portraits of persons close to him. He made some art specifically to support social causes with which he was in sympathy. He found a new, better lighted studio and shared the space with other artists with whom he took satisfaction in communicating.

In his therapy Charles developed more ability to think and to verbally articulate his thoughts and feelings. He realized that as a child he had no help to learn to think about his situation and understand his overwhelmingly painful feelings, and had no choice but to induce a kind of narcotic trance in which somatic sensations and affects he did not understand motivated him to re-play traumatic scenes he had not been able to control. As therapy progressed Charles would tell me from time to time that he felt he was awakening from a nightmare.

Bob Dylan

Bob Dylan is a legend in the world of folk music and poetry. His creations and the act of expressing them publically moved and gave voice to the feelings and beliefs of the generation that grew up in the Sixties, and other generations as well. Little credible biographical material about him is available, as virtually no one other than former wives, who are understandably reluctant to share intimate details, claims to have known him well enough to offer definitive insights about the workings of his mind. The discussion that follows draws heavily on the authoritative biography *No Direction Home* by Dylan's long-time acquaintance Robert Shelton (1987), and the documentary film of the same name produced by Martin Scorsese (2005). It concentrates mostly on the five years, 1960–1965, following Dylan's twentieth birthday. I have also included some quotes from personal communication with Warren Colman, editor of the *Journal of Analytic Psychology*, who is also something of an expert on Dylan.

In *Blowin' in the Wind*, one of his best known songs, Dylan tells us that "The answer, my friend, is blowin' in the wind." In a concrete and rambling interview in the October–November 1962 issue of *Sing Out*, when he was 21 years of age, Dylan explained the song as follows:

> There ain't too much I can say about this song except that the answer is blowing in the wind. It ain't in no book or movie or TV show or discussion group. Man, it's in the wind – and it's blowing in the wind. Too many of these hip people are telling me where the answer is.

He is describing a concrete state of actualization; it's not symbolic, it is what it is. The lyrics to his songs contain a number of references to wind and breath, with its ancient spiritual connotation. Interviewed in the Scorsese documentary, the Beatnik poet Alan Ginsburg calls Dylan, being and blowing, a shaman.

Dylan mesmerized audiences. His performances had the quality of self-induced states of ecstasy. Films reveal how he sings with eyes closed. As his total body syncopates, he blows into his harmonica, held by a special attachment next to his mouth, and his hands play acoustic guitar or piano. There seems a sensory-perceptual-motor identity or actualization with the world about him, and the quality entrances audiences. Friends describe how he intuitively and emotionally absorbed the ambience or spirit around him and gave voice or breath to it. His childhood friend Harry Weber likened such activity to that of "a primitive person" (Shelton, 1987, p. 69). Dylan was asked on countless occasions whether he considered himself spokesperson for a movement, and he always denied it. Shelton describes the way he created as like an altered or drug state: "The words seemed to come from somewhere else. . . memory. . . unconscious mind" (ibid., p. 70).

Colman (personal communication, 2010) comments that: "The quality of trance-like emotion in his early performances is common to the blues." He adds: "This is probably where the blues links up with shamanism. I believe there is also some evidence of Cherokee influence on the blues and several blues and rock greats have Cherokee blood I'm told." Links on Google indicate that there is a significant association between Cherokee tribes and blues music.

Dylan's sense of identity did not seem stable. He was notorious for giving many and widely varied accounts of his life and background that had little if any relationship to facts of his upbringing that have gradually been uncovered. It is as though he were living out a discontinuous, unintegrated series of dream vignettes. Almost no one who has been part of his life really claims to have "known" him. It was many years before the public became aware that his real name was Robert Zimmerman, that he grew up in a conventional family in a small Minnesota town, and that his father was a furniture salesman. Suze Rotolo, one of the first significant young women in his life, and one of a very few people Dylan believed knew him well, said of the persona "He is mystifying. Most of it he created, and then added to. . . . He has a whole cloud around him" (Shelton, 1987, p. 133). He assumed different personas at different stages of his life and career. At the beginning he learned about Woody Guthrie and according to his friends and himself almost literally took on a Woody Guthrie identity. It was the beginning of several voice transformations. First he made Guthrie-like vocalizations. Many years later he sounded very much like Johnny Cash, another idol with whom he collaborated. Such shifts in identity, illustrative of the discontinuous holistic or undifferentiated quality of PMA, are very different from the mature selective process of identification that has lasting value in the development of personality.

Fellow folk singer Dave van Ronk remarked to Dylan that his song *A Hard Rain's a Gonna Fall* is "heavy on symbolism" and Dylan is said to have responded: "Huh?" Dylan himself described his work as an expression of what no one had thought or done before. In number eight of his *11 Outlined Epitaphs* (2003/1964), he writes: "If it rhymes, it rhymes/ if it don't, it don't/ if it comes, it comes/ if it won't, it won't," a clear statement of actualization, not symbolism. Poem ten of another series of eleven written in the same year is a statement that there is no contradiction, opposites are identical: "You ask me questions/an' I say that every question/if it's a truthful question/can be answered by askin' it" (Shelton, 1987). Much of what he wrote and sang achieves its effect not by symbolic communication of ideas but by moving his audiences and evoking in them an inarticulate emotional resonance – a primordial response.

As Dylan's fame grew so did his reputation as an ornery cantankerous person. When he was asked by the press and critics to explain who he was, what he believed, and what his music was about he would insist the music spoke for itself and deny there was any special message he was trying to convey. The transcripts, many reproduced in Shelton's book, are classic examples of people talking at cross-purposes. Interviewers, sometimes skillful and many other times woefully insensitive and clumsy, questioned him thoughtfully about symbolism, hidden meaning and logical connection; and Dylan, sometimes patiently but most of the time with barely concealed exasperation and sarcasm responded concretely (it is what it is) or tangentially according to some non-logical process. The interviewers concluded that for some unfathomable reason Dylan was deliberately being hostile and obfuscating, and perhaps to some extent this was true, but perhaps much of the time his mind was working in a qualitatively different way than theirs.

During the decades following the five incandescent years of Dylan's productivity at the beginning of the Sixties there have been numerous efforts by respected figures in the worlds of literature and music to place the creative significance of his work in perspective. I claim no expertise on this subject but will cite a few comments from Shelton's (1987) book that seem to elaborate the nature of mental activity underlying his contributions. Christopher Ricks, Professor of English at Christ's College, Cambridge University, comments that since the death of Robert Lowell Dylan has become "the best American *user* of words" (italics mine) and adds that "he's got more than words to use." Eugene Stelzig of the SUNY English department writes of Dylan's "songpoetry" that he is in the Romantic tradition of "the artist as a seer/prophet." The editor of Robert Shelton's biography, Gabrielle Goodchild, commented about Dylan's novel, *The Tarantula*, that it is "a circus of dreams" in which he uses "language of concurrence, coincidence and contradiction," and that "language is pressurized into producing a new and purposeful energy" (Shelton, 1987, p. 236). Shelton himself has this to say about Dylan's non-symbolic use of words to pressure and to move others:

> The dream-hallucination as mirror of reality: The priest-seer-artist
> dreams of a reality that lies outside ordinary time and space yet mirrors

the everyday world. . . . For surrealist artists, dreams, imaginings, even hallucinations, natural or chemical, have helped broaden and deepen the scope of art. . . . The artist, as dreamer-in-chief, lends structure, shape, and color to the visions he will, at some point, share with his audience. . . . Innumerable Dylan followers have assured me it is *impossible* to understand much of Dylan's 1965–1966 work without dropping acid.

(ibid., p. 270)

He goes on to liken Dylan's work to that of Blake, Coleridge, Rimbaud and Baudelaire, who "give existence and substance to that 'other world'" (ibid.).

During this period Dylan wrote *Mr. Tambourine Man*, a song that Shelton believes is an expression of Dylan himself, "a sandman for adults, a spirit who draws us out of our daily parade to escape. . . playing a song for me, taking me following, casting me under his dancing spell. . . . Listening to him, we are quite ready to go anywhere. He lets me forget about today, and tomorrow he'll have yet another song for me" (ibid., p. 275). In describing *Visions of Johanna*, Shelton quotes Bill King as saying in his doctoral thesis (*The Artist in the Marketplace*) that *Tambourine Man* is Dylan's finest poem and comments that he "constantly seeks to transcend the physical world to reach the ideal where the visions of Johanna become real" (ibid., p. 322). The folk singer Richard Farina made this insightful comment about Dylan: "What he says and what he does are the same thing. His expression is precisely what he is. . . . I don't believe that I understand what is going through his mind" (ibid., p. 327).

Absence of reflective comparison and contradiction is one of the qualities of PMA. Shelton comments repeatedly about Dylan's mercurial, change-able, chameleon-like, moment-to-moment contradictory quality. This is a commentary on the lack of integration or continuity in Dylan's expressions. Colman (personal communication, 2010) says:

> I think one of Dylan's strengths is that he doesn't discriminate between good and bad – he "knows too much to argue and to judge" (*Love Minus Zero/No Limit*, 1965). This fosters his creativity since he allows everything through – another indication of him being particularly in touch with PMA. However, I would say that the artist, Dylan included, is more like the shaman than the psychotic in that the work involves a particular kind of integration between PMA and what Jung would call "directed thinking."

Yet thought and symbolism do seem to play a part in Dylan's life and work. Colman (ibid.) says: "Although he/she needs to be especially in touch with PMA, any successful artistic work involves considerable shaping and development." In referring to Dylan's work he adds:

> I would argue that a great deal of this is certainly symbolic – lines like "we sit here stranded, though we're all doing our best to deny it" on *Visions of Johanna* (1966) and more clearly, "She was born in spring, but I was born too late" on *Simple Twist of Fate* (1974). On the other hand the multi-layering of imagery seems to stem more directly from PMA (as I understand it) – e.g. "jewels and binoculars hang from the head of the mule" (also from *Visions of Johanna* and later recreated as a literal visual image for a Rolling Stones album cover).
>
> (ibid.)

Was Dylan actually some sort of shaman? The shaman has mastered transit between thought and PMA. He consciously and thoughtfully commences a journey to the world of spirit and ancestors by inducing trance or ecstasy, gathers information, exits from such a journey in a controlled way, and returns to thoughtfully impart the knowledge for the constructive use of the social community. Or, he or she guides a troubled person through such a personal journey. Dylan certainly had some degree of disciplined, integrated control over entry into and exit from his PMA states, both in writing music and poetry and in when, where and how to present it. He uses his capacity for PMA to induce ecstatic states in others, to arouse frenzy and hysteria that are not well controlled by thought. He does take the audience through a journey with an ending, but it is more like a drug experience than a learning experience. He does not use thought to bring back knowledge gained from PMA and impart it thoughtfully to the community; his purpose is more to induce reciprocal primordial states in himself and his audience, whom he may have looked upon as a bit too wedded to the world of rational thought. Available accounts of his off-stage life raise questions about the maturity of his general mental state, that is, how much of his daily social and interpersonal behavior was also determined by PMA. He moved many in the larger community in ways that were personally meaningful to them, some constructively and others not so, but he made clear it was not his thoughtful intention to do so; he took no personal responsibility for his effect on others, nor did he see his calling as doing good for a larger community.

We have traced a path involving shamanism and creativity that will culminate in the ensuing discussion of psychosis. There are fundamental similarities among the three that involve heavy reliance on PMA, as well as fundamental differences regarding the times, places and purposes of primordial expression and its regulation by or dissociation from thought. There may be an underlying constitutional difference between some persons who become shamans, creative, or psychotic, and others who become none of the above. The developmental outcome of such constitutional sensitivity may relate to the attitude of the interpersonal and social environment to these characteristics. The "product," and how it is looked upon by and received by the social community, may depend upon the kind of integration or dissociation between PMA and thought that is developed, and upon whether the product or expression is received as an enhancement to community life or as a disruption and drain on resources.

Chapter 13

Psychosis

"What is psychosis? Can you explain that to me?" Papa Wiramu, the elder and a *Tohunga* in Te Whare Marie, a Maori cultural healing group that operates in conjunction with a psychiatric clinic in Wellington, New Zealand, challenged me in a direct and friendly way. His concern was understandable insofar as the Maori, like many other spiritual cultures colonized by the west, have been scarred by the medical tendency to define persons who hear voices, have visions, and practice telekinesis, teleportation, astral projection, dream-hopping and spiritual healing, as psychotic, medicate them, and thereby disrupt their personal cohesion and the cohesion of the communities in which they live.

The western perspective on psychosis suffers from contextual bias – the tendency of the culture to privilege logical thought. The psychoanalytic subset of western culture is further biased because its database for understanding normal as well as psychotic mind consists of persons in treatment for significant psychopathology. It tends to devalue and label as pathological the phenomenology of primordial mental expression. Spiritual cultures, in contrast, place a high value on PMA, including experiences that westerners might label irrational and superstitious if not outright hallucinatory and delusional. However, such cultures integrate PMA with thought in a dialectical way that provides controlled access to it, both entry and exit, and utilize the result in the service of establishing and maintaining cohesion and harmony in the collective community. In spiritual cultures the shaman is the guide and interpreter between thought and PMA in the service of the community. While the kinds of mental activities that are called psychotic in western culture are not so labeled in spiritual cultures, such cultures do identify persons who are out of harmony with the community, nature and the ancestral world, and attempt to heal them.

It is important to attempt to comprehend the nature of psychosis in a way that transcends a particular cultural context. Psychosis, spirituality and creativity share a predominance of primordial mental activity, but there are crucial differences among the three. The severity of the psychosis is directly proportional both to the extent of PMA and to the degree of dissociation of primordial mental activity from thought. In other words, PMA comes to have a life of its own. Another way that psychosis differs from shamanism and from creativity is that the result is not used in the service of the social group or community. In psychosis the community or social group is required to be at the service of the individual, whose unregulated and hence maladaptive expressions of primordial mental activity render him or her more or less disabled.

Theoretical background: Historical perspective

In his *Anthropology* Immanuel Kant anticipates some of the ideas about the difference between primordial mental activity in psychosis and ordinary thinking that Freud articulated more than a century later:

> The only universal characteristic of madness is the loss of *common* sense and its replacement with *logical private sense*. . . . For it is a subjectively necessary touchstone of the correctness of our judgments generally, and consequently also of the soundness of our under-standing, that we also restrain our understanding by the *understanding of others*, instead of *isolating* ourselves with our own understanding and judging *publicly* with our private representations, so to speak. . . . For we are thereby robbed, not of the only, but still of the greatest and most useful means of correcting our own thoughts, which happens on account of the fact that we advance them in public in order to see whether they also agree with the understanding of others; for otherwise something merely subjective (for instance, habit or inclination) would easily be taken for something objective.
>
> (Kant, 1798, p. 113)

Freud began to formulate his understanding of psychosis in *The Inter-pretation of Dreams* (1900). He writes that "we are working towards the explanation of the psychoses when we endeavor to elucidate the mystery of dreams" (1900, p. 66). He maintains that the mental activity in psychosis is the same as that in dreaming, and that dreams are a mini-psychosis. He adds: "My explanation of hallucinations in hysteria and paranoia and of visions in mentally normal subjects is that they are in fact regressions – that is, thoughts transformed into images" (ibid., p. 544). He notes that the same reduction in censorship that triggers the primary process that in turn leads to the work of dreaming can also occur under pathological conditions in waking life, leading to a state of "hallucinatory regression." He goes on to state that: "To this state of things we give the name of psychosis" (ibid., p. 568). In his late life summary of his work he returns to the central relationship of the mental activity underlying dreaming to that of psychosis, stating: "A dream, then, is a psychosis with all the absurdities, delusions and illusions of a psychosis" (1940, p. 172). Important as these observations have proved to be, a dream is not a psychosis. Dreaming meets the requirement of PMA that is dissociated from thought, except in the unusual instances of lucid dreaming (Chapter 11). However, because of the motor paralysis that accompanies REM sleep there is no action, hence no disruption in relation to the community; everything takes place in the mind. In his 1915 paper on the unconscious Freud writes that the psychoses are narcissistic conditions in which the affective basis of attachment (what he called libidinal cathexis) necessary to form the transference that is required for the process of a psychoanalysis is unavailable because of an arrest/ fixation at the earliest stage of psychosexual development (which he described in 1900 as the primary process). As he did not practice in mental hospitals Freud's knowledge of more disturbed persons was second hand, through readings such as Schreber's memoirs and from colleagues such as Tausk, Abraham, Ferenczi and Jung. This conception of psychosis is of an arrest at or regression to the form of mental activity characteristic of dreaming and of the very onset of life.

Freud was not the only one in his time who believed that dreaming and psychosis are related. Jung wrote: "The psychological mechanisms of dreams and hysteria are most closely related to those of dementia praecox" (1906, p. 78). In his classic (1911) text on Dementia Praecox, Eugen Bleuler remarked on the similarity between the mental activity of the schizophrenic and that of the dreamer, and stated that schizophrenic thinking, especially its delusional aspect, operates by rules that distinguish it from waking thought.

Almost half a century later, Bion (Chapter 3) elaborated a conception of psychosis as failure of the normal process of dreaming, which metabolizes raw experience into thought, and fulmination instead of a destructive process of mental splitting and evacuation; an abnormal dreaming process very similar to Klein's paranoid-schizoid position. My clinical experience is that persons who are recovering or recovered from a psychotic episode often characterize the experience as having been like a dream, a nightmare from which they were unable to awaken. Kolberg (2009) interviewed nine persons who had recovered from psychotic episodes and seven of them described the experience as like a waking dream.

Freud and Klein's models of primordial mind as it functions in psychosis – the primary process and the paranoid-schizoid position and phantasy – describe the same mental phenomena – a concrete, body-referenced mind that is sensory-perceptual, auditory-visual and psychomotor; that is undifferentiated in the sense of not observing ordinary distinctions between self and other or world; that is immediate, discontinuous and stimulus-bound; and that lacks a thoughtful, reflective self and symbolic capability.

Freud and Klein both believed that infants and children are psychotic: innately biologically destructive, intolerant of instinctual frustration, aversive to reality, and defensively distorting of experiences of reality they find unsupportable. The psychotic process involves creating a more palatable sense of satisfaction or goodness. To describe the primordial mind and psychosis Freud explicitly uses the term hallucination, and Klein uses such terms as paranoid, schizoid and manic. Both their theories at times speak of primordial mind as qualitatively distinctive from thought and at other times as though it is simply a variant of thought.

Freud concluded that the primary narcissistic fixation in schizophrenia makes it impossible for the analyst to develop a working collaboration and for the patient to form a transference, precluding the possibility of psychoanalytic therapy. The problem of forming a relationship can be understood in another way, namely that the mind of the schizophrenic is functioning largely according to primordial mental activity that is not integrated with thought, and we ordinarily and meaningfully communicate with others through thought-based language. Freud was able to work with primordial mental activity in dreams precisely because the dreamer had become a waking reflective subject, able and willing to integrate the two experiences and translate the dream into thoughtful language. Despite Freud's pessimism a number of clinicians working in hospital settings – beginning with Tausk, Abraham and Jung – in Freud's own time, and especially Klein and those influenced by her, have demonstrated it is possible to make therapeutic relationships with such persons, probably through some attunement to the primordial wavelength in conjunction with some capacity for thought on the part of the psychotic person.

I am indebted to my patient Jacob (see Chapter 14) for bringing to my attention the following excerpt from a 1936 article by F. Scott Fitzgerald that could come out of Freud's description of the primary process, Klein's of the contrast between the paranoid-schizoid and depressive positions, Bion's of the uncontained mind that lacks alpha function, Matte-Blanco's of symmetrical logic, and I conceive of as the disintegration or dissociation between thought and primordial mental activity:

> The test of a first-rate intelligence is the ability to hold two opposed ideas in the mind at the same time, and still retain the ability to function. One should, for example, be able to see that things are hopeless and yet be determined to make them otherwise. So there was not an "I" anymore – not a basis on which I could organize my self-respect – save my limitless capacity for toil that it seemed I possessed no more. It was strange to have no self – to be like a little boy left alone in a big house, who knew that now he could do anything he wanted to do, but found that there was nothing that he wanted to do.

Psychosis and primordial mental activity

The psychoses are characterized by 1) a basic disturbance in the affective attachment configuration, as described in Chapter 4, leading to an implicit or procedural distortion of the fundamental affective relationship to others; 2) a preponderance of the primordial mental activity that processes the affect; 3) dissociation (lack of disciplined and controlled integration) of PMA from thought; and 4) the maladaptive way in which PMA is used in a particular socio-cultural context.

The balance of these factors, each of which is variable, determines the variety and severity of psychotic expression. The so-called neuroses are for the most part disorders of thought; internally experienced states that torment the sufferer and evoke empathic and sympathetic distress in those who care about that person. The psychotic disturbances involve literal enactments that make the interpersonal and social environment suffer. The psychotic spectrum in western culture ranges in severity from mild manifestations that have varying degrees of contextual-social acceptance including sociopathic, borderline and narcissistic personality conditions in which people are destructive to themselves and destructively impose their wills on others, often just in their close relationships but sometimes in mass displays of cultism, dogma hate and prejudice; to the major psychoses including schizophrenia in which people are no longer able to adapt socially and interpersonally or to take basic care of themselves. Activity in psychosis also spans a wide spectrum. Extremes of psychosis might be looked upon as states of trance (catatonia, negative symptoms) or ecstasy (affective storms). Catatonia involves paralysis of verbal and motor expression that is strikingly similar to the state of sensory-perceptual identity and motor paralysis that Freud first noted in his discussion of dreaming. At the other end of the spectrum of activity a charismatic leader specializing in ecstasy expresses belief in a forceful, compelling way that moves others into a shared state of ecstasy or mass delusion. The hysteria or frenzy leads to cult phenomena, demagoguery, persecution, and social horrors like genocide. Adolf Hitler came perilously close to success in recruiting others into his primordial mental world and rageful enactment of world destruction in the service of a utopian delusion of purification and creation of a new race.

Table 13.1 summarizes some of the salient characteristics of PMA in psychosis. The driving force of psychosis is raw somatic affect rather than the identifiable emotions that characterize thought. This phenomenon was named alexithymia by Sifneos (1975) and described also by Nemiah (1978) and De M'Uzan (1974) among others. The expression itself is not reflective but is sensory, perceptual, and, except in the extreme of catatonia, involves action, the motor system. The affective experiences are amorphous dysphoric states like somatic emptiness (a hole inside to be filled); global, sour, unhappy mood; protracted states of depression and despair; destructive,

Table 13.1 Primordial mental activity and psychosis

What motivates mind	Alexithymia. Driven by somatic sensation and unprocessed affect
How meaning is experienced and expressed	Concrete, psycho-somatic, sensory-perceptual and auditory-visual, motor-enactive except in catatonic states
Nature of personal narrative	Unintegrated, discontinuous. Stimulus-bound. Immediate moment is the whole or totality of experience. Without time and memory
The center of experience and expression	Undifferentiated, global or holistic with regard to inside and outside, self and other. Center of agency outside the corporeal person (paranoid, referential)
Absolutism/relativism	Belief, certainty, "magical" certainty that what is believed is actually happening. Conflict is interpersonal not intrapsychic and involves enactment of undifferentiated aspects of self
Expression, communication, learning	Concrete and literal. Active expressive mode and receptive inductive mode (learning). Exerts/experiences peremptory force or pressure, push and pull
Relation to thought	Dissociated
Language – morphology sometimes affected (neologisms)	Uses information including words concretely and formalistically but linguistic syntax and grammar are preserved
Development	Learns disturbed procedural pattern in attachment phase and subsequently expresses it. Thought is limited and dissociated

tantrum-like enactments suggestive of rage; the spectrum of anxiety, panic and dread, and psychosomatic states including migraine headaches, skin disorders and gastrointestinal and genitourinary problems. Although no one who observes a person in the throes of acute schizophrenia doubts that distress is being experienced, the nature of the emotional suffering is not known to and borne thoughtfully by the person in the way that an empathic observer might imagine. A common resistance to treatment is the reluctance to do the work to identify and bear painful emotions, and many successfully treated persons have told me that the kind of suffering related to acknowledging and bearing one's emotions is much more painful and difficult. What can make the work bearable is the accompanying sense of personal integrity and control, and the capacity to direct one's life in emotionally rewarding ways.

In psychosis external reality is undifferentiated from intrapsychic (subjective) reality and, in contrast to the collective sharing of PMA that characterizes interactions in spiritual cultures, the experience is idiosyncratic not consensual. There is experience without an integrated differentiated self to think about it. What is experienced and enacted is a happening, a sensory-perceptual event rather than an experience of the mind. It may help to understand this by contrasting the *experience* of dreaming itself with the recasting of the dream in language on awakening in order to think about it. Often we wake from dreams believing what we dreamed actually occurred. In psychosis there is no awakening or thought, and the experience is the reality.

While the observer notes delusions and hallucinations and infers that the person is unable to appreciate reality, it follows that the subject experiences his or her mind as omnipotent, possessing power to alter the world. Psychosis is the ultimate example of the subjectivity of one's world view. Along with the fact that painful emotions arising from awareness of one's real place in the world are not experienced, the result is a kind of self-induced form of narcosis or anesthesia.

PMA in psychosis is literal rather than figurative; it is concrete and enactive. In its expressive mode it exerts force and pressure to actualize beliefs. The person does not abstract, represent, symbolize and reflect on ideas and emotions, which would imply awareness that his or her world view is subjective and relative, so there is nothing to communicate and no exchange of meanings. Such concrete expression and enactment of belief exerts pressure on others to lose personal boundaries and to enter into the subject's delusional system. This form of collusion is commonly encountered in cult phenomena and instances of mass hysteria due to induction of ecstatic states. Klein called milder instances of this phenomenon projective identification and she considered it a defense rather than a different way of perceiving. In more severe instances, such as schizophrenia, the magic of primordial mental activity is wrought in isolation, and the person can have a sense of omnipotence while being unable to care for him or herself and requiring institutional care. The literal quality of mind along with undifferentiation of self from other leads the person to feel assaulted or persecuted by externally misperceived aspects of his or her own mind and contributes to phenomena such as paranoia and ideas of reference.

In the psychotic state ordinary rules of logic, causality, time and space are not appreciated. There is no sense of passage of time; the moment is everything and there is no remembered past or anticipated future. While schizophrenic persons often obsess, giving the impression they are in conflict within themselves, such paralytic obsessions tend to be about whether to do or not to do, and are not about psychologically incompatible ideas. Complex internal mental states such as comparisons, contrasts, psychological conflict and ambivalence, and choices are not experienced. Contradictory opposites are not distinguished. A thing can simultaneously be its opposite and the solution often turns out to be another iteration of the problem.

That the process I am describing is radically different from thought and the expression or reception of thoughts in communicative language might seem inconsistent with the fact that psychotic persons are usually quite capable of talking and writing, if sometimes in ways that are strange and idiosyncratic. Language and aspects of culture have been assimilated in a formal or literal sense, for example vocabulary and grammar, but these are employed concretely as objects that exert force or pressure, both expressively and receptively, rather than abstractly as representations or parts of thought. The concreteness of the schizophrenic mind has been remarked on by many (Klein, 1930; Segal, 1957, 1978; Searles, 1962; Harrow *et al.*, 1972). The relationship of PMA and language is explored further in Chapter 15.

Illustrations of PMA in psychosis

Detailed illustrations of the theory I have proposed are found in the chapters to follow. For now I offer a few brief examples. In the course of a discussion about personal responsibility with Caroline, the schizophrenic woman who provided and helped me to understand the clinical material that is the basis for Chapter 15 on language, I made what seemed to me an obvious logical causal statement to her. I connected her uncontrolled attitude about spending money in order to immediately gratify wishes with her very limited resources, and expressed concern she would soon run out of funds. She responded in a matter-of-fact way, saying: "I'm going to buy a $100 pair of desert boots because they keep my feet warm so I won't be so distressed in the next few months."

Another time she told me that because she was afraid she would waste a $20 bill she needed on something she might have an immediate impulse to buy, she had put it with her battery jumper cable in her car where she couldn't touch it except in an emergency.

One Christmas Caroline gave me a decorative wine stopper as a gift. In response to my question about why she had done this she revealed that she had observed wine bottles in my recycle bin and concluded I was an alcoholic. Her father's alcoholism, one of the manifestations of his pervasive psychosis, had been a major family problem leading to his eventual self-destruction, and the family had been unable to get him to stop. She went on to tell me that she was afraid she might lose me, and she was determined to put a stop (stopper) to my drinking. This was not a symbolic gift but a magical action.

The following vignette illustrates absence of contradiction, undifferentiation of self and other, concreteness, and dissociation of PMA from thought. After many years of therapy Caroline had developed a realistic responsible part of her personality. Nonetheless she still functioned much of the time in PMA dissociated from thought, living in a dream world of uncontrolled pursuit of immediate gratification heedless of the fact she did not earn enough money or have sufficient savings to support such a lifestyle. She was rapidly approaching the point where her resources would run out, but she continued to live as though she were a reasonably well-to-do woman. We had talked about numerous plans and potential solutions but there was no continuity between her statements and her actions; she did not sustain her sincere resolutions much beyond the moment they were made. After repeated insistence on my part she had more or less come to accept the necessity of putting her remaining funds in a trust controlled by one of her family members. Against my better judgment I agreed to her request for yet another "last chance." She agreed that the following hour she would bring in a specific list of the kinds of excessive spending and travelling she did that would be forbidden, and during the two-week period that followed if she violated the agreement in any way then the trust would be drawn up. She appeared very sincere and thoughtful during this discussion.

She was late for the following appointment and explained that during lunch she had begun thinking about her situation and ended up day-dreaming. She took out a list of kinds of excessive expenditures – long car trips, clothes, books, CD buying, meals out, entertainments, etc. Inci-dentally and without affect, in the middle of discussing how she owned far more coats than she needed, she informed me she had just purchased another one and had gone to pick it up before her appointment, the implication being that this was the reason for her lateness. Then, after adding she had planned not to tell me, she added that she had just been on another buying spree. I said that was the last straw, no more chances, and it would be necessary to make the trust agreement. She became enraged, saying I had broken *my* word and that she had said she would start tomorrow not yesterday. I pointed out it was she who had broken her word, that her action had symbolic significance and that it was not just a concrete issue of which day she would start, and that this had happened once too often. She vacillated, one moment enraged at me for not giving her a chance and claiming that she could control herself if given the chance and the next moment telling me she had not even realized she was going to go on the latest binge, and if given more opportunity she would probably break the agreement the day after we made it.

The aspect of PMA involving expression or forcing and impression or feeling forced is illustrated by three vignettes. Caroline was in the habit of mass-mailing inappropriate and bizarre recitations of her personal business to a large group of persons from her past and present life. She had once told me she believed she was forcing herself into their mailboxes so they would take care of her. "Mailboxes," incidentally, was not a symbol.

For many years we had observed that when I began to experience some success encouraging Caroline to think about painful issues rather than indulging in the typical wishful belief that they did not exist, she would make a facial expression I construed as a yawn. We had come to see this as an indicator of her resistance to being influenced by me. On one such occasion I asked her to tell me more about what this expression meant. She replied: "I'm opening my mouth because I want you to go in and find my feelings."

Adam was referred to me when he was in his mid thirties with a diagnosis of paranoid schizophrenia after many hospitalizations in the course of the preceding decade. In the course of getting to know him he told me an interesting story about growing up that seemed to illustrate the concrete pressuring quality of PMA as a vehicle of deep learning and its relationship to belief or delusion. At age twelve he was taken by his mother to a therapy group for families of alcoholics. There, as he tells the story, it was "revealed" that his father was an alcoholic who had physically abused his mother for many years. The therapist, according to Adam, remarked that in such families there is always a scapegoat and asked who the scapegoat was in Adam's family. He recalls his mother remarking that he had been. Adam grew up believing that it was his job to take care of his parents and their problem, which meant to suppress all the feelings he had because his parents were not capable of tolerating them, and be a "good boy." In his adult life he was unable to assert himself appropriately and instead would act like there was something the matter with him, leading him eventually into the mental health system. He developed fluid grandiose delusions surrounding ideas of being Christ, or having a special relationship to him, or else that he was the victim of international plots and conspiracies of the highest order. It seems that he was functioning in PMA at the time of the therapy session he remembers, and believed that the therapist was concretely informing him that his was the role of suffering victim, not that he was being helped to understand in a symbolic reflective way the nature of interactions in his family.

Kay, a professionally accomplished middle-aged woman, gave me permission to include this entry from her diary. It was written after many years of therapy and a growing capacity to think and reflect on her mental activity. Kay had two hospitalizations in her early twenties because of suicidal ideation, hallucinations and delusions. The context of her entry was her tendency to obsess about whether or not to undertake an almost hour-long trip over winding hilly roads to my office in icy, snowy winter conditions. In this instance she had decided to remain at home and have the session to which she refers by telephone:

> When I looked out the window after we ended our conversation I saw that the trees were encased in ice and opined (I'm looking for another word than "thought") "I was RIGHT." So, without knowing it, I was still worrying about whether or not I had predicted correctly about icy conditions. Somehow, this need to be RIGHT is related to my difficulty

thinking and making as fully informed as possible decisions. If I could accept that one can't know anything about the future with 100 per cent certainty I'd be freer to think and take my own thinking seriously and act on it rather than just acting or not acting (paralysis). You said that I needed to be in an accident before I could think/know/believe that I was in danger of getting into an accident. YES. This feels absolutely right. I need to be extremely sick (temperature over 102) before I know I am sick at all; I need to be audited by the IRS before I accept that I really have to file income tax returns. What goes into my needing to be IN the situation of concern before I am sure that I am ABOUT to enter the situation? There is something about needing to feel SURE. Why? Because a hostile voice within challenges my reasoning, my thinking, and does so by asking in an attacking voice: "Are you absolutely SURE? Isn't this a little self-serving?" This is my mother. . . I remember year after year feeling disappointed that she didn't make/buy me a birthday cake but "forgetting" immediately so the next year anticipating a celebration and being disappointed. I was complaining that my mother hadn't gotten me a cake and a friend said, "but she never gets you one" and I said "huh?" and she reminded me of the previous number of years and finally I had a past in mind when I thought about the future. What we're talking about. . . is a kind of visual-motor "chaining." I go from one activity, stimulated by a visual sense, to another, and only with great effort can I direct myself to my desk to think about what is important. Not thinking keeps me from clarifying and making more organic the meaning of our conversations. Like when I asked if talking about sexual feelings was a kind of enactment. Only by asking the question and then by thinking could I know that our conversations are not a kind of unacknowledged enactment but an acknowledged conversation about reality toward the end of my own development. What I resist is being grounded with awareness in the true anguish of my past and the realization not only of what I have missed but what I may become aware of yearning for too late. The past is not past to me and the future is not future. If the past were past, it would be over; if the future were future, I could plan and hope.

At this stage of her therapy Kay had acquired some capacity to think about her PMA. What she describes is concrete sensory-perceptual-motor actualization in which there are no comparative distinctions and no passage of time. It is what it is and there is nothing to think about. She is not actually schizophrenic, however, because unlike the back ward occupant who can imagine herself a deity in an impoverished even horrendous setting Kay requires an external resemblance in formal or superficial characteristics as a template for her concrete actualization. She describes a state in which actual experience or happening is required in order to validate knowledge of reality. The back ward schizophrenic no longer requires or cares about actual experience; his or her reality is totally undifferentiated as in a dream.

Next I summarize an entire hour and relevant parts of two subsequent sessions from my work with Brandon. At the time of these sessions Brandon was in his early fifties, married, and inconsistently dedicated to an art career that had brought him some success. When he first consulted me, decades previously, he was withdrawn and socially isolated in a state of non-verbal misery, seriously suicidal. He was supported by a substantial inheritance, living in a basement apartment, engaging in repetitive ritualistic disassembling, cleaning and reassembling his motorcycle. In our early sessions he was nearly mute and was convinced (accurately, as we learned after many years) that he had no thoughts. In fact much of his mental experience was somato-psychic, for instance internal burning sensations that, much later, we identified as "burning rage," and amorphous states of misery and sourness that seemed to amalgamate rage and hopeless despair. He used and experienced words not as vehicles of communication, but as things with which people manipulated and harmed one another, and understandably he received my feedback as a hostile attack. Early in the process of learning to think and feel he depicted his mental state in a drawing of a man cleaving himself to pieces with an axe. He specialized in finding women as withdrawn as he, with whom he could engage in non-verbal subtly sexually sadistic relationships the exact nature of which he withheld from me so that he would not have to talk about and think about them. It was years before he could begin to formulate and verbalize thoughts and feelings rather than mindlessly enact a state of hopelessness, withdrawal and intense somatized rage that took the form of attacks on himself and withdrawal from a world that was not differentiated from himself and hence defensively perceived as hostile, attacking and untrustworthy.

The hours I recount came after many years of work and achievement of some limited capacity to think about his still extensive periods of dissociated PMA. Because he lived at a distance from my office we alternated between face-to-face appointments and telephone sessions. The first hour was a telephone appointment. It took place during the week following the Thanksgiving holiday. When he was a boy Thanksgiving had been a time when his mother typically got drunk and lost control of her rage in gross and often indecent assaults of which Brandon, her youngest child, was the victim of choice. It had also been the time of year in Brandon's early adolescence when his father committed suicide with a pistol after a lengthy period of depression and hospitalization.

The first hour began with a long silence, something I had come to understand as a reliable signal that he was in a primary mental state of somatized non-verbal rage and despair associated with the undifferentiated sense that I was critical and angry at him as well. Brandon eventually interrupted the silence to say that he realized "something's going on." He realized over our holiday separation that he had missed me (such an awareness was a relatively recent development). He next recounted how he struggled to be active, thoughtful and caring while entertaining his wife's dysfunctional family, most of whom he did not especially like, and to distinguish painful memories of childhood holidays as mental events to be remembered with appropriate feelings of distress rather than mindlessly acted out in the form of rage and withdrawal. While immersed in this struggle he had realized that he wanted to see and talk with me. Another lengthy silence ensued, finally interrupted when he informed me that, although he knew my phone number quite well, he had found himself dialing the phone number of his deceased mother instead. At this point he began to talk and to think about his holiday more comprehensively, elaborating his struggle between withdrawing and experiencing rage somatically, globally hating himself and the world and succumbing to powerful urges to have aggressive sex with his wife on the one hand, and talking with her about his thoughts, feelings and memories on the other. Her family is too much like his own he concluded, and his efforts to think, communicate and take more initiative were only partly successful. He became progressively more thoughtful and communicative and remarked that he needed to get out and make some friends. As the hour drew to a close he said he was confused that this regression had occurred at a time when he believed he had had a thoughtful and constructive weekend and wanted to talk with me about it.

Later the same week Brandon began his session by remarking: "My father's death is coming up soon." When I repeated aloud his literal words he was shocked and amused. He had been thinking about talking to me about the upcoming anniversary of his father's death. We agreed that he seemed to be literally living in another place and I encouraged him to try to find words to describe his state of mind. He said he had been walking around all day in a daze or state of shock, looking at the walls. The remainder of the hour was characterized by a collaborative struggle to help him resist the pull toward a dream-like enactive state, and to talk about it and remember instead. In the course of our discussion he told me about the effort he and his wife were making to adopt a child and the difficulty he experienced waiting patiently for the agency to respond to their application. In the course of his narrative he began to look wide-eyed, lost, and incipiently tearful, and talked of his sense that they had forgotten about him. I remarked that he was repeating the experience of being left all alone by his father (and mother), and he burst into tears and began to talk about it. He then talked of plans to take an infant care class because he needed to know something about such things as how to give a child a bottle. Once again he looked dazed and said he felt as though he didn't know what he was doing.

I knew from previous conversations he had learned a good deal about child care by caring for nieces and nephews, and was not as ill-prepared as he believed. I commented that it is very difficult for a child not to have a parent who cares and knows how to meet his needs.

Two sessions later he reported a dream in which he was climbing up the outside wall of a large stone cathedral accompanied by the minister. Suddenly the railing broke and he fell, dangling over the side and clutching it. The minister encouraged him to climb back up but did not attempt to rescue him. In the discussion that ensued he realized that the cathedral imagery was undifferentiated. It condensed what he had come to realize as his father's hypocrisy – formally practicing religion while being emotionally disengaged from it – and his sense of betrayal when his father sent him away to a boarding school with a religious name and tradition that had a prominent cathedral next to the campus, and shortly thereafter committed suicide. He also associated the cathedral to one that was in the city where I had previously had my office, and to some of our recent discussions of how he might begin to see church communities as opportunities to meet people, socialize and make music. He recognized that the dream actualized his struggle about mentally going over the edge into a state of regression or hanging on to being thoughtful. He related the dream to his passive and revengeful wish that I magically make it so that his painful childhood would never have happened, and his struggle to accept that "all" I could do was help him to learn to have a mind of his own and to take better care of himself. Being outside the church enacted his lifelong sense of isolation and alienation and simultaneous sense of imprisonment in a small withdrawn place, like the bedroom of his childhood and other places in his life where he had "holed up." In boarding school the church was across the street from the campus and the students were forbidden to go beyond campus except for the services. His father had left him at school and there was no way out other than psychological withdrawal.

In these hours Brandon vacillates between two forms of mental activity, sometimes actualizing both in dream and during waking hours the sensory-perceptual-somatic-motor state characteristic of his childhood, and other times thinking about it. In the dream, opposites and differences are depicted as an undifferentiated unity; there is no distinction between past and present and hence no sense of time.

The realistic ability to reflect and contrast that is characterized by appreciation of the relativity of time, differentiation of memory from present, and a sense of continuity in the face of change, is largely absent in the mental activity of psychotic persons. This is reflected in many ways. There may be a subtle sense of being disoriented in a "place" that is also familiar, being neither here nor there, being formally in the present while acting or enacting something that is not accessible to thought or memory. The session in which Brandon dialed his mother's number rather than mine, and commented without awareness that his long-dead father's death would be coming in a few days, illustrates this quality of experience. Psychotic despair, one of the elements that makes effective therapy with such persons difficult, has the same timeless quality; things are and will always be the same, even when there is objective evidence of change.

The development of psychosis

How does a normal mental process, primordial mental activity, come to be the foundation of psychosis? Judging from studies that have confirmed REM activity *in utero* the neural circuitry responsible for PMA seems to be fully formed and operative at birth. In contrast, the neural circuitry and psychological capacity for thought and thought-related language matures gradually over the first decade of life. In the normal course of development thought comes to have superior adaptive value in many situations for the growing child and eventually the adult, especially in western culture. In all cultures, however, it gradually comes under the integrated regulatory control of thought – as to times, places and contexts of expression. In western culture the integration for the most part involves suppression and relegation of PMA to sleep and dreaming, although it may be employed selectively in socially sanctioned phenomena such as spirituality, creativity and parenting, and persist in some other ways and situations that are not so obvious.

In spiritual cultures the balance of the two mental processes may tilt more in favor of PMA, and there may be less suppression of PMA; the process of integration involves controlled entry and exit between thought and PMA for community-sanctioned purposes under the discipline and guidance of the shaman. What determines maturity is integration between these two forms of mental activity and selective adaptive employment of the result in the community in which the person must function. In spiritual cultures the shaman is a model of mental health and maturity, having been trained to face and grapple with the subjective demons of a PMA state of dissolution of self and boundaries that may be experienced as demonic torture and dismemberment, along with experiences of voices and visions. The shaman learns to master the experience and develop the capacity to willfully transit from thought to PMA and back in a controlled and disciplined manner.

In western culture maturity also involves disciplined control of PMA by thought, but for the most part the control is exercised by suppression rather than thought-regulated utilization. There is no single figure who exemplifies the maturity the shaman represents in spiritual cultures. Perhaps it is best represented by some creative artists, those who are in touch with and gain information about themselves from their dreams, some mothers who manage the transit between realms in the course of their child rearing, and those individuals who have mastered the kinds of extreme stress and trauma that would ordinarily induce psychosis.

The integration–dissociation variable is probably influenced by constitutional as well as environmental or interpersonal factors. These particular sensitivities were discussed in Chapter 11. Interpersonal factors that predispose toward psychosis begin at the earliest attachment phase of development (described in Chapter 4). Contemporary iterations of attachment theory emphasize the concept of implicit or procedural learning and knowledge, and link disturbed attachment to adult psychotic pathology, especially borderline personality disorder. This association is especially notable in the work of Fonagy (Fonagy, 1999a; Fonagy and Target, 1996; Fonagy and Luyten, 2009). Mary Ainsworth (Ainsworth et al., 1978) derived a "strange situation" experiment and classified infant behavior into four affect-based attachment categories: secure, anxious/avoidant, anxious/resistant and disorganized/disoriented. Lyons-Ruth (2003) and the Boston Change Process Study Group (2007; Stern et al., 1998) have formulated a model of disorganized attachment, a form of very early affective conflict that is external rather than intrapsychic in the sense of being interpersonal or relational. If caregivers behave in ways that are rejecting and attacking, and distort the meaning of infant initiatives by responding to them with dissonant or inappropriate affects, the consequence in the infant is anticipatory procedural learning or reflexive dysphoric affective responses that may be adaptive in the dysfunctional family context but ultimately maladaptive and self-destructive in a more normal social context. Rhythm or dysrhythmia is an important element. The infant who is responded to in ill-timed, inappropriate, disruptive and hostile ways probably assimilates such a pattern in a deep somatopsychic way, and learns to reproduce it.

In summary, the earliest learning experience, deeply and somatically assimilated via primordial mental activity, involves frustration of basic need, hostile non-synchronized caregiver responses to infant need signals, as well as distorted, inappropriate responses. This somatically misshapen attachment template comprises the implicit or procedural knowledge that is carried through life, and on which PMA draws or models subsequent relationships. I would like to reiterate, however, that implicit or procedural knowledge of itself is insufficient to account for psychotic pathology. It is the substrate on which primordial mental activity draws. In the emerging psychosis the pathological implicit knowledge is processed at the levels of learning and expression by PMA, and the PMA in turn elicits further disturbed responses from the interpersonal environment. The result is antithetical both to development of thought and to the learning of disciplined control of the relationship between thought and PMA.

For approximately two decades after Sullivan's landmark books (1953a, 1953b) an extensive family therapy literature flourished that describes in clinical detail some of these pathogenic family configurations. The family environment is sometimes overtly traumatic but frequently it subtly invalidates thought and mature adaptation, distorts reality and the emotional meaning of experience by a combination of coercion and neglect, and supports and rewards immature mental activity and behavior. In such a psychotic family structure parents are threatened by the child's autonomy and its potential to expose family problems so they undermine the child's development of the capacity for mature thought, and through their own PMA coerce the child to express and enact repudiated destructive aspects of themselves. They overlook and rationalize the child's problems and infantilize him or her in a way that fosters disturbed behavior. With little capacity for realistic adaptive thought and self-control and the path to autonomy closed the child may learn to accept the rewards of passivity. These include avoidance of the mental work of self–object differentiation, mental representation, integration, recognition and control of emotion, and use of language to communicate – the characteristics of mature thought. The natural enthusiasm and curiosity with which the child approaches the challenge of learning to think and to use thinking to actively and constructively adapt may be replaced by an attitude of *hebitude* (a term derived from Greek, meaning mental lethargy, the root of hebephrenia), which characterizes psychosis. Primordial mental activity, however maladaptive from an external "objective" perspective, may persist as the mental expression of choice in order to create a delusional sense of mastery, a magical sense of omnipotence, in the face of what would otherwise be a state of helpless entrapment.

The next steps in development of psychosis occur in late adolescence and early adulthood, when the socio-cultural expectation is that the person separates from the primary family and achieves some degree of autonomy with regard to work and formation of a new family. The pattern involving thought and PMA that was adaptive within the family environment in which it originated is maladaptive in the larger social-cultural context.

Such psychotic family units are held together by denial, as portrayed in the fable of *The Emperor's New Clothes*. The prevalence of denial in families of psychotic persons is documented in an extensive family therapy literature of half a century ago (Robbins, 1993). Investigators of the family background of schizophrenics who are unaware of this mechanism and lack the orientation to study family dynamics in depth have promulgated the erroneous belief that schizophrenia is an illness of late adolescence and early adulthood that develops in a hitherto "normal" person from an unremarkable family background. Such denial of pathology in association with low developmental expectations and reward for immature behavior serves to conceal the pathology from view until late adolescence or early adulthood. What "worked" in such a family environment is exposed as psychosis in the larger culture when the person is unable to meet expectations for independence, education, and formation of close relationships with others.

For example, the parents of Rachel, a young woman I have written about at length elsewhere (1993), would not acknowledge the existence of any premorbid disturbance or any family problems whatsoever during half a year of regular social work interviews following her hospitalization, during college, for florid psychosis. Even more striking, her parents were convinced that there was nothing abnormal about her psychotic state, despite feedback from hospital staff about her catatonic posturing and her hallucinations. Her father remarked to me: "Any of us would act the way she does if we had to be in a place like this, with all these crazy people!" Eventually Rachel's parents admitted having observed similar behavior in Rachel as far back as her early teens, but even then they managed to discount its pathological implications. Father, for example, insisted that her hallucinating was no different from his habit of talking to himself. After a year and a half of intensive family work extensive family problems were gradually uncovered that some years later led to her parents' divorce.

A similar account is to be found in the gripping family biography written by Elizabeth Swados (1991) entitled *The Four of Us*, centered around the chronic schizophrenia of her older brother Lincoln. Everyone in the Swados family was aware of the facts of Lincoln's disturbance from the time he was quite young, but they construed it not as illness but as the expression of an exceptionally gifted and creative individual, and hence encouraged it by blaming others who might react differently. Swados concludes her remarkable account with the statement that: "The easiest way to understand his schizophrenia was to believe it didn't exist. . . . My true beliefs centered around my esteem for my brother's gifts. He was a difficult genius who would prove himself to his opponents" (ibid., p. 30). He eventually committed suicide.

Walker and Lewine (1990) conducted a study in which experienced clinicians were shown home movies taken during the childhood of five persons who became schizophrenic to determine if they could distinguish the child who was at risk from his/her siblings. They were able to do so in four of the five instances. What was particularly intriguing about their report was an incidental comment about the "pilot" patient they studied to determine whether their project was feasible. Viewers of home movies had no difficulty identifying him as the abnormal sibling. His parents, however, not only stoutly denied that there had been anything abnormal about him as a child, but asserted that he had been the best adjusted of their children!

The exposition of PMA in psychosis continues in the next two chapters. Chapter 14 contains first-hand accounts of the nature of psychotic mental process from persons who have developed some capacity to think and reflect about it. In Chapter 15 the linguistic aspects of primordial mental activity are explored and illustrated with detailed clinical material. In

Chapter 16 data are presented from neuroimaging studies in support of the hypothesis that psychosis is a manifestation of a qualitatively distinctive form of mental activity that seems to share common features with dreaming.

Chapter 14

Thoughtful reflections of psychotic persons

Autobiographical and biographical accounts of personal struggles with psychosis abound in the "scientific" and popular literature and even the entertainment media. Daniel Paul Schreber's memoir was the subject of Freud's (1911b) monograph and the basis for some of his speculations about paranoia and delusion. Joanne Greenberg wrote the hugely popular fictionalized account of her work with Frieda Fromm-Reichmann, *I Never Promised You a Rose Garden* (1964), under the pseudonym Hannah Green. Recent accounts that have received much attention include Sylvia Nasar's (2001) biography of the genius mathematician John Nash, which became the subject of a movie, and the psychiatrist Kay Redfield Jamison's (1997) autobiographical account of her manic-depressive illness.

Most such writings recount the subject's struggle first to become aware that he or she is psychotic. The struggle takes place in the context of believing the illness is an affliction of which the person is victim; one that is presumably of organic origin and in that sense external to the basic organization of the personality. The presumed task is to learn to cope with this illness as one would with diabetes or cancer; to regulate and suppress symptomatic manifestations so that they interfere minimally with "normal" life, primarily using educational techniques or behavior modification along with medication. The underlying assumption in such writings is that the psychotic mental process itself is meaningless and epiphenomenal to the underlying organic process.

A more recent strand of first person accounts comes from persons who call themselves "voice hearers." They have sought and found a community of others who have struggled with similar experiences and the stigmatizing way society deals with them in the form of diagnoses such as schizophrenia (Lampshire, 2009; Lambrecht and Lampshire, 2009; Randall *et al.*, 2008). Many of these people do not believe that they have a psychosis or mental illness at all, but see themselves as being as "normal" as anyone else and needing to accept and control the unusual experiences and capacities they possess.

In Chapter 11, I explored possible constitutional underpinnings for some of these experiences and in Chapters 9 and 10 discussed the problem of distinguishing spiritual shamanic phenomena from psychosis. I have suggested that psychosis is the product of dissociation of PMA from thoughtful regulation so that it manifests itself in ways that are contextually maladaptive and destructive to the individual and to his or her inter-personal relationships, and the community. Maturation and health by contrast involve regulation of PMA by thought. A central distinction in evaluating the struggles some people report is between integration that involves a kind of understanding of the meaning and significance of pri-mordial expressions by the thoughtful aspect of mind, such as Jung (2009) achieved, and a kind of dissociation and control by thoughtful mind that treats the primordial aspect of mind as an alien external affliction. As noted in Chapter 10 it is not always easy to discern when a person has actually achieved thoughtful control and when that person may be deluding him or herself. This chapter includes two first person accounts of such a mature integrative process.

Most of the clinical data used to illustrate psychoanalytic theories of psychosis come entirely from the perspective of the author, who is using them to support his or her ideas. The reader will never know what the patient's side of the story might have been and whether the patients whose lives are described would have agreed or disagreed about the accuracy of the accounts or the formulations themselves. What follows, in the spirit of collaborative authorship, are two remarkable first person accounts of the mental process underlying psychosis. They illustrate many of the char-acteristics of primordial mental activity and the struggle to achieve a mature integration of PMA and thought and a more effective sense of self-control based on understanding and acceptance. At the advanced stage of therapy during which the accounts were written both persons, to whom I have given the pseudonyms Lisabeth and Jacob, had become actively involved in the collaborative process of studying how their minds work and had actually done some writing independently or contemplated the prospect. Both had observed I was writing a book, and both responded enthusiastically when I suggested they might want to contribute something about the knowledge they had acquired not simply to recognize descrip-tively that they had been psychotic, but also to reflect on and think seriously about the mental processes involved. There is no definitive way to prove that the reports are not just meaningless repetitions of things they heard me say to them in the course of therapy. However, much of the data that Lisabeth adduces to support her own ideas about the psychotic workings of her mind came from verbatim entries in a diary she kept during the early years of her therapy. I am grateful to both of them for their permission to use the material, which is presented alongside my own description of their problems.

Lisabeth

Lisabeth's story illustrates primordial mental activity characteristic of a less severe psychotic condition. She maintained enough distance from others and had sufficient capacity to utilize thought in situations that did not involve emotional intimacy that her profound disturbance was not apparent to most people. She remained closely tied to her mother and brother and isolated from and frightened of other people. She had not had an intimate or even a sexual relationship until her early forties when she became involved in a destructive lesbian relationship, which was the first and only time she ever slept a night with another person until well along in our work when she was in her early sixties. She requested therapy because she felt unable to end the relationship, unable to sleep at night, and intolerably burdened by the discrepancy between the way she had to behave in her work and the way she felt inside, which was near continuous panic and terror with strong suicidal urges. Meanwhile, in her very challenging career, Lisabeth was experiencing increasing success. She was highly valued and appreciated for her skills planning and executing complex programs that required working closely with a community of people both individually and in groups but she experienced no satisfaction or sustenance from her accomplishments as they were based on compliance with perceived expectations rather than on a foundation of inner emotional self. She let no one know what she really thought or felt, because she was terrified others would get to know that in "reality" she was nothing but excrement, and reject and attack her in the way she believed she deserved. When she was not working Lisabeth spent much of her time alone and withdrawn.

Not long after beginning treatment Lisabeth was able to separate herself from the troublesome lesbian relationship that had motivated her to consult me, but my wish to believe that this was a sign of the success of our work was short-lived, for it soon became apparent that she had taken me as the new partner for her adhesive possessive behavior. She began to eat and drink excessively in order to anesthetize herself and fill a sense of emptiness, anxiety and doom.

Lisabeth was a remarkably perceptive person. She noticed everything, and was soon making detailed and finely nuanced observations about me and what she could observe about my life. However, these were undifferentiated from or fused with a belief system she had about me. She made quasi-delusional fabrications that were rationalized and tenaciously maintained even if there was no data to support them. Her beliefs had the surface quality of idealization. I was a perfect person, the greatest at everything – knowledge, ability, accomplishment, wonderful family. But the dark underside of these ideas, as I realized after the sense of having been flattered wore off, was that she made me out to be inhuman – someone who had no feelings, needs or problems. That way she did not have to care, even as she believed I did not care about her. As is characteristic of PMA these beliefs were realities to her, associated with actions that seemed to her rational and justified, rather than ideas to be reflected upon and thought about. For example she did not believe I needed money so she made a serious case that I ought to treat her free of charge.

Her belief system was essentially that people exist on a binary linear scale; at one end are those who are "perfect," the greatest at everything, living a life of problem-free bliss, with all needs met and never a painful feeling. At the other end are those who are defective, worthless and full of problems, concretely equated with being excrement. Her mother and brother, neither of whom sounded all that extraordinary judging from her descriptions, and most of the time me, were at the perfect end of the scale whereas she perceived herself almost literally as excrement and was utterly convinced that was how I thought of her. Her basic belief that she was excrement was concrete and somatic including the sensation of knots in her stomach, and she regularly had diarrhea in my waiting room bathroom prior to sessions. Sometimes, however, she was on the other side of the scale. In her lesbian relationship with a very disturbed partner, for example, she allowed herself to be used and verbally abused while, as we discovered, harboring a secretly arrogant belief that she was superior.

Soon after beginning therapy there were signs that her life was stabilizing and improving in quality, but she claimed to be getting no sustenance from our relationship. She steadfastly maintained that we did not have what she called a "real" relationship. She experienced me as a false-self, pretending to care about her but actually offering her nothing more than artificial "technique" while I secretly looked down on her with contempt from my psychoanalytic Mount Olympus because she was full of problems and hopelessly defective and I reserved my caring for those in my personal life. My interpretations to her were often experienced as criticism and confirmation of her worthlessness. She bristled when I would refer to our relationship as "therapy" for in her personal lexicon being in therapy was synonymous with being defective. Needless to say, this made it difficult for her to take away anything from the comments I made to her other than criticism and rejection. In response to her critical belief that beneath what she perceived as my facade or pretense of caring, I was actually being hostile and critical, I would say that she made me feel as she did, that nothing I said or did was ever right.

Although Lisabeth's reactions to me were affectively (somatically) intense and pressured, she was frightened and contemptuous of feelings and unable to bear and identify them, another aspect of PMA. Sometimes she cried and choked so much during sessions that she literally believed she was about to die or the world was coming to an end. It slowly became evident that the predominant feeling associated with all her beliefs was rage, either directed in critical attacks on her own person leading to self-hatred, or at me for any reminder that we were separate individuals. When she was not aware of the rage she felt a physical inertia she sometimes called being tired, as her mother had apparently labeled her depressive state, and other times referred to as "being entropic." On other occasions she experienced migraine auras. She was enraged at the idea that I was withholding from her what she imagined was the perfect and emotionally effortless existence that I possessed. This perfect life was for her literally the only good life, and if only she could get it from me concretely she believed it would make up for what was missing in her, or she would no longer be herself but instead be me. The exact nature of the solution was never entirely clarified. This holistic lack of differentiation and boundaries is another characteristic of PMA.

She seemed consumed with the idea of being or becoming me and literally tried to get into every facet of my life in hopes of getting what she was convinced that I had. At the same time she was terrified of any actual contact with me. She went to great lengths to avoid face-to-face encounters with me outside of the office, yet between sessions she spent much of her non-working time tracking or stalking me. She would stand outside the building where I worked for long periods of time hoping to get a glimpse of me through the window. Later, when I had moved my office to my home, she sat in a snow bank on a frigid winter evening peering through the windows. Another time she used binoculars to try to see into my house. She searched through a wastebasket in the office bathroom for something I had written that she seemed to believe would be of immense value. She prowled through an unlocked building on my property when I was on vacation. Through personal research she discovered my publications and when and where I gave lectures. After getting my permission she attended conferences where I made presentations, and phoned me at inappropriate times. All of this was a desperate effort to discover in the most literal sense what I had that she was missing and hopefully get it from me. For someone so socially attuned and astute in her outside life and work she was for the most part unaware that there was anything unusual or inappropriate about her behavior. In short, as is characteristic of PMA, she was *psychologically* unable to differentiate us and appeared to be trying to actualize a kind of delusional-hallucinatory experience of identity (not identification) with me. Her attachment to me was such that for periods of time following the final session that preceded a separation she literally felt that her arms and legs were amputated, that I had concretely taken essential parts of her with me.

At the same time that she was preoccupied with the conviction that she did not have a real relationship with me and was not getting the real "stuff," it became evident she was deriving some benefit from our relationship. Characteristically she would begin an hour in a state that combined inarticulate misery, negativism and confusion with utter certainty about the accuracy of her beliefs. Gradually she would become more open and engaged, and to her never ending surprise, feel better when she left. So I often found myself making variations of a generic comment to her: "What you *believe* about me and my life is more real to you than what actually goes on between us during our time together." After some years of treatment, when she was learning to think about herself and to identify and bear her emotions rather than blindly continue to function in PMA she responded with simultaneous amusement and asperity to my questioning about the accuracy of one of her beliefs by saying: "Don't confuse me with facts."

Lisabeth was in treatment for many years. By late middle age, she had acquired a considerable ability to think about herself, to identify, bear, and put in perspective her feelings, and to distinguish an inner life of *fantasy* from reality. She no longer experienced everything somatically, nor was she so driven to try to actualize her mental content. She began to develop enough of a sense of self-worth that we could reflect about her excremental sense of self as an idea or belief and not as a concrete reality, and she began to feel happy and satisfied with her own activities and relationships. Caring about me as a separate person largely displaced the urge to consume (and destroy) me. In fact caring and loving, feelings she had not previously experienced, became a central focus of her feeling good about herself and about an expanding meaningful social life. When she was around 60 years of age she began to date seriously for the first time. She found and eventually married a man with whom she had the first experience of heterosexual intimacy in her entire life, got married, and derived great satisfaction from their relationship as well as from a maternal role in the lives of a nephew and niece, and a grand-maternal role with her husband's grandchildren.

In the later stages of our work Lisabeth reminisced about the way she used to be, and she recalled how during the winter she would find where I had parked my car and literally follow in my footsteps in the snow. However tempting it might be to think of this as a metaphor it was not. She remarked: "I wanted to find out everything about you, and then I tried to be and do what you were and did." Note that she did not say she tried to be *like* me. Despite her obvious growth and the enhancement of the quality of her life she adamantly resisted any suggestion that our relationship might ever end. *Termination* was experienced in PMA and literally and immediately meant to her the experience of annihilation, being lethally terminated. The very utterance of the word produced an immediate eruption of convulsive body feelings and a terror so great that she felt that (not "as though") the world was ending. She tried to convince me that termination was not an expectable part of therapy as a route to independence and autonomy, but should be optional. We were able to work on that, as well.

Two vignettes from Lisabeth's therapy illustrate the problems she had experiencing herself as a separate autonomous person and conceptualizing, bearing and sustaining her own thoughts and feelings. We had missed a couple of sessions because I was out of town for a few days, and when we re-convened she seemed somewhat disorganized, anxious and, as slowly became evident, angry. Associations gradually linked her mental state to our separation, and she then talked about it more directly. She recounted having driven around the community in which we both lived and only then realizing with a sense of distress that I was not there. As she could not concretely see me she felt empty and could not emotionally experience me as a caring presence. I suggested we discuss where I "am" for her, specifically whether it depended on immediate concrete sensory-perceptual attachment or whether she could keep in mind caring feelings and positive memories. As we talked she began to experience such feelings and her mental state improved.

During another hour soon thereafter, following a long weekend separation, she remarked after sitting down that her chair was further away from mine than usual. If this was indeed the case the difference was fractional. Without pause to reflect she proceeded to try to move it closer. I asked her whether her feelings about me were far away or close and she soon realized that she had managed to eliminate feelings of caring about me and our relationship. Immediately she felt better and moving the chair was no longer an issue.

In my preface to Lisabeth's story I noted that primordial mental activity seemed to dominate her life. In the later stages of her treatment it was mostly confined to dreaming. In the early stages of her treatment she dreamed, for example, of being an undifferentiated larval creature immersed in some sort of fluid, or a naked body sleeping behind a glass barrier being admired by others outside. In contrast, in the later stages of her treatment she told me a dream following a very satisfying adventurous trip she had taken with her husband that had involved the choice to take some time away from her therapy, something she would never have done voluntarily in the past. The trip had involved some wilderness camping and the related special arrangements necessary for discharging toilet functions had much preoccupied her. She and her husband had been the oldest persons on the trip. She had been very proud of how well they were able to do the strenuous activities but had found herself competitively furious at the experience of *falling behind* younger people. She had been especially attentive to the single women, without partners, on the trip. Other immediately relevant background information has to do with work we had done on the issue of separation from her mother, a woman whose distant, uncaring, condescending attitude had been masked by a social facade not unlike the one Lisabeth initially presented to me and she had believed I was manifesting toward her. Her divorced single-parent mother had infantilized Lisabeth and her brother while subtly demeaning them in relation to herself and "teaching" them that any manifestation of feelings was immature. She had not prepared them in any way for independent living, with devastating effects on brother as well, as he spent his entire life living with her.

In the dream Lisabeth was on a trip or a journey with an older woman as guide. The group needed to catch a boat to ferry them to their destination and the older woman reassured them that they need not worry, there was plenty of time. When they got to the dock, however, the ferry had left. In the next sequence of the dream Lisabeth was menstruating and tending to herself while a little girl looked on with concern. Lisabeth explained to her that she need not worry, for women sometimes have a bit of post-menopausal spotting. We understood the dream to be an enactment of her experience of having missed the boat in life because of her lack of an independent self and mindless dependency on her mother, a position in which her mother was deemed perfect and omniscient and Lisabeth had been *left behind* or *fallen* into the role of a *behind* or excrement, and that her sense of being excrement had led her to *waste* her menstrual cycles and potential as a mother. What I should like to emphasize is that aspects of the dream like *missing the boat* and being *left* or *falling into the behind position* and menstrual bleeding (waste) were not symbols or metaphors but concrete sensory-perceptual actualizations, which differed little from the PMA that had characterized the transference of her earlier years of therapy.

In the latter years of her therapy Lisabeth composed the following reflection on her mental activity, using years of diary entries to validate the accuracy of her memory:

Within the first few sessions of therapy I started to list words on small pieces of paper – "hopeless," "helpless," "fear of falling apart," "I hate me," "miserable," "why doesn't he help." I see these jottings as expressions of my then fragmented mental state and overwhelming sense of fear, hopelessness and despair. I requested therapy because I had developed severe insomnia, wanted to end a possessive lesbian relationship and couldn't "get rid of" the feelings of despair. I attributed my desperation to an impending job change and inability to escape the lesbian relationship – it was merely a temporary aberration; I would be in and out of therapy in a year. Given my level of desperation it is stunning I was so out of touch with the depth of my disturbance and thought it merely a temporary state.

As therapy progressed I ended the jottings and decided to keep comprehensive journals of my thoughts and feelings – I was struggling toward a more organized mental state, trying to put the pieces together. I maintained this activity for many years often writing daily. I have reviewed much of these writings to help me remember and verify the following recollections and reflections. Words in quotes are taken from those journals.

In my work (CEO of a non-profit) I was admired and cared about, considered an excellent leader and supervisor, a fine public speaker and planner, a person who could think strategically and analytically as well as mobilize the organization and larger community around shared goals. I didn't believe any of it. Inside I felt like a "fraud," "a failure," frightened and paranoid, convinced I would be fired. I kept these feelings hidden, tried to dismiss them, and lived in terror that someone might find out. I became increasingly overwhelmed by the dissonance between how I felt inside and the growing success in my work. I felt "split" between my work-related persona and an "entropic," paranoid and dysfunctional mental state where I described myself as feeling like an "inchoate mass," wanted to crawl in a hole, see no one and eliminate all feelings. I did not have a clue about what was going on.

Entropy was always lurking in the background but on weekends I would "slip into it" full-blown. I would be exhausted, frightened, withdrawn, and wanted to die. I believed I was a terrible person and felt as if "it" – the state – was visited upon me. I only wanted something or someone to make "it all go away." I had to force myself to undertake the ordinary tasks of living – grocery shopping, housecleaning, visiting a friend, etc. After such weekends I would arrive at work feeling in a fog. I can recall pushing and struggling inside my head to get out of the "fog" – to make my mind readjust to the circumstances. In retrospect it was similar to awakening from a dream but more difficult. [She tried to dissociate and suppress the PMA, but her paranoid ideation indicates her efforts were not entirely successful.] After I succeeded in forcing myself to re-enter the working world I would feel relief from my intense pathos – it would seem to dissipate – I was "better." At the time I did not realize that I was struggling to disengage from a mental return to a non-thinking and miserable childhood state. I was only aware that re-entry on Mondays was excruciating and that work seemed to serve as a relief.

When I felt "better" I was better. "It," the intense dysphoria, was gone. I was always shocked when "it" returned. "Where did it come from?" "Why doesn't it go away?" "What's wrong?" I had no capacity to understand that my mind was generating these "states" – I did not think; I acted. I had no internal emotional awareness. I was not able to reflect upon or identify what feelings (e.g. loss, rage, love) might be driving my actions, nor did I even know what feelings were. To me feelings were a global state where I felt either hopeless, helpless, and anxious (often expressed somatically), or "better." I had no capacity to identify, reflect upon or bear feelings. I was full of rage, did not know it, nor could I have tolerated the knowledge. Likewise, I was unable to tolerate feelings of dependency or caring. Early on in therapy Dr. Robbins became a target of my rage.

After merely twelve sessions I thought I was "in love" with him. I was unaware that my sensations were not love, but a possessive clinging driven by rage and envy. I thought I wanted to be with him 24/7 but in reality I avoided any outside encounters – essentially I could not stand to be near him. I was convinced that he lived in an "ideal" world where he had no problems or difficulties, was the object of the world's and his family's adoration, "had everything and saw me as a nothing." He floated effortlessly through life; I was excrement. Reflexively my thoughts about his perfect life and my nothingness would spiral out of control. I would become increasingly angry. I never asked, "Why am I thinking this?"

The thoughts were fact, so real that I began to find out all I could about him (track down journal articles he authored, attend his presentations with his permission, sit outside his office building to get a glimpse of him, drive by his house, and more). Not because I admired and loved him. I wanted to destroy, capture and be him, although I did not know it. I thought I was making a special connection with him (I was unaware of my ignorance about and aversion to real emotional connection; what went on in the consulting room was inauthentic). At the same time I wanted to know if he was real, whatever real was. Was it someone who had no feelings and problems or someone who did? Any evidence of his having to undertake a normal act of living – going to the bank, changing the oil in his car, etc. – was essentially a shock. [When she trespassed into the building on my property while I was away she discovered equipment for changing oil.] My God, I would exclaim to myself, he actually does such and such. Yet I ignored any evidence that his life was not perfect. [I had to move my office from my home because I was in the throes of a divorce.] The more I undertook these activities the more I felt orphaned, dysphoric and in an all-consuming rage – more evidence that I was excrement. I became my verbal representations of how I felt – the words were not metaphors. I didn't feel like "The Little Match Girl"; I was she, a waif. When I felt like an "inchoate mass," I was an "inchoate mass," ugly and non-human. When in an all-consuming rage I was the ugliest thing on earth: rage itself.

Interspersed with entropy and rage I began to develop a nascent positive attachment to Dr. Robbins which was intolerable. I could only express it somatically. When I thought about him between sessions or looked at him during sessions I would experience a sensation that felt like an "electric shock" shooting through my body. I would cringe, suck in my breath, wince and turn my head to the side in order to try to escape the sensation. It was a dramatic autonomic response.

Later, when I began to have sensations of being nurtured and cared about I would experience short-lived euphoric states. At these times I believed I was physically connected to or part of Dr. Robbins and

experienced a global feeling of elation not attached to any understanding that I needed him and that he was becoming indispensible to
me. I would merely be in a dream-like state where all was now perfect –
briefly I became invincible. Shortly, however, I would destroy any hint of
"good feelings," go into a rage and mercilessly attack him as uncaring.

Given my inability to understand, develop and sustain emotional
connections without concrete contact, any separations from Dr.
Robbins were agony, especially summer vacations. Four years after I
began work with him I experienced the most painful and desperate of
these separations. He had told me that I could call him if I was having
trouble, yet I could not. I sat by the phone staring at the phone number
thinking that he would be angry, dismissive and not want to be
disturbed in his perfect life. These thoughts became fact. I lost all
contact with any positive relationship with him – I had dismissed him. I
went to bed for the night deeply depressed when suddenly I was
compelled to go to his house. I had to act. I got up, put on my clothes
and went. I was driven with no conscious awareness of what lay behind
my actions except a desperation that I could not see him, know what he
was doing, or control and possess him. While on his property I felt a
temporary somewhat mystical connection to him and remember saying
to myself, "he would want me to be here because it makes me feel
better and he would want me to feel better." I had no sense of reality,
that I was not connecting with him at all, that I was trespassing, or that
he might be angry at my transgression. The next day my despair
intensified to the point where I called him to tell him what I had done. I
was shocked when he said I had violated his trust. The day after our
conversation I wrote in my journal:

> "The aftermath of this action has been devastating. I'm really
> shook up by it on the one hand, but not on the other. There are
> moments when I cover my face and cannot believe I did what I did
> – I'm so ashamed. I feel as if I can never go back to him or fix the
> terribleness of it. At others I think it was and is my right – he is
> part mine and what belongs to him he should share. I choke up
> with the wish to be part of his family. It is so painful. I am so
> confused. Here is this person [me] with all this responsibility and
> respect who is trying to write two inspiring speeches [which I was at
> the time], on the other there is this person who is dying inside –
> who can't inspire anyone especially herself who goes trespassing on
> her shrink's property because she is so crazy. I feel like I can't
> stand it anymore."

I am sure that if I had remained connected to our relationship and been
able to phone him when I was in such a desperate state I would not

have become so utterly lost. The genuine contact and ensuing discussion would have helped me to think about our real relationship and to recognize that I missed and needed him.

As therapy progressed I began to develop the capacity to have and reflect upon identifiable feelings and thoughts. I developed a deeper interest in words and their nuance, wrote increasingly lengthy reflections on my now more tolerable feelings, and began figure drawing and sculpting. I claimed I could feel the neurons in my brain making new connections. One day I exclaimed, "I know what's wrong with me, I never learned to feel!"

I no longer go into "entropic" states. At times, however, I still have feelings that at first seem to come from nowhere. I have to work to undertake a conscious inquiry into them. For example, recently, when my spouse and I arrived at a vacation spot I unexpectedly felt angry and lonely. I tried to ignore and dismiss the feelings. (I had been looking forward to our week away. How could I possibly feel otherwise?). In the middle of the night I awoke and decided to think more deeply. My thoughts drifted to the place of my childhood where my family vacationed every summer. To the family our vacation spot was "holy ground" – it was the centerpiece of each family member's life and mythology (my brother, mother, and me). As I reflected on my feelings in the present, I realized I had mentally returned to the past – I was actually at that childhood vacation spot with my mother and brother. Instead of understanding that I was remembering how I felt as a child, I was actually there. As a child I had no awareness that I felt lonely and angry, such feelings were "bad" in my family. I was expected to love that childhood vacation spot – it was the perfect place; no other could match it; no one in their right mind would ever want to be anywhere else. If I thought otherwise I would have been out of my mind. And so I was! Not because I thought differently but because I didn't and couldn't.

Jacob

Next I share a first person account of primordial mental activity written by Jacob, in his later sixties, after many years of therapy. Jacob's psychosis first became evident in late adolescence. He had begun graduate school in mathematics and his talent was attracting special interest from his professors. He developed a crippling delusion based on the belief that he could prove it is possible to divide by zero. It drove him relentlessly and obsessively to destroy any truly productive efforts. Jacob made all his major efforts and relationships into impossible problems or destructive belief systems, using his intelligence in conjunction with rage he was totally unaware of to rationalize destroying any constructive efforts, and attacking anyone who tried to care and reason with him. In this case he eventually became so agitated he had to drop out of school. While in retrospect it would seem that he should have been hospitalized, instead he returned to his parents' home and began the first of seven fruitless attempts he made at psychotherapy and psychoanalysis. He relinquished aspirations most dear to him, especially his evident talent and interest in mathematics, as he had destroyed the pursuit of other abilities and interests in life since childhood – athletic, musical and literary. Even so, his unusual intelligence and abilities enabled him to sustain a life that was outwardly reasonably successful despite a level of disturbance that might have disabled another person. He found work that was much less creatively demanding and was able to find a woman of apparently saintly tolerance to marry and with whom to have a family, although, as we shall see, he treated her abusively, as he did anyone who tried to care.

His mind was a place of violent sadomasochistic *phantasy* about body parts and sexual and excretory functions, his own and those of women, and he lived in a constant state of terror of imminent death from a variety of imagined horrible illnesses. He believed others were trying to destroy him and he constantly found fault with and attacked anyone with whom he became involved. He had no awareness of his rage and fear. While he never inflicted major physical harm on anyone, his relationships with others were characterized by major and relentless verbal abuse and belittlement, and in a similarly poorly rationalized way he was obsessed with his own body parts and sensations, leading to self-abusive preoccupations such as compulsive masturbation to the point of injury to his penis that caused blood to appear in his urine, manipulation of his anus and preoccupation with his excretions. His belief that he had a fatal illness attached itself to one symptom after another, and kept him preoccupied with doctors, whom he did not trust and feared were out to harm him. He had serial sadistic relationships with women in which he possessed and controlled their bodies and made them do his bidding in matters so bizarre as having one woman dress in undergarments that had belonged to his mother. He was plagued by powerful homicidal fantasies and impulses toward those close to him and paralyzed by obsessions about whether he would or wouldn't, could or couldn't. He was aware of feeling physically cold, despairing and alienated from a world that he believed to be unmitigatedly hostile to and not understanding of him. Jacob believed that his outlook and behavior were entirely normal and justified by the way he was treated by others and anyone who attempted to question him was dismissed as crazy and dangerous, and subject to verbal attack. In particular he had no conception of how angry and uncaring he was.

His therapists were mostly psychoanalysts. Some of them apparently tried to placate him, something I could readily understand in light of the relentless verbal attacks he was prone to make and his tendency not to allow anyone else to talk, but others tried to help him think about himself, albeit judging from his own retrospective account with little success. Of the seven therapists he saw before encountering me, the most meaningful experience was with an internationally reputed Kleinian analyst who seemed to have cared about Jacob and to have tried in ways that were sensitive and understanding to encourage him to control his relentless abuse. The analyst had to end many sessions early, ejecting Jacob because of his behaviour. Finally and sadly he told Jacob that his assaults were striking a personal vulnerability related to his own childhood, and shortly thereafter, following on one of Jacob's particularly virulent attacks, he abruptly terminated their relationship.

In his later fifties Jacob decided he had to try therapy again and was referred to me. He was in a state I can best describe as total despair and paranoid alienation from the cold, inhuman, lethal world he experienced around him. The early years of our relationship were characterized by his belief that I would not let him "finish" and say what was on his mind, by an endless litany about body parts and functions, and by relentless and often openly abusive assaults on me for an endless litany of wrongs I was doing to him and that he was convinced that I had done to him in prior sessions. His stream of talk was continuous and pressured, and he rejected any intervention on my part, even so much as a question, which he experienced as a lethal suffocating assault on his very being. He used his considerable ability to rationalize his behaviour as normal and justified and he responded to any attempt on my part to suggest it was unusual as hostile and critical. He seemed totally unaware that I was a human being who might have feelings and at times he was quite convinced that I was crazy or some kind of dangerous monster. His elephantine memory of my seemingly endless transgressions always contained an element of truth, however lifted out of context and distorted. His behaviour often reminded me of a caricature of psychoanalysis, about which he had accrued considerable knowledge; one in which he was "analyst" and I was the patient whose badness had to be rooted out, validated and expunged. Any effort I might make to halt or limit his paranoid, often abusive but tightly rationalized rhetoric in order to get a few words of my own in edgewise usually elicited an angry reproachful response. He would conclude that I was not allowing him to finish what he needed to say and was not listening to him or understanding him, and then initiate fresh assaults on me for all my problems and failures to understand him and treat him well.

After our sessions I often found myself pacing the floor of my office trying to contain myself and control my anger and sense of impotence. During our sessions when he accurately intuited any hint of frustration much less anger from the tone of my voice it served to corroborate for him what he already "knew," namely how hostile and dangerous I was. I asked him to tape record sessions and listen to them privately in hopes he might gain some insight, but instead he used the recordings to intensify his search and destroy mission with regard to my badness. He was full of sadistic fantasies about me and my family members and would anticipate seeing me with such fantasies as throwing lye in my face, throwing me down the stairs, and more. We accumulated much evidence in the course of our work, both emotional and intellectual, of the underlying basis of his problems in his relationship with his mother. Although the insights sometimes seemed to make a deep impact on him they had limited effect on his behaviour, which was entirely lacking in caring and almost entirely lacking in comprehension of what was actually transpiring between us.

Meanwhile, there was accumulating evidence that outside the consulting room his work, relationships, and state of satisfaction were improving significantly. He did not connect any of this with his therapy or the idea he might be depending on me and I might be helping him. Indeed he rejected any suggestion along these lines I might occasionally make. Instead he took entire credit for the insights that seemed responsible for the changes, even insisting he had in some way known these things all along. After some years and on rare occasions when pressed he would begrudgingly and in hostile tones acknowledge that this was the first helpful therapy relationship he had ever experienced.

Very gradually he became increasingly able to think and to reflect about his mental states and to begin to sort out and differentiate the past from the present, and the contents of his own mind from his convictions about the minds of myself and others. For many years he was adamant in his belief that he had loved his mother and that she loved him. This belief persisted in the face of innumerable detailed recollections of incidents in which his mother had controlled and assaulted his body and restricted his freedom. These incidents were recounted with little awareness of his feelings, and he rationalized them with the idea that she loved him and was simply helping to treat the awful lethal disease or badness in him. He was totally unable to comprehend these from an adult emotional perspective or to connect them with his fixed lethal view of the world. As he tried to become aware that his diffuse rage had been turned in hatred against himself and others, and to realize that he did not know how to feel caring for himself or others, he would report simultaneous somatic sensations of having a breast and of smirking, both of which seemed associated with being infiltrated with and over-whelmed by his mother's identity and rage. Such incidents would presage his turning on others much as it seemed she had turned on him as a child.

Jacob had a breadth of knowledge that included a certain familiarity with Freud's writings, an interest that had been enhanced by his lifetime in therapy, often with psychoanalysts. During a search for personal infor-mation about me on the internet he discovered a paper I had written about dreaming and the primary process. He realized that my description fit his mental activity, and he began to use the concept to help him to understand his mind. He became preoccupied with what he came to call his "aphasia" when it came to finding words of his own to describe his most important mental states and his feelings. This was in striking contrast with his unusually large vocabulary and interest in literature. In this aphasic state he was especially inclined to interpret any effort I might make to help him in word finding as trying to force words in his mouth and down his throat, suffocate him and make him "suck up" and lose his identity.

The session that follows is taken from the eighth year of his therapy. Jacob began with a lengthy discourse about an art exhibition he had seen the previous day that he believed I should see, interspersed with moments of awareness that he was emotionally disconnected from me and the here and now. He interspersed this disquisition with comments about my lack of expression when I greet him and his belief I inhibit my emotions. These were accompanied by criticism of me, delivered in a hostile tone of which he was unaware. The criticism mounted in response to my occasional mildly delivered comments about his lack of connection and his perseverating with the art exhibition, and he told me that I was being "too strong." He talked about his difficulty accepting the insight that he was paranoid that he himself had volunteered in a previous hour. He spoke of being aware that he needed to identify, think about and contain his rage, and his realization that as a child he felt forced to turn anger that should have been expressed toward his mother in on himself instead. He realized he had committed a kind of psychological suicide in order to maintain a sense of connection with his mother who relentlessly attacked and criticized him. He went on to say that he never had even the modicum of self-esteem necessary to hold this idea about his mother's abuse and the associated feeling of rage in mind, and instead had to convince himself that others were trying to destroy him so he might get rid of the rage. He described how difficult it is for him to have "faith" and "believe" these ideas. When I encouraged him to think about and elaborate the nature of this difficulty he reverted, with some asperity, to the belief that I was coming onto him "very strong." Toward the end of the hour we began to talk about his struggle between containing and thinking about this idea on the one hand, and entering a state where he could not make distinctions or hold in mind his feelings on the other, and about the ease with which he stopped thinking and began to act concretely according to the belief that he was being abused.

The remainder of the chapter consists almost entirely of Jacob's reflections about his psychotic mental activity. I have interpolated comments relating his remarks to PMA in brackets. I begin with his responses to a series of questions I asked. The first is when and how he had become aware he was psychotic:

> Prior to my therapy with you I never was told that I was psychotic. The closest to being told such a thing was Dr. X (the Kleinian analyst)

telling me that I had a "characterological disorder" not a neurosis. He mentioned that there were technical differences between the two terms (neurosis and characterological disorder), but didn't want to elaborate. I had no idea that a characterological disorder might be psychotic.

Even though you explicitly told me that you thought I suffered from a psychosis, I really never seriously considered this as a statement of truth. At times I thought you were "crazy" to be making such a remark to me. Like all things challenging my psychotic relationship with my mother, I turned it around, so that I was sane and everyone else was insane. It took me many years to really believe that I was suffering from a psychosis. In that time I saw how unstable I was; how fragmented my thinking was; how my identity (world view) moved back and forth; my dissociations, etc.

Next I asked him for his thoughts about the nature and cause of psychosis, and specifically whether he had experienced hallucinations and delusions:

The essence of psychosis is a deep belief that the problem is elsewhere: in the externalization of motivation, feelings, and behavior, all based on delusional beliefs. In my case I suffered from paranoid thinking caused by my dissociating feelings that ultimately were too painful for me to harbor in my own mind. [He is talking about undifferentiation, lack of integration, being affect-driven and unable to thoughtfully identify emotions.]

The only hallucination of which I am really aware was the sense of smell of smoke, most probably representing a sense of asphyxiation from the squashing of my mother [concreteness and sensory-perceptual actualization possibly related to synesthesia].

The truth is that I had delusions most of my life, but it is not until recently that I have become aware of them. My main delusion is the belief that my mother loved me, and my reversal of responsibility for all things which challenged that belief [inability to experience contradiction; undifferentiation of opposites].

The causes of psychosis are beliefs too painful to admit are mine. In response to this are delusions to change this reality, and an externalization, dissociation, of those fragments too painful to hold in my mind. Coupled with this is paranoia or an externalization of motivation for these personally damaging feelings. Associated with this psychotic thinking, is a real fragmentation of my mind, so that things are extremely difficult to be held as a cogent unit for thoughtful consideration [lack of differentiation, integration, and ability to identify emotion].

Next Jacob describes what he calls the primary process. Note his comments about language – concrete and forceful; not symbolic.

That the primary process is a language before language, at first sounds like a contradiction of terms. For while this language appears to have words found in the language we use each day, its words are subordinated shadows of feelings in dreams. This truth colors the desperation and helplessness I experience in its use, both in its connection to my present and past. In the present, expression is substantially limited to a vocabulary that is inadequate to either thinking or discussion. So how it feels in real-time is permeated with the rage and sense of being overwhelmed and unable to express myself. Yet it is the impotence of the past, my absence of verbal ability to respond to the attacks of my mother, that underlies the use of the primary process now. For me the primary process is a tool for acting out a most painful and disintegrated period of my childhood, using a primitive pre-verbal (pre-thinking) language with words dictated by primal feelings, rather than the reflection of my mind.

The primary process is a language so coarse and blunt that it suffers from a vocabulary incapable of real description; that is to say its essence is defined more by what is missing than present – primarily all tools of thought: metaphor, association, and reflection. It is in this absence of real thought that the attempt of communication occurs. It is hardly surprising that a prominent feeling in many of my episodes of primary process expression is aphasia – a loss of language. Stated differently, I might say that I end up using non-metaphoric words. In ordinary parlance, we would call words lacking thought and metaphor "concrete." In speaking this language, I somatically, in my torso and arms, feel the bluntness, heaviness, lack of expression, and inadequacy of this absolutely concrete vocabulary. My experience of relating in the primary process is thus a clash of two worlds, the primal feelings of dreams versus the nuance of present day reality.

This experience feels incredibly frustrating – the painful expression of blunt, concrete words in a world of complex, nuanced ideas and feelings. I literally feel this within myself (somatically) as a rather heavy and frozen environment. This is quite consistent with the inability to use metaphor or associate ideas. And this is nothing other than the inability to think. So with very few words at my disposal I actually have felt like an animal grunting out blunt sounds, forced to contend with a more dexterous opponent. In my mind's eye I literally feel and see a vacuous image, as if trapped in a small world of emptiness – the emptiness of a universe of no words, in which, on the one hand, I am forced to express my feelings, but on the other hand know how unequipped to do so I am. As mentioned above, rage enters this arena from two sides: in present time, the utter inability to articulate my feelings; and as an echo of the past, my impotence in responding to my mother.

I will give four examples of my experience with the primary process. The first illustrates almost a direct expression of undifferentiated rage and self-inadequacy. The second, a suicide attempt, is most dream-like and delusional. The third illustrates the symptom of aphasia while feeling impotence in responding to an overwhelming challenge. The fourth example is very close to the nexus of the central forces of my psychosis. It overlays one upon the other, most if not all of the problems that forced me to this delusional framework of thinking. It is my hope, that a full understanding of this last manifestation (translation to description and thought) will open the door to a liberation from its jaws.

With the inability to think, action is immediate within the primary process. This action is compounded by the drive of rage – both internal and external. Associated with rage is a destructive drive, directed both to myself and to the outside world. The first example took place when I was 12 or 13 years old in a summer camp. In the course of a basketball game on an outdoor gravel court, in a desperate and rageful attempt to play against another kid and overcome my feeling of low self-esteem, I dove to get a ball he had in his possession. I actually left my feet, approaching a horizontal orientation in the air, and then crashed and skidded along the gravel court, deeply gouging out my knee. Before I jumped, I never stopped to consider the damage in store for my knee, though I was sure it would happen; it felt as if my world had shrunk into focusing only on performing this behavior. Thought about the outcome of this behavior was totally absent. At the time I was totally unaware that driving this primary response was a feeling of rage at myself (acted out in hurting myself). Looking at it now I can see that I dissociated to the person with the ball, characteristics of unfair athletic advantage (a good basketball player) that in my mind justified my anger in fighting back; my action created an external object to destroy – the boy with the basketball. But the feeling of the action was like being in a tunnel, totally cordoning off the remainder of the world (reality). In this sense it belonged solely to my mind like a dream, totally independent of time.

The second example is more desperate and delusional. Playing running bases, running from curb to curb in order to beat a throw across the street, as if running from base to base I attempted to run past an approaching taxicab that I absolutely knew would hit me. I can still remember the thought that there was no way I could beat the car. But reality didn't matter, and thus awareness was lost. I was in another world, one of dreams and magic. The image in my mind was that

I would somehow find a way to fly – totally delusional. There could hardly be a better example of the primary process as a wish fulfillment, a dream. In gross terms it was an attempted suicide. Yet it was much more.

Using the guise of worrying that I would be hit by a car, my mother had forbidden me to ever play in the street. In my mind I was going against her "rules" by playing there. At that instant when I decided to run I accepted the delusion of flying to escape my own personal crisis of not being free. In simpler terms suicide was freedom. Only now can I see the rage I was carrying in response to the unyielding criticism of my mother, which had become internalized in my own fragmented psyche. My delusion of flying was both an acceptance and escape of that internalization, an attempt to free myself from myself. Most central and startling is how I shut out thought and reality, and the absolute primacy of my action. I spent three weeks in the Hospital. On admission I had an out of body experience, where I imagined that I stood on the side of the steps and watched others carry me on a stretcher up the front steps through the front door of the hospital.

Common to all these examples is some trigger that initiates activity in the primary process. Always present, and manifest to some degree, are impotence and rage. This third example took place at a business meeting. I was a manager, and I was challenged concerning a person I wanted to hire. For some reasons, my candidate appeared to be lacking a stellar reputation. As it became my time to provide a defense of my candidate to my superiors, I felt overwhelmed, trapped, and impotent. Being overwhelmed and impotent I was driven by deep rage, directed both internally and externally. All words left my mind except one. I knew that my candidate had experience with state government and after an agonizingly long pregnant silence I said something like the single word "state." I had lots more to say, but my mind was totally blank. I was locked in this primary process straitjacket. I had lost all capability to think; I had literally lost my mind. I felt embarrassed as if someone else had commandeered my body, soul, and mind; I was helpless, totally impotent.

This fourth example of primary process is one which has been most chronic during my current therapy (I am not sure if I had this somatization prior to therapy with Dr. Robbins, though I surely had others). Its manifestation is the feeling that I have a woman's breast on my right side, at the very site of my right breast. My major feeling is that my body is deformed, a strange feeling at my breast and right arm, with an image in my mind of the deformation on my right chest. Along with this vision is a feeling in my right arm of wanting to push this deformation off my body. As the uncomfortable feeling of this breast persists, so continues my overall awareness of the image of this deformation and the tense feeling in my arm of wanting to rub this breast away.

Central to the essence of this woman's breast on my body is the sense of it being foreign: my deep desire to push it away, wipe it off. When I feel this somatization, I have an image of this breast being superficial on my chest like a skin lesion or blister. This breast, however, can not be pushed off, only superficially stretched or altered. Thinking about it now, I am astonished how dreamlike is this experience, somatic and concentrated. And I am also amazed how much of me is imbued in this process. Wrapped within this manifestation is my taking in the spirit of my mother, accepting it, feeling it as an externalization but an implacable permanence, hating it, and trying to remove it, as if it were a skin lesion I could slough away.

It is amazing to me how concentrated and undifferentiated my feelings are inside the "cloud" of this manifestation of primary process. (I borrow the word "cloud" from computer jargon, where it is used as a "big picture" description of networks without worrying about their confusing details.) For present in this instance is not just a breast, but the bodily feelings of this addition to my body being both unnatural and unwanted; and the associated feelings in my arm, a sensitivity and tightness, with the feeling of wanting to dispose of this addition, as it appears in my image of it, which I carry in my mind. The feeling to remove it occurs in my right arm, which is unnaturally stiffened and touching the right side of my torso. It feels as if I, a fish, were to use its fin to push something off its body. On reflection it's interesting that somehow my fingers are not part of this process. Perhaps the absence of fingers is consistent with my deep feeling of impotence and being incomplete.

It is only recently that I've given any real thought to translating from one language to another: primary process to reflective (metaphoric) English. [Awareness of the need to learn to think and to integrate and thoughtfully comprehend the PMA experiences.] This manifestation primitively represents my fragmented lack of self, the mixture of my mother and myself. The tenacity of the breast's grip on my body (more my mind) prohibits me from moving it off my body. I've never had the feeling or image of successfully pushing off the breast from my body. Instead, I see myself pushing against the breast in a downward motion. But I can only push the breast down or stretch it, never remove it.

At the same time as this breast is permanent, it is also totally unwanted. Translated into simple language this means: I've internalized my mother with her destruction toward me, and this is the configuration of my psychotic psyche. Part of this primary process configuration is the undifferentiated rage that results from being in such a self-destructive mindset. By undifferentiated, I mean that this rage is there, but I'm unaware of it; it is not directed toward any one person, but ready to be unleashed without any self-control. The other feeling hidden in this "cloud" of primary process is that of impotence to the self-destructive internalized mother. In real life this can act-out as my victimization, providing internal license for releasing undifferentiated rage through a paranoid dissociative externalization. On the other hand, empathy with my impotence as a child and the real victimization to my mother's rage can be liberating.

Until recently I had not understood the relationship of my attempting to remove the "unwanted" breast to my attempting to shed my rage to the outside world. Both the breast (understood as my internalization of my mother) and my rage are permanently mine, but unwanted. Yet there is no way to shed them and make them go away. At best I must understand them, be aware of them, and control them. But the analogy between the breast of the primary process and my rage is striking.

The breast primary process manifestation has become a common background state of mind for me. In order to move from this thoughtless world of primary process and psychosis to one of thought and sanity, my job is to keep this state of mind in the foreground – use my mind to create a bridge of translation from the primary process to a coherent description in a language of feelings and thoughts. Reflection must keep me aware of my feelings of impotence, compliance, lack of self-esteem, and blazing rage. I'm hopeful, after continual work of building this bridge, that new synapses will develop that will initiate thoughts and feelings rather than the reflexive and stifling behavior of the primary process.

This is a moving account of inability to command language and thought, to articulate emotions, and hence to communicate with others. What he calls the primary process is reminiscent of states in which one is aware of being trapped in a bad dream and tries unsuccessfully to waken and call out to others. Jacob describes the state of concrete, sensory-perceptual-somatic-motor actualization of undifferentiated, unintegrated mental states that cannot be thought about, producing actualizations and delusional beliefs. He describes the timeless quality, neither here nor there, the inability to experience contrast and contradiction.

Next I asked Jacob to describe himself prior to our therapy and how he felt he had changed:

Before therapy I was totally unaware how psychotic I was. I lived totally in the domain of primary process thinking. I spent most of my day involved in deep compulsive dialogues with myself, usually concerned with the topic of being squashed. I believed that one of the poles of these dialogues inside myself belonged to someone else (some

psychological agent representing my internalized mother). Needless to
say these dialogues spilled outside with rage all the time. I "knew"
there was something wrong, but had no internal handle that it might be
me. All responsibility was dissociated to the outside. Most unfortun-
ately, I released enormous amounts of rage to the outside, as a way of
clearing my body (note the primary process) of such painful feelings. In
short I lived with a paranoid frame of mind – in quite a narcissus
complex. I'd say it took many years within therapy before any substantial change from this frame of thinking took place.

   My marriage was falling apart. What brought me to therapy was the
belief that somehow I could manipulate therapy to vindicate myself
from the charges of being at fault.

Note here the somatic gastrointestinal actualization process, being
squashed and excreting. As I described, he did try to "manipulate therapy"
in order to make me the "bad" patient. Next I inquired about therapeutic
process: what had helped and what did not in his various therapies, what
was involved in making a therapeutic relationship, and what advice he
might give to someone trying to work with a person like himself.

   I think what helped me the most was learning how paranoid I was and
how the dissociative mechanics of this thinking totally prohibited any
productive relationship from being established between myself and the
therapist. All therapies in the past failed because the therapist became
the one upon whom I dissociated my thoughts. It only took about eight
years to overcome this obstacle. WOW!!

   My advice is to stop as quickly as possible the cancer of therapy that
I describe below. Therapy doesn't start until this is controlled. One
major process within psychosis is what I would call the dissociative
compulsion argument. This process is monomaniacal and crippling to
all attempts at dialogue. It occurred in my head out of therapy and as a
destructive force inside therapy. It totally captivates all energy and
totally paralyzes any functionality. It totally destroys the freedom and
functionality of a patient and a doctor. In reality, this is a conflict gone
awry (or perhaps haywire is a better description). In my case, this was a
reenactment of squashing by my mother, a core issue for me. Squashing
someone is taking someone over (suffocating them) with forced feelings
and behavior and thereby forcing their impotence and rage. I would say
that this process crippled any professional help with which I was
involved, until recently. Only when this is controlled, can the patient
relate with the doctor and not his dissociated rendition of the doctor.

About two years later Jacob added the following:

In the past two years I have moved closer to owning my own conflicts rather than acting them out; owning and controlling the rage which has driven my lifelong destructive impulses. A central example of this new space of understanding is the reduced frequency of unwelcome somatic sensations of having a breast, which has largely been replaced by feelings and comprehension of being enmeshed in the swirl of a destructive identity with my mother, resulting in my sadistic retaliative acting out as reflexive behavior.

Chapter 15

Language, thought and communication

The fact that there are qualitatively different mental processes – thought and primordial mental activity – has important implications for how we understand language and communication. There is considerable controversy about what constitutes language and communication, and whether language and communication are isomorphic with thought and symbolic capability. To increase the complexity of the problem there is controversy about the relative roles of nature (the brain) and nurture (the culture) in determining language and communication. In this chapter I review some of this controversy and introduce three examples – the language of the Piraha, the tribe described in Chapter 8; dreaming; and schizophrenese, the speech and writing of a schizophrenic person – to illustrate my contention that there is a language of primordial mind and a language of thoughtful mind, that they are different, and as a consequence that there are two different kinds of communication.

Background of the controversy about language

It seems self-evident that the nature of the human brain constrains language, thought and culture, but does it fatefully determine them? Does culture determine mental process, language and communication, does mind determine culture, or is there a complex gray area in between? Theorists begin with different ideas of first cause – brain, thought, language and culture. Beginning with the brain, Berlin and Kay (1969) believe that it determines thought, language and culture. A less extreme position known as universal grammar is held by Chomsky (1957, 1975, 1986), that brain fundamentally constrains thought and language. Culture and environment can modify but not fundamentally change the universal elements of language. Working from the other end of the causal spectrum Whorf (1956) and Sapir (1921) believe that it is language that determines our perceptions as well as the nature of thought. Urban (1986) goes further and maintains that language determines culture as well as thought. Everett (2008) takes the extreme position that culture is primary and fundamentally determines language and thought.

The postmodern era is characterized by debate within many disciplines between those who believe in universal principles and those who are relativists and see everything as a product of context. In linguistics the debate centers around the concept of recursion, which some believe is a distinguishing feature of hard-wired grammar common to all languages. The debate has recently centered around the Piraha, the small Amazon basin tribe whose culture and mindset were described in Chapter 8. Universalists (Chomsky, 1957, 1965, 1986; Hauser *et al.*, 2002; and Jakobson, 1956) and the psychoanalyst Lacan (1953) believe that there is a neurologically based grammar or tree structure common to all languages. But contextual relativists, including two former disciples of Chomsky, Pinker (1994) and Everett (2005, 2008), believe that within certain neurologically determined constraints the way in which a culture views its world basically determines its language.

Recursion is a concept derived from mathematics and philosophy that relates to feedback. It has been applied somewhat loosely to language. Pinker (1994) states that recursion is a procedure that invokes an instance of itself. Everett (2008) describes it as self-referential. One element is nested or embedded in another of the same type. It requires referencing or remembering what has gone before, in time or in narrative chaining, sequencing or association of ideas. The dog that John owns wandered through the field until John called him and then he ran back to get his treat. The clauses refer back to John, John's dog, the dog itself and what the dog did. Recursion seems to be the self-referential or subject-chained narrative quality of language. Evidence of recursion in language includes such things as finding clauses or phrases or sub-sentences embedded in others, structural relationships between pairs of sentences, or two possessors in a sentence. Ideas are located or subordinated within or branch from others. Abstract and symbolic capabilities depend upon recursion insofar as they are referential concepts.

Recursion is an aspect of thought as well as of language. Referential aspects of thought include the ability to multi-task, to hold in mind more than one thing at a time, to cross-reference and weigh ideas or states of mind relative to one another in logical or causal sequence. Examples of recursion relevant to psychoanalytic theory include achievement of representational constancy and the capacity to reflect about one's mind and to experience intrapsychic conflict and ambivalence. But recursion is not a feature of PMA.

The relationship between language and thought

Piraha language does not seem to be recursive and Piraha mental process and communication do not seem to reflect commonly accepted characteristics of thought, as outlined in Table 5.2 (see p. 55). In Piraha there seems to be repetition, reiteration and contiguity, based on the concept of immediacy, that now is everything, that there is no differentiation of time past, present, or future – qualities that are characteristic of primordial mental activity. Those who maintain that language is hard-wired and that there is a universal grammar common to all language believe that Everett's observations are flawed and biased, but they have as yet been unable to prove it. Some have suggested that the issue may be semantic rather than syntactic, that Piraha speech omits coordinating conjunctions, a problem that linguists refer to as parataxis. It is a moot question whether such a hypothesis simply represents the subjective effort of the observer who speaks "ordinary" language to make sense of these arcane utterances. I illustrate this challenge later in the chapter when I describe my work with Caroline. The problem that has been highlighted in linguistics may be larger than what constitutes language. Is there more than one mental process, hence more than one basic kind of language, and more than one form of communication?

The linguistic debate about universalism and recursion, then, is a specific instance of a larger question about whether there are qualitatively different mental processes, qualitatively different languages that reflect them, qualitatively different ways of communication as a result, and whether culture and mental activity are fundamentally related. Are thought and language aspects of a unitary isomorphic entity; is thought the only user of language, and does all language depend on thought? Vygotsky maintains a unitary hypothesis that thought and language are intimately related both developmentally and existentially, and that they are linked by meaning. He asserts that "meaning. . . belongs in the realm of language as much as in the realm of thought. . . since word meaning is both thought and speech, we find in it the unit of verbal thought we are looking for" (Vygotsky, 1934a, 1934b). He believes that thought and language emerge conjointly from an initial Piagetian sensorimotor phase: "In the beginning was the deed. . . The word was not the beginning – action was there first" (1934a, p. 255). Next in terms of development he describes egocentric or predicate "inner speech," in which, by virtue of its solipsistic nature, subjectivity is implicit but as yet unformulated in terms of a thoughtful concept of self. Ultimately social speech develops, with concepts of self and other:

> We can confidently regard it [inner speech] as a *distinct phase of verbal thought*. It is evident that the transition from inner speech to external speech is not a simple translation from one language into another. It cannot be achieved by merely vocalizing silent speech. It is a complex, dynamic process involving the transformation of the predicative, idiomatic structure of inner speech into syntactically articulated speech intelligible to others.
>
> (ibid., p. 248)

In this position he seems to equate language with meaning, and to outline a sequence of development involving transformation from an earlier phase. I am of the opinion that the early stage of development to which he refers is not a precursor of thought but is a different primordial mental activity that persists and that uses language in a different way.

There are others who believe that thought and language are related to one another, but not necessarily aspects of the same thing (French and Fromm, 1964; Seeman, 1970; Chaika, 1990; Chaika and Lambe, 1985). They note how difficult it can be to find the right words to express thoughts, and argue that because particular thoughts and experiences can be cast in many linguistic forms the two are similar but not identical. What this argument suggests is that thought and language may be two qualitatively different processes that are related by analogy, which is the conclusion I propose.

Communication and its relationship to language and thought

Another debate has to do with the nature of communication and its relationship to thought and language. But what constitutes communication? Dictionaries commonly define communication as an essential element of language, but such definitions do not specify that it requires the use of words. The presence of symbols, signs, gestures, or the like – that is, of other representational elements – is deemed sufficient.

Surprisingly, not all linguists adhere to the dictionary definition. Some believe that the presence or absence of communication is not a defining feature of language (Akjamian et al., 1984). When attempting to ascertain whether a form of expression that sometimes uses words is a communication it is important to recognize that miscommunication is still a form of communication. Conscious intent may differ from actual effect, and conscious intent from unconscious intent. If two people attempt to communicate, for example, and the language chosen is a second language for one of them, the intended meaning and what is actually conveyed (if the conveyor speaks the chosen tongue poorly) or understood (if the person whose second language it is happens to be the recipient) may be very different, and neither party may comprehend what has happened. Another form of miscommunication may be the use of a shared language by one party to deliberately deceive the other. The fact that the meaning of these exchanges remains in essence opaque to or misunderstood by one or both parties does not alter the fact that a communication has taken place.

I think it useful to broaden the definition of communication to include communication of meaning through thought-based language and communication through affective induction or concrete impact. When words are used concretely to forcefully express beliefs or convictions that are not subject to reflection (dogma), when words are used performatively, as expletives or objects with the intent, conscious or not, to exert force in the world and to move people, then it is likely that the accompanying mode of mental expression relates to primordial mental activity rather than to thought. Such expression may be dissociated from thought as is the case with psychotic phenomena, or it may be intentional and integrated with thought, as when a person gives a speech designed to move others to act rather than to think. Because language that articulates meaning in the form of reflective communication of thought and language that exerts force or conviction both utilize formal aspects of words, grammar and syntax, the essential differences between the two are readily overlooked.

The relationship of dreaming to language, thought and communication

What does dreaming (Chapter 6), which is a manifestation of PMA rather than thought, have to tell us about language and communication? I doubt anyone would argue that we communicate while asleep unless we are capable of lucid dreaming, in which case the communication is coming from the thoughtful part of mind. However, insofar as the PMA that underlies dreaming also underlies various waking human behaviors it may have something to tell us about a particular kind of communication that occurs in waking life that is unrelated to thought.

In Chapters 2 and 6 I considered the relationship of dreaming to thought and language from the perspective of symbolism, and concluded that while there has been confusion and lack of clarity about the nature of dreaming it does not appear to be a symbolic activity. This is not a widely held point of view. Freud wrote in various places that dreaming contains the essential elements of language, especially hieroglyphic-like symbolism decodable by association. In other writings Freud described the primary process in dreaming as concrete, undifferentiated and sensory-perceptual – very different from language defined as an aspect of thought. Lacan (1953, 1968) believes that the symbolic order, the language order, and the law or social order are in many respects indistinguishable. Insofar as language is an inextricable element of the social order, it is inherently symbolic. He maintains that both the unconscious and dreaming are language structures.

> The dream has the structure of a sentence, or, rather, to stick to the letter of the work, of a rebus; that is to say, it has the structure of a form of writing, of which the child's dream represents the primordial ideography, and which, in the adult, reproduces the simultaneously phonetic and symbolic use of signifying elements, which can also be

found both in the hieroglyphs of ancient Egypt and in the characters
still used in China.

(1953, pp. 57–58)

In his description of language and dreaming, to which I do not pretend to
do justice in this brief summary, Lacan draws on Freud's concept of
primary process (principles of condensation and displacement) and seems
to conclude that dreaming is a symbolic activity.

Jung also wrote about dreaming as language, sometimes as a symbolic
vehicle but at other times as a very different linguistic process, "something
like a text that is unintelligible" (1954, p. 159). He wrote that "the manifest
dream picture is the dream itself and contains the whole meaning of the
dream" and that "the best way to [interpret dreams] is to establish the
context. . . free association will get me nowhere" (1954, p. 97). "I therefore
proceed in the same way as I would in deciphering a difficult text. . . dreams
generally have a 'dramatic' structure" (1959b, p. 367). The idea that a
dream has a dramatic structure would seem to imply that it has a thoughtful script and hence is part of the thought system. However, at the same
time Jung seems to be describing an interpretive process using thoughtful
analogical reasoning, for example likening a dream in which the dreamer
has the experience of venturing into a field to the issue of vocational choice.
The implication is that the dream is constructed by a process different from
thought but related to it by analogy.

My opinion about dreaming, language and thought is more like Jung's.
Since the dream experience is of happenings, since elements are associated
by contiguity (and then, and then) rather than logical narrative sequence,
since the dream is concrete and subject and object though differentiated in
formal characteristics are undifferentiated in meaning, dreaming would
seem to lack the quality of recursion that is a feature of the kind of
language that is related to thought. I suggest that recursion is a characteristic of thought, that thought is not necessarily identical either to
language or to communication, and that neither thought nor communication need necessarily be restricted to the realm of the symbolic.

Freud's assertion that dreams are not intended to be understood seems to
mean that although they have unconscious meaning they are not communications in an intentional sense. There are a few analysts who maintain
that dreams are communications (Lacan, quoted in Dor, 1998; and Kanzer,
1955). They argue that mental life is inextricably interwoven with the social
world and relationships, and social and relational elements are present in
dreams, therefore dreams are communications. The assumption is that if
the dream is symbolic and meaningful, since the dreamer is embedded in
social relationships it must be a communication. It seems likely that such
reasoning is a product of confusing the dream as experienced with the
dream as translated into thought after awakening and then in some

instances communicated to others. It is true that some dreams are about actual communication to another person, but as the dreamer is asleep, others are not present in awareness, and the experience is a kind of hallucination, it would seem that the experience is an undifferentiated presentation of the mind of the dreamer rather than communication.

From a somewhat different perspective French and Fromm write that:

> The logic that we miss in the dream work is the syntactical logic of speech – the syntactical logic that is essential for the framing and testing of propositions and reasoning from them. Speech was designed primarily for communication. When we dream, we are not particularly interested in communicating our thoughts to others or in reasoning from propositions. Therefore we can dispense with syntactical logic.
>
> (1964, p. 162)

In other words, dreaming is not an effort to communicate and dreams are not characterized by recursion.

To conclude, dreaming can inform us about the nature of thought, language and communication if we consider that dreams take place while asleep, and we look not at the dream itself but at the process that produces it. From that perspective I conclude that analysis of dreaming helps us to understand that there is a process – PMA – that is qualitatively different from thought and is the foundation of both a language and a form of communication that are also very different from thought.

Language and communication in schizophrenia

Schizophrenic disorders of language, thought and communication first attracted the interest of psychiatrists at the Burghölzli sanatorium in Switzerland at the turn of the twentieth century. These included Kraepelin (1896), Jung (1906), Stransky (1905), Bleuler (1911) and Freud's disciple Tausk (1933). Beginning with Klein (1930), a handful of analysts, among them Katan (1939), Segal (1950, 1956, 1957), Bion (1955, 1957, 1959), Searles (1965), Arieti (1974), and others whose work is inaccessible to a non-German or non-French-speaking reader (Schilder, 1942; Storch, 1924; Gerson, 1928; Bobon, 1962), also became interested in the subject. Since the neuroscientific view of schizophrenia as an organic illness whose verbal manifestations are meaningless epiphenomena gained ascendency about four decades ago psychoanalytic interest in the meaningfulness of schizophrenic speech and writing has correspondingly waned.

The psychoanalytic debate about whether schizophrenic speech and writing constitute language has focused on the question of whether symbolic capability is missing entirely, whether symbolism is arcane and opaque, or whether words can be used in a way that is simultaneously symbolic and concrete. I reviewed in Chapter 2 that although Freud believed that the primary process is the basis both of dreams and of schizophrenia and that schizophrenic language is concrete, he nonetheless vacillated about whether dreaming is concrete or symbolic. Jones (1916) must have sensed Freud's two voices on this subject, and tried to explain how the process could simultaneously be both. The Kleinian position has perpetuated this confusion which ironically seems to express the principle of absence of contradiction that characterizes the primary process as well as PMA. Klein maintained that phantasy, the basis of schizophrenic language, is a concrete somatic-psychic process. Segal states the distinction succinctly when she comments on her patient's "failure to distinguish between that which was thought of and that which was" (1950, p. 269). Yet Klein herself (1930), Segal (1956, 1957, 1978), and others (Katan, 1939; Burnham 1955; Searles, 1965; Arieti, 1974; Werner, 1948; Goldstein, 1944; and Cameron, 1944, 1963) have asserted that schizophrenics are stimulus-bound and concrete, and that they cannot abstract, generalize, or form concepts and categories. In a reasoning process like that of Jones, Klein (1930) introduced the term "symbolic equation" to suggest that language could simultaneously be concrete and symbolic, and Segal (1957, 1978) elaborated this idea. Kleinian interpretive practice often treats psychotic utterances as symbolically decodable.

Harry Sullivan (1953a) was of the opinion that schizophrenic and ordinary language are qualitatively similar in all respects, including symbolic capability, but that what makes schizophrenic language seem different is its unusual *use* of symbols. However, a substantial body of opinion among psychiatrists, psychoanalysts and psychologists, as early as William Alanson White (1925), is that what separates schizophrenic speech from ordinary language is a specific defect in symbolic capability. Building on Freud's (1900) primary process mechanisms of condensation and displacement the psychologist Von Domarus (1944) coined the phrase "predicate identity" with reference to how words are treated concretely as objects, chained by formal or superficial characteristics rather than by abstract or symbolic meanings, and not related to the subject who utters them. The result depicts an idiosyncratic solipsistic universe that expresses wish or belief and is unrelated to the person's actual place in time and space.

Although Freud did not treat schizophrenics, during the period early in his career when he was still preoccupied with the primary and secondary processes and the relationship between dreaming and schizophrenia, he wrote about a patient of Tausk who

> complained that her eyes were not right, they were twisted. This she herself explained by bringing forward a series of reproaches against her lover in coherent language. "She could not understand him at all, he

looked different every time; he was a hypocrite, an eye-twister, he had twisted her eyes; now she had twisted eyes; they were not her eyes any more; now she saw the world with different eyes."

(1915, p. 197)

His analysis: "Here the schizophrenic utterance exhibits a hypochondriac trait: it has become 'organ-speech.'" He goes on: "A second communication by the same patient was as follows: 'She was standing in church. Suddenly she felt a jerk; she had to change her position, as though somebody was putting her into a position, as though she was being put in a certain position'" (ibid.). She was able to tell Tausk that her lover's behavior had put her in a bad position, a conflict between her sense of herself and her wish to be as he wanted her to be. He writes: "Tausk's remarks depicted the words 'putting her in a false position' and her identification with her lover. I would call attention once more to the fact that the whole train of thought is dominated by the element which has for its content a bodily innervation" (ibid.). In this clear description of primordial mental activity Freud seems to believe it is a communication that can be understood if the listener can hear it as enactment with analogy rather than as a thoughtful symbolic utterance.

In summary, there has been considerable controversy about whether schizophrenic speech and writing meet the criteria of language and communication, as conceived of as thoughtful symbolic processes. I believe that schizophrenic verbalization is not a thoughtful symbolic process and I will illustrate that it is the most vivid waking example of a language and communication based on PMA.

The language and communication of schizophrenia

How does the model of PMA, in dissociation from thought, help to understand schizophrenic language? A schizophrenic person perceives the world from within a solipsistic framework that uses words whose formal characteristics differentiate self from other, but does not distinguish what is in the mind from what is in the world. Such a person uses words and sentences as concrete vehicles to exert force or belief coercively, not as vehicles to transmit meaning, and similarly hears the utterances of others as forceful coercive impressions or persecutory assaults, paranoid ideas of reference. Communication occurs but not by thoughtful exchange of meaning; the medium is literally the message. Schizophrenic language is not recursive. Paralytic obsessive rumination is one of its manifestations, and it is different from weighing of different ideas and choices. There is reiteration or contiguity with little evidence of awareness of sequence, passage of time, awareness of contradiction, or recursive referencing of units of meaning to

Table 15.1 Language and communication in thought and PMA

	Language of thought	Language of PMA
Pragmatics: Motivation	Emotionally based ideas and somatic sensations	Somatic affect. Alexithymic
Grammar, Syntax, Morphology	Intact	Intact including vocabulary, masking undifferentiation and concreteness. Exception: neologisms made by affect-driven undifferentiation
Semantics: Abstraction	Choice between symbolic to convey meaning or literal to exert force.	Concrete and literal. Non-representational. The thing itself. Immediacy and belief
Semantics: Differentiation	Differentiated into meaningful categories	Holistic and collective. Verbal designations (names) mask ideational undifferentiation or unity of persons and things
Semantics: Referentiality and recursion	Reflective, recursive, comparative, contrasting	It is. Belief. No comparison, contrast, recursion, reflection
Semantics: Narrative reference and sequence	Self as recursive reference. Time-referential. Integrated. Causal logic and sequence	Affect-driven snapshots linked by contiguity. Timeless and unintegrated. Self only a formal designation
Pragmatics: Communication	Primarily exchange of ideas and meaning	Peremptory pressure and force both in expression and impression (learning). Words are things

other ideas. Some characteristics of language used for primordial expression in contrast to language used for thoughtful communication are summarized in Table 15.1.

Caroline and the language of schizophrenese

I presented some vignettes from Caroline's therapy in Chapter 13. She had been given a DSM diagnosis of chronic schizophrenia during the course of numerous hospitalizations spanning the decade or so preceding my first encounter with her. She was in her early forties at the time of the verbatim examples of speech and writing that follow, and had been in psycho-analytically informed therapy with me for about a dozen years at the time. Prior to my first encounter with her, all sorts of treatments – pharmaco-logical, psychological and electro-convulsive – had been administered by a variety of institutions and caregivers, to no avail.

Caroline had become catatonic and immobilized following graduation from college. In the ensuing years she manifested the classic symptoms of schizophrenia, including flattened and inappropriate affect, postural rigidity, delusions and hallucinations. Over the years before I met her she was in and out of hospitals. Once she had to be tube fed, bathed, and carried to the toilet. Another time she bit and nearly severed her tongue. On another occasion, under the delusion that she was about to be electrocuted, she tried to act on a hallucinated command to jump out the window and escape. She repeatedly formed delusions about special romantic relationships with her doctors in which they would take total care of her.

I met her after her transfer from a well-known hospital accompanied by a note from the former attending psychiatrist saying that she was "a pathetic young woman." She showed little ability or inclination to take more than the most basic care of herself. Shortly thereafter she ingested a massive dose of medications stolen from the nurses' station, inducing a near-fatal coma that lasted several days. Many years later she was able to tell me what it was all about. Her psychotic and alcoholic father had recently died as a consequence of self-destructive behaviour. In her growing up he had neglected or threatened Caroline's expressions of need and capacities for thoughtful emotional expression and constructive coping, and bribed her with money as well as license or permission to do anything she wished without having to face the consequences, and without having to learn to take care of herself in the world outside the family. She was apparently in an inchoate rage that he had abandoned her in the hospital and not removed her from the situation without consequence as he had done in the past. Caroline had engaged in a delusional competition with another seriously self-destructive patient for the attentions of a prominent male doctor and his staff based on the belief that whichever of them was most disturbed would get totally taken care of by him. She had experienced the emergency room physician's ministrations to her on the gurney as consummation of her desires, and she subsequently developed a delusion about that physician and pursued him shamelessly and inappropriately for many years thereafter.

After two years of four times per week therapy and establishment of a suitable medication regimen Caroline was able to leave the hospital, never to return, and to manage a marginally independent existence, supported by substantial trust funds. She did not like to work and she did not feel she had to, so she had never learned to do it well and she never had more than part-time, entry-level employment. Her inappropriate behaviour and continued messing up of relationships, responsibilities and opportunities seemed to be her way of proving the truth of her oft-repeated mantra "nothing good will ever happen." At the same time she used much of her money and time to pursue immediate gratification in the form of consumption of food and material goods and leisure trips. Caroline was driven by impulses for self-gratification, did not take into account the consequences of her behaviour, and did not form close relationships or sensibly manage her personal finances. Nonetheless, her capacity to work remuneratively and to take care of herself very gradually improved and she began to develop some serious interests and experience some sense of personal meaning and satisfaction. Even as her trust funds diminished, and regardless of obvious facts to the contrary, she acted as though she was a wealthy philanthropist and claimed that doctors who had treated her in fact had personal romantic interest in her. She believed she did not have to abide by the same social conventions and limits as others. She maintained an unshakeable belief that it was the responsibility of others to take care of her, and when something went wrong she invariably found persons out there, including myself, who she could convince herself were to blame and hence make targets of her uncontrolled, tantrum-like rage.

After about a dozen years of therapeutic turmoil we developed islands of thoughtful communication that were interspersed with her still bizarre and often destructive behavior. She became more able to recognize and talk about her underlying beliefs, attitudes and behaviors but this thoughtful part remained for the most part dissociated from her mindless and limitless pursuit of self-gratification. When confronted with the contradiction between the latest of her recurrent promises that she would reform and be constructive and her endless irresponsible and destructive behaviour she would typically get angry, rage at me for not caring about her, and conclude the discussion by saying: "I'm going to do it anyway."

I became particularly interested in the peculiarities of her language, something that most of the people around her seemed either not to notice or to interpret in some way that made sense to them. When, try as I might, I could not comprehend what she was saying, I began to inform her that she was speaking *schizophrenese* and to insist that she translate particularly arcane utterances into comprehensible English. In characteristic fashion she informed me that it was my responsibility to understand her. Finally, in a state of some desperation, I portrayed myself to her as a student, asked if she would teach me, and took out pad and pen. With her permission I began to record both her utterance and the subsequent dialogue in which she attempted to express what she had said in a manner that I could comprehend.

What follows is a verbatim transcript in which she talked about what I gradually realized had been a day of irresponsible, out of control behaviour involving playing pool (an activity she had done with a recreational therapist during her hospitalization) while waiting for repairs on her car which had been damaged due to her careless driving habits. The question marks represent places where I asked her to tell me more about what she meant:

I had time to kill. Rack it up and pocket 'em. Sock it and rock 'em. Clear the table. The only table that had monkey business to it. [?] E. [a staff member in the hospital, whom Caroline idealised] and I used to play pool. [?] Judgement Day. I've got so many balls and I have to put them in the pocket. Get the eight-ball in and you're out. I've got to shoot straight from the hip, and keep both feet on the ground. Just straight shots coming from the heart. People have things racked up against you but you keep on shooting, and if you make a racket like me it gives them more ammunition. [?] Now you *really* think I'm crazy. I racked 'em up and then I bought a root beer. The guy said, "You can't drink that here," and then we talked about getting 50 per cent off lodging in [a distant resort]. I said that late September is the best time to go there [laughs]. [*What are you laughing about?*] Well, it's not a short walk to get there, and I have $16 in my wallet. They don't want unethical behaviour in the bar. So I think about going there; I build up in my mind places to go. I start out thinking I'm going to clean the apartment. Then I do these other things. Then I start thinking when I don't that it's the fault of the landlord and others. Then I ran out of time and I had to go to work; I was late again. [*What about the resort?*] It's a *Closetland* place [a reference to a movie about a woman who turned to fantasy in order to endure torture]; no problems there, everything is fine.

In this excerpt Caroline moves between primordial mental expression and reflective thought. She experiences the pool table as the "real" world, of which she is magically the omnipotent arbiter and master. She literally and magically believes that by putting balls in the pocket she is ridding herself of her problems, killing time (in primordial mental activity the passage of time and its significance is not recognized) and killing people who offend her so that there is nothing she needs to be responsible for and work at. What might appear to be low-grade metaphors or similes–clichés such as "shoot straight," "shoot from the hip," "rack 'em up," "rock 'em and sock 'em," being "behind the eight-ball," "killing time" – are concrete undifferentiated conglomerates of words, perceptions, actions and affects, magically experienced as an actual happening. From her effort to translate and our subsequent discussions I infer that, had she been able to express her state of mind in more mature thought and fantasy rather than the magical omnipotence of primordial expression, she might have said:

The Day of Judgement has come for me. I'm very angry at myself for all my monkey business – wasting time and dismissing the efforts of staff back when I was in the hospital, damaging my car, not being financially responsible, not cleaning my apartment or being on time for my appointments, and treating life like a game I practiced when I was in the hospital. By making so much destructive noise I give others ammunition to use against me. I've really got myself behind the eight-ball. I wish I could get rid of this unhappy situation and get my feet back on the ground. But I'm in a rage at having to be responsible; I just want to kill more time, blame others, wipe the table clean of all my problems and imagine I'm at a resort on a perpetual vacation.

Had she expressed herself in that way Caroline would have had to think about what was "on her mind," identify her emotions and bear responsibility for them. Primordial mental activity enables her to create a reality that conforms to wish and belief, and disregards logic, time and causality. She believes she can magically alter the past and create a wished-for future. Wishing makes it so. By not differentiating self from other and experiencing the distress of her life as though it were out there she rationalizes a kind of emotional excretion in lieu of thinking about her rage.

In her state of psychic undifferentiation Caroline had no sense of personal privacy or boundaries. Just as she believed her words and gestures magically altered reality, so she construed the words of others as commands or intrusions. She repeatedly sent duplicate batches of twenty to forty letters at a time to casual acquaintances or figures from her distant past. These consisted of mindless recounting of details and complaints about her life. I gradually learned this evacuation of mind was based on the belief that she was literally giving others her problems.

Schizophrenese appears to be more or less normal syntactically (Andreasen *et al.*, 1985; Matthysse, 1987). A sentence that seems bizarre to the listener may actually be syntactically sound. Caroline read me the following inscription that she had written in the front of one of her books:

C. C. [her initials]. For a friend having a start at a pearly new larger place. To a larger print. What's a crop? Slow reader from Carolina who pearls not. Ultimately she had a problem. A "no J." problem. Last chance world knits A., for a friend what, L., from a friend, C. C. O. T. V. promise.

To my amazement, when I initially transcribed this into my computer, my word-processing program, which mercilessly critiques what I would like to believe are perfectly acceptable sentences, had nothing to say except that three lines are predicate fragments lacking a subject, something that in a less bizarre writing sample might from a semantic standpoint seem unremarkable. The words are linked by contiguity and lack meaningful logical narrative sequence.

From a morphological standpoint things are more complex. Word forms are generally observed except in the instance of one of the most striking features of schizophrenic speech, the use of neologism. In some instances the issue is semantic, and the word may be used for an idiosyncratic purpose by condensing or not differentiating meanings. Here is an example from well along in Caroline's therapy, when she had become capable of thinking and communicating with me about her utterances. While talking about her difficulties maintaining focus, initiative and perspective in her search for a more responsible job she told me she had come up with a term to describe herself, "batted" in the eye, but she wasn't sure that "batted" was a real word in the sense she was using it. She told me that bats hang upside down, and reverse the normal cycle of day and night. Then she recalled that we had talked about how she construed positive things like taking care of herself and accomplishing things she could be proud of as negative, and her expectation that others should be responsible for her and entitlement to rage at them when they were not, as positive. "I'm not battered," she remarked, "but I'm batted because I shut my eyes. I didn't keep my eyes open in my job search and as a result I misconstrued things. I didn't like what people said to me [constructive advice and suggestions]; it felt like they were hitting me and I shut my eyes. Not my real eyes, you know; my psychological eyes." Then she recounted a memory from her childhood involving her mother, who had literally and psychologically seduced her into a state of shared fantasy, withdrawal, and inertia, and said: "I used to get pink-eye [infection] a lot as a child and mother would fill this eye cup with a solution and I had to hold it over my eye for a while. I found that it felt good, in fact that I liked the sensation of not seeing, of hiding." At this point I said to her that if she was thinking and talking about how she tended to confuse positive and negative, up and down, and living in reality vs. fantasy, why did she choose a word she made up that could not be shared or communicated to others? She responded: "It's a way of hiding. If I make up a word that is removed from others' understanding of the English language then I can stay in the dark myself." The reader might also take note of the forceful concrete expressive and impressive quality of her utterances.

In other instances a new word may be created by undifferentiated blending or stringing together of morphologically unremarkable elements by acceptable ordinary language rules or processes such as the use of affixes, compounding, onomatopoeia, proper noun transformation, clipping and blending. For some time I believed that Caroline was not very bright. One of the observations I misinterpreted in order to reach this conclusion was her very limited vocabulary and the frequency with which she used neologisms or we encountered words whose meanings she did not know, and sometimes confabulated. What she did tend to do was to take words she already knew and make neologisms by combination or undifferentiation, assigning them unusual meanings based on some quality or significance related to a private concern or wish, so that the new word expressed a belief or concrete reality. Once again the neologism appears to serve the purpose of concretely exerting force rather than conveying meaning. As time went on she was able to talk about her aversion to the "reality" of differentiated, meaningful and communicated language. Her writing was similarly idiosyncratic. She eventually began to take literature courses. She got feedback that she took aspects of the assignment that had personal meaning to her and wrote disjointed assertions of her beliefs rather than trying to assemble and communicate to the teacher her own thoughts about the text she had read with the expectation of receiving thoughtful feedback.

As previously noted, many prominent linguists agree that the presence of recursion is an essential structural criterion for language. Schizophrenic utterances are linked to a subject and to the speaker but only in a formal or concrete sense; they are not organized around a thoughtful, reflective, centered sense of self and subjectivity, nor do they have a thoughtful narrative quality. Schizophrenia is a state of self-centeredness or egocentricity in the solipsistic sense of the term, in distinction to the more mature self-centeredness that is based on the capacity to have a thoughtful reflective sense of self. Schizophrenese is a language of predicates or objects that are not narratively linked to a self functioning in a world differentiated from others, but linked instead by superficial or formal qualities to the person's beliefs or actions.

Turning to semantic and pragmatic aspects of schizophrenese, Heinz Werner and Bernard Kaplan remark: "One cannot conclude from the fact that the schizophrenic person may exploit conventional linguistic forms in his utterances that he actually uses or regards language in the same way as does the normal" (1963, p. 257). From a semantic perspective schizophrenese is characterized by an absence of the ordinary distinctions between word, thing, bodily process, affect and action, and its relation to the subject is different, as well. It is an immediate language of the body and its concrete impact, particularly motor (throwing, hitting), respiratory (breathing, talking and blowing, as in the felicitous expression "mind blowing"), gastrointestinal (vomiting and defecating), and orgasmic ("fucking one's brains out"). Here is Caroline's description of printmaking: "I was pounding it down, oozing out my black insides on paper." She told me: "I want to run and run and run away from the painful feelings. I feel like I can split off, disintegrate, and get away from them. This is what schizophrenese is about."

A commonplace and perhaps too readily accepted definition of psychosis is that it is defensive – a refusal to accept reality. This is a bit like saying that the sleeping dreamer denies reality. It assumes a thoughtful mind in conflict in which one part defends itself against another that is capable of awareness of a differentiated external "real" world. While there is usually some small but dissociated capacity for realistic thought and adaptation, such conflict occurs only in more advanced stages of work with schizophrenic persons like Caroline, and then it seems to have to do with the choice about whether to do the hard work of thinking, feeling and adapting, or to take the easier way out afforded by PMA. Prior to that, words and language are primary non-defensive things of action that are believed to have magical power to change events. Loewald describes "the magical compelling power of words. . . . Language in its primordial form has the power or the significance of *action* for the *speaker*" (1980, p. 202). In less severe psychotic states, where there is some capacity for thoughtful adaptation and some awareness of an external world, the words exert force on others in order to co-opt them into the delusional world of the subject. In more severe instances, like schizophrenia and, for example, the back ward Messiah, the magic is done in isolation and what others do seems of no consequence.

In ordinary discourse speaker and listener recognise the symbolic import of a concrete-sounding statement such as "I have a special pipeline to the boss", or "Let's smoke a peace-pipe." The metaphor serves as emphasis or highlighting of a key idea that is being talked about. In contrast, Caroline once literally handed me a section of plumber's pipe – a gesture so pregnant with meaning yet impregnable to my interpretive skills that it would have been easy to conclude that the pipe was an arcane symbol. When I questioned her about it, however, she was able to tell me that she *was making* a connection with me. In other words, the pipe was just a pipe, but in the language of belief and actualization the action was fulfilling a wish. On another occasion she gave me a gift of a wine stopper. It turned out she was concerned I might be an alcoholic like her father, and she literally believed this would *stop* me. Whereas a suitor might metaphorically and passionately declare love by saying "I give you my heart" or sing symbolically about how to deal with painful problems as in the folk lyric "Pack up your troubles in your old kit bag and smile," Caroline told me that when she mailed her Valentine's card with a large heart on it to a large number of casual and former acquaintances she believed she was giving herself to others she looked upon as more willing to assume responsibility for her than she was for herself.

Many concepts have been proposed to describe the undifferentiated aspect of schizophrenic speech. Ironically, they resemble schizophrenic neologisms in the sense that they are idiosyncratic to the author and are not built upon by others. Caroline herself proposed that this is "combination thinking," a phrase remarkably similar to the term *combinative thinking* proposed by Johnston and Holzman (1979). Other terms include *condensation* (Freud, 1900; Stransky, 1905), *contamination* (Stransky, 1905; Jung, 1906; Von Domarus, 1944), *combinative thinking, syntactical substitution* and *telescopage* (Lecours and Vanier-Clement, 1976), *interpenetration, overinclusion* and *metonymy* (Cameron, 1944, 1963), *primary aggregation* (Arieti, 1974), *predicate identity* (Von Domarus, 1944), *dedifferentiation, parasemantic, polysemantic,* and *holophrastic* (Werner and Kaplan, 1963).

Von Domarus' (1944) concept of *predicate identity*, the central characteristic of what he calls *paralogical thinking*, is of particular interest. Von Domarus utilizes Vygotsky's definitions of subject and object, or predicate: "Vygotsky calls the subject of a sentence that about which something is said, and the predicate that which expresses what is said about the subject; subject and predicate are for him psychological, not grammatical terms" (1944, p. 111f). Predicate identity means that two elements unrelated to the subject and unrelated by meaning are treated by the schizophrenic subject as though they are identical (not *are associated*) because they share a quality that fits the person's belief. "The paralogical thinker finds identity of subjects whenever and wherever he finds identity of predicates" (Von Domarus, 1944, p. 113). Von Domarus cites the example of a patient who believed that Jesus, cigar boxes, and sex are identical. They shared the quality of being encircled (halo, cigar band, holding). The delusional belief of a schizophrenic that an unrelated woman is her mother, for instance, may result from making an identity of the predicate fact that both that person and the patient's mother are women.

I was told about a patient who maintained that men are grass. A detailed analysis revealed that the subject of belief was death, and the predicates "men" and "grass" were treated as identical because they share the characteristic of dying. What is interesting is how easy it would be to express some of these beliefs in thought. For instance, if we insert the word *like*, the statement becomes "men are *like* grass." The syllogism "men die, grass dies, therefore men are *like* grass" might even become poetic, as it is in one of the most moving parts of the Brahms *German Requiem*. In schizophrenese one might say "Johnny is a weed," based on the qualities of rapid growth. In this concrete paralogical assertion "Johnny is growing fast, weeds grow fast, therefore Johnny is a weed." Expressed in symbolic thought one might simply say "Johnny is *growing like* a weed."

Werner and Kaplan (1963) report an example from the work of Tuczek of a patient who used the term "the sent" to denote the color white. The underlying process was that snow is white, and snow is sent from God. The meaning of many otherwise arcane schizophrenic associations can be grasped if one can determine the predicate quality that aggregates them. Caroline commenced an hour by looking at my shoes and commenting: "It makes me angry that you always have neat shoes and I don't." I commented that I had noticed that her feet were beginning to move. She said: "Our feet move together," and added that she would like me to hug her. I asked why and she said: "I want to be in your shoes." She then realized she was not having a wishful fantasy or talking symbolically, but attempting to create a literal belief that she was me by means of predicate identity but could not quite manage it.

The semantics of schizophrenic utterance provide insight into delusion and the formation of neologisms. Delusions are fixed beliefs precisely because in the mind of their creator they are literal actualities and there is nothing to be thought about or questioned. As for neologisms, Caroline once remarked: "I've got it set up at work so no one can refrain from *authoriting* me. They tell me what to do. It pisses me off." When I inquired if she believed *authoriting* was a legitimate word, she said she supposed not. I then asked why she did not say what she meant in acceptable English. She replied that it would compel her to face feelings of shame at loss of dignity and control over her own life. By not accepting the existence of an ordinary language word to express her feeling state she managed to repudiate the reality of her responsibility and to avoid the feelings about it. I do not think this was a specific unconscious attempt to defend herself against unconscious conflicts over passivity and irresponsibility so much as it was part of a general effort to avoid the work of thinking. This is another example of the identity of words, things, and actions. If the word is the real thing, and she can substitute a neologism, then she can delude herself that the thing or the problem no longer exists. It is easy for the analyst who is struggling to understand the patient to gloss over the idiosyncratic aspect of the word in favor of what appears to be the underlying meaning, as one might do with some of the peculiarities of speech of someone not fluent in one's native tongue. In this instance it would be easy to assume that Caroline really didn't like having others tell her what to do. This form of communication combines the patient's *delusion* with the analyst's *illusion* to create a *collusion*.

The pragmatic aspect of language relates to communication. Is schizophrenese a communicative language? What is the relationship between communication and intention? The schizophrenic person's utterances communicate to others like any other verbalizations. Though they have an effect on the hearer, and usually a powerful one, it does not follow that there is intent to transmit *meaning* to another separate person or indeed that there is thoughtful intention of any kind. Rather, the verbalizations are efforts to actualize in the interaction the subject's internal affect-driven state of affairs. The success of such a delusional activity is a *folie à deux*. When Caroline became capable of some thought she realized that her schizophrenese functioned to mislead and deceive, but as she did not hitherto "know" this, no communicative intent was involved. In order to function as a vehicle of communication, contextual elements and related linguistic assumptions – personal, social and cultural – must be sufficiently concordant in speaker and listener – the "music," so to speak, that accompanies the words. In the case of schizophrenese these assumptions are idiosyncratic to the speaker or writer and there is no thoughtful communicative intent. If concordance is defined in the sense that Klein defines projective identification, however, as induction of a mental state that the respondent can act upon or think about, then there has been a communication. Here is what Caroline says about it:

I get away to a place where my *own* words are real but other people aren't; I can't be touched by them. I guess I'm finding a closet land, a private place where I escape to my own words to avoid other people's touch that threatens me.

She seems to be telling us that she experiences the words of others in schizophrenese as concrete coercive impressions; again a kind of communication but probably not what the interlocutor intended.

In an apparently idealizing letter Caroline referred to one of her former doctors, whom she surmised was Jewish and on whom she had a delusional fixation, as a "kite." Judging from the absence of an overt response from him it would seem that he had dismissed the letter, as he did much of her writing to him, as yet another example of her insanity. Little did he know, as she eventually rephrased it to me in ordinary language, that he had once enraged her by telling her she was "higher than a kite," or that her father had often referred to Jews as "kikes." She invented an undifferentiated neologistic epithet that condensed what he had called her with her rage in such a way that she could throw it back at him without being thoughtfully aware of what she was doing and without his having any idea what she was doing, and hence without consequence to her.

Caroline once said: "I give people the breathing they need. I make a case to take care of me. I respire them. With every breath I give them responsibility." 'Respire' is a neologism made by the ordinary morphological processes of clipping and condensation of the physical process of respiration and the work-related concept of responsibility. This is an affect-driven undifferentiated amalgamation of respiration and responsibility that in Caroline's mind forces herself inside others. On another occasion she made a similar statement from a gastrointestinal perspective: "I'm mad today. I had to put in limits and boundaries and not spill my guts. There are lots of snakes inside me and I want you to eat them for me." In reference to an episode of vomiting during a meal with her family when they questioned her about instances of her irresponsible behavior, she commented: "I couldn't bear the feeling of having taken all those courses, wasting money, scattering my time, and I had to get rid of them. I was throwing up the feeling."

Whereas ordinary language serves to heighten reflective emotional self-awareness and selectively communicate this to others, who might in turn provide feedback that would further heighten self-awareness, schizophrenese functions in lieu of thinking, communicating and receiving communications of meaning, and apprehending social reality. It is coercive both expressively and receptively. Often when I would encourage Caroline to couch a schizophrenese utterance in ordinary language by asking "what do you mean" she would reluctantly acknowledge that she herself was unaware of what she intended. As Caroline said, she did not use metaphor because "metaphors take more responsibility; they are more connecting." Named emotions as motivating forces are missing in schizophrenia. The "wording" is affectively driven. Schizophrenese short-circuits the necessity to know, think and feel. This is not defensive, however, until the person is capable of thought and aware that there is a choice. Caroline once said: "I want to run and run and run away from the painful feelings. I feel like I can split off, disintegrate, and get away from the painful feeling." She concluded: "This is what schizophrenese is about."

Despite its strange and colorful quality, schizophrenese is neither a language of conscious awareness (reflection) nor of unconscious conceal-ment (repression), both of which as I described earlier in the book are aspects of thought. It does not support mental representation, symboliza-tion and reflection. A neurotic patient might refer to her habitual and inappropriate tendency to confide personal affairs to others using the unconscious symbolism of a phrase such as "spilling my guts." If ques-tioned, she would have the sense that she had said something worth reflecting *on*, thinking *about*, and analysing the symbolic meaning *of*. The reflection might also lead to the uncovering of an unconscious meaning to the phrase as well – perhaps a repressed conflict or memory. When Caroline used the expression about spilling her guts she not only believed there were snakes in her intestines that she needed to give to me (although she could reality test the idea if pressed to do so), but also referred to an earlier occasion when she had vomited to rid herself of unwanted feelings.

In psychoanalysis with someone who is not psychotic the analyst might suggest that the patient's behavior and associations indicate that she viewed her problems as a mess she believed she could dump onto or into the analyst, and the patient might respond to the interpretation with associ-ations to oral or anal fantasies and memories. When Caroline says "I send it ('my mess') to responsible people. . . I'm filling up their mailbox. . . I word my way into a relationship with letters," she is *doing something* and not speaking metaphorically or thinking. Whereas an ordinary person might be aware of the underlying fantasies and conflicts, Caroline literally believes that she is excreting her gastrointestinal self, which is identical to her words, into others. One might say that she is expressing phantasy, in the Kleinian sense, with the caveat that this is a language of closure that leaves no unconscious symbolized meaning to be interpreted or thought about.

The pragmatic aspects of schizophrenese are closely related to delusion and delusion-related deception, that is, deception of the thoughtful observer that is not thoughtfully intentional on the part of the perpetrator. These processes enable the subject to avoid the effort of having to think and feel, and consequently to bear and realistically adapt to psychic distress conse-quent to the conflicts and dilemmas that comprise ordinary life. It must be emphasized that the process is not the mind's effort to avoid re-awakening of awareness of hitherto thought and then repressed conflict; it is the avoidance of the work of thinking and feeling itself. Schizophrenese enables a person to believe (delude him or herself) that he or she has omnipotent control over the world. The language is felt by its user to possess the power to undo, reverse and eliminate the reality of what would otherwise be painful thoughts and feelings. It is a language of psychic alchemy or delusional omnipotence (Burnham, 1955; Frosch, 1967; Glass, 1981). As Caroline put it: "I fool myself into thinking it didn't happen." Speaking ordinary language, she referred to schizophrenese as "the language of wish and desire." With her knitting, a game of pool, a walk around the lake, or detailed letters to others, she creates a universe that she can describe and act upon with the conviction that she is effortlessly altering events, problems and associated feelings, both present and past.

Ordinary language also employs reversal, but in an entirely different way and for an opposite purpose. By its stark contrast with the shared and implicitly acknowledged context, such reversal in ordinary language serves to highlight or *accentuate* the feeling the speaker wishes to convey. A thoughtful Caroline, for instance, might say: "If only I could change what happened in the past by getting all the balls in the hole except the eight ball now!" The delusional reversal of schizophrenia, by contrast, eliminates the necessity to differentiate mind from reality, to bear painful thoughts, feelings and memories, and to adapt to a consensually validated world. An ordinary person, faced with a painful situation, might transiently find solace by constructing heroic fantasies and becoming in imagination someone able to surmount any difficulty, someone invulnerable to pain and hurt. Schizophrenic language, by contrast, lacks the "as if" capacity inherent in the use of metaphor that is required to construct such a fantasy, and instead there are delusions of omnipotence or of messianic suffering. In place of a world that is imperfect, in progress, and requiring thought, bearing of distress, and adaptation, schizophrenese articulates a world that is already seamless and complete.

To summarize, there are two qualitatively different kinds of expressive and receptive language, one based on primordial mental activity and the other on thought. The differences are for the most part semantic and pragmatic, to a minor extent morphological, and not at all with regard to grammar and syntax. The difference determines how the language employs learned elements including words, grammar and syntax. Both communicate, but in different ways. The language that expresses thought is reflective, representational and symbolic, and communicates by conveying and receiving meaning. The language that expresses PMA is a concrete vehicle of impression and induction related to belief or certainty. If the participants in an interaction are each using a different form of mental activity there will be no consensus, but that does not necessarily mean nothing has been transmitted or communicated. Both languages communicate. Whether a specific example of the language of PMA is deemed pathological, as in the instance of schizophrenia, or a culturally normal expression, as in the case of the Piraha or of creativity or spirituality, depends on the social-cultural context in which it is used, the degree of integration with or dissociation from thought, and on the socially adaptive synchrony or maladaptive asynchrony of the communication that ensues.

Chapter 16

Neuroscience of primordial mind

Finding evidence to support the hypothesis that a common mind model underlies such disparate phenomena as attachment, dreaming, spirituality, shamanism, altered states of trance and ecstasy, creativity, psychosis and more is difficult. While finding a common neural circuitry for some of these superficially disparate phenomena would offer major support for a unifying mental process model such as I am proposing, it would at best be corroborative. On the other hand, in such an ambiguous situation it is all too easy to succumb to the simplicity of organic reductionism and conclude that if the neurobiological data are not there or are equivocal then the psychological theory must be dismissed.

Using neuroimaging technologies it is now possible to study brain function and mental activity concurrently, and look for correlates. Brain functioning during dreaming, the prototype of primordial mental activity, has been extensively studied. Neuro-metabolic activity has also been studied in schizophrenic persons. Those studies are in a far more preliminary stage than similar studies of dreaming, and they are fraught with problems related to diagnosis and methodology. Nonetheless, the results are intriguing and suggestive. Cortical and sub-cortical mapping studies of infant and child development and attachment behavior are also being conducted, and some of the findings seem to correlate with Freud's theory of the primary process.

The mind–body problem

Before discussing these findings I would like to place them in the larger context of the mind–body problem. What is the relationship between the psychological system of mind and meaning that is the focus of traditional psychoanalytic study and the organic system comprising brain function that is the focus of neuroscience?

As with so many things, Freud was not always clear or consistent in his position about the mind–body problem, and overall it shifted in the course of his career though not decisively. In his 1895 *Project for a Scientific*

Psychology he formulated the primary process in terms of hypothetical brain functioning and stated his goal of eventually reducing all mental functioning to neurology: "The intention is to furnish a scientific psychology that shall be a natural science: that is, to represent psychical processes as quantitatively determinate states of specifiable material particles" (1895, p. 295). He reiterated this wish in various forms until as late as 1920 when, during the re-formulation of his instinct theory, he wrote: "The deficiencies in our description would probably vanish if we were already in a position to replace the psychological terms by physiological or chemical ones. . . we may expect it [biology] to give us the most surprising information and we cannot guess what answers it will return in a few dozen years to the questions we have put to it" (1920, p. 60). At the same time, in the years following the *Project*, there were increasing indications of another point of view, a systems perspective that is stated most clearly and decisively in his final writings:

> We know two kinds of things about what we call our psyche (or mental life): firstly, its bodily organ and scene of action, the brain (or nervous system) and, on the other hand, our acts of consciousness, which are immediate data and cannot be further explained by any sort of description. Everything that lies between is unknown to us, and the data do not include any direct relations between these two terminal points of our knowledge. If it existed, it would at the most afford an exact localization of the processes of consciousness and would give us no help towards understanding them.
>
> (1940, p. 144)

This comment, half a century before the advent of neuroimaging, is remarkably prescient.

Freud's inconsistency is characteristic of the vicissitudes of the age-old mind–body debate, and specifically the place of a theory of mind in the broader context of the relationship between body and mind. Such an eminent scientist as Sir Francis Crick, co-discoverer of the structure of DNA, has unabashedly stated the monist reductive position that: "'You,' your joys and your sorrows, your memories and your ambitions, your sense of identity and free will, are in fact no more than the behavior of a vast assembly of nerve cells and their associated molecules" (1993, p. 3). Writing in the 1920s Adolph Meyer (1958) proposed the concept of psychobiology, a coordinated biological, psychological and social approach to understanding a disturbed person. George Engel (1977, 1980) worked with persons with diagnosed medical illnesses that might have a psychological component (psychosomatic) and proposed what is known as the biopsychosocial model. His emphasis was on understanding the contributions of psychological and interpersonal/social factors to an organic illness. In other words, his model assumes that the phenomenon under study is essentially organic in origin, so that the role of psychosocial factors is to modify the expression of the basic biological process. His model is not one of a system or systems in a hierarchical relationship to the biological. While these models are more sophisticated than Crick's, each is basically organically reductive.

Mind and brain are qualitatively different systems in complex relationship to one another (Robbins, 1993, 1996). As different systems they have no linear causal relationship. It is more like the relationship of foundation to superstructure; the brain establishes parameters and a pattern but as they are not aspects of a single system of interconnected "parts" mind and brain do not have linear causal connections that can be understood by simple construction and reduction. The brain-mind problem is part of a larger problem having to do with the levels or systems that comprise human phenomena, and their interrelationships. This is the subject of Chapter 17. For now, while neuroscience cannot validate psychoanalytic hypotheses in the sense of proving their validity, the analogical correspondence or lack of correspondence of its findings can add or subtract significant support.

Neuroimaging

While Freud's (1895) attempt to create a neuro-psychological model of mind seems archaic and fanciful to contemporary ears, he was, as we all are, a product of context. It was fully a quarter century later, in 1924, that the first functional neuroscientific technological imaging device, the EEG, was invented. For those not familiar with neuroimaging in its contemporary guises the major technologies are radioactive isotope emission tomographies (PET and sPECT) and magnetic imaging (fMRI). sPECT measures cerebral metabolism, defined as blood oxygen transfer, using radioactive isotopes. It can also be used to measure binding sites for neurotransmitters such as dopamine and serotonin. fMRI records cerebral metabolism defined as oxygenation by measuring the differential magnetic field produced by deoxyhemoglobin and oxyhemoglobin. Along with the potential of these exciting new technologies is the question of how to understand their limitations and interpret their findings. For example, these technologies require the subject to be still within the confines of an apparatus many "normal" persons find claustrophobic and in the case of fMRI very noisy.

Infancy

There is some suggestive evidence that a qualitatively different form of mental activity predominates in infancy. As REM sleep has been documented in the fetus during the third trimester of pregnancy, it would appear that PMA occurs from the very beginning of life. Chiron, Jambaque, Nabbout, Lounes, Syrota, and Oulac (1997) have demonstrated that the infant brain differs from the adult brain insofar as the right hemisphere is dominant.

Dreaming

Dreaming, the phenomenological prototype of primordial mental activity, has been the focus of numerous neuroimaging studies. There is more or less general agreement among investigators of REM sleep using PET (Maquet et al., 1996; Nofzinger et al., 1997; Braun et al., 1998; Hobson et al., 2000; Solms and Turnbull, 2002) with regard to comparative patterns of cerebral activity during dreaming as contrasted to wakefulness, and the findings have been corroborated by studies of the effect of various neurological lesions on dreaming by Solms (1997) and Solms and Turnbull (2002).

Until recently dreaming was believed to occur exclusively during REM sleep, and the brain stem (Pons), which seems to be the essential instigator of REM sleep, was believed to trigger dreaming, a conclusion that is difficult to reconcile with Freud's ideas of unconscious instinctual motivation. Experiments on rats by Hobson (1999) led to his proposal of the activation-synthesis hypothesis, that dreaming is nothing more than a brain-stem-initiated reflex activity, and that the content of the dream is intrinsically meaningless. However, recent neuroimaging studies (Cavallero et al., 1992; Braun, 1999) show that dreaming is not exclusively associated with REM cycles, and sleep and dream laboratory studies have confirmed that, while it is less frequent, people do dream during other stages of sleep. Another finding that is inconsistent with Hobson's hypothesis is that most persons whose Pons has been removed (Feldman, 1971) continue to dream. Other neural mechanisms can also activate dreaming. Cavallero and Braun each describe a variety of trigger mechanisms, of which the REM state is the most frequent, that activate sensory-perceptual areas in the posterior forebrain and are anatomically distinctive from the frontal lobes, which play a central role in waking thought and associated motor activity.

Hypothesizing from neuroimaging findings, Panskepp (1998) has proposed that a dopamine-based "seeking system" in the ventral tegmental area of the limbic system, which projects to the hypothalamus, nucleus accumbens, anterior cingulate gyrus, other frontal areas and the amygdala, may generate dreaming. Solms and Turnbull (2002), Hobson (2009), Hobson et al. (2000), Maquet et al. (1996), Nofzinger et al. (1997) trace a dreaming pathway involving amygdala, hypothalamus, and upper brain stem that they call the rage and fear system, and another involving the anterior cingulate gyrus of the limbic frontal lobe and the upper brain stem that they call the panic system, to go along with Panskepp's seeking system. Such findings are consistent with psychoanalytic theories of motivation – both Freud's pleasure principle and Klein's emphasis on innate rage. They also broaden the palette of motivation to include such affects as fear. They support the hypothesis that raw, unrepresented somatic affect generates PMA.

Areas of the brain that are active during dreaming include posterior forebrain limbic-paralimbic structures, some of which (lateral hypothalamus, amygdala, orbitofrontal and cingulate cortices) are in the frontal and temporal lobes; ventral parts of the visual cortex at the occipital-temporal-parietal junction, which are involved with more abstract interpretive activity; and a particular part of the parietal lobe associated with spatial sense (the operculum). Areas that are less active during dreaming than during wakefulness include most of the parietal cortex and especially the supramarginal gyrus; the posterior cingulate cortex; primary environmentally connected perceptual elements of the visual cortex; the frontal parts of the limbic system, which are involved in reflective thought; the dorsolateral frontal cortex, which is the gateway from thought to action; and, possibly of greatest significance, the prefrontal areas, which are essential for complex cognitive processes and language.

Both Solms and Turnbull (2002) and Braun (1999) have stated that the findings from neuroimaging studies of dreaming are consistent with some but not all of Freud's model of the primary process. However, Braun's understanding of Freud's model of dreaming and the primary process is based on the passages in which Freud relates it to thought and to symbolism, not to a qualitatively different process. His interpretation of neuroimaging studies supports the hypothesis of a different process. He writes:

> Condensation and distortion represent the crux of the "dream work" – camouflaging threatening material by transferring the latent into the manifest content. This process should require considerable mobilization of the brain's symbol-making machinery. . . . And if there is any single region of the brain felt to be essential for self-monitoring, abstraction, and symbolic encoding, it would be the dorsolateral prefrontal cortex, a region in which activity plummets at sleep onset and in which functional inactivity is destined to persist throughout the entire sleep cycle. . . . Furthermore, other heteromodal areas that play an established role in semantic processing and might be expected to participate in Freud's secondary dream work – perisylvian regions including the posterior middle temporal gyrus and the inferior parietal lobule – are relatively inactive during REM sleep as well.
>
> (1999, pp. 199–200)

He notes that there is "no clear mechanism for some of the secondary processes proposed by Freud; that is, screening of impulses emerging from the unconscious, censoring these impulses or wishes, and encoding them in obscure but acceptable dream symbols" (ibid.). His conclusion is similar to mine in defining PMA: "That there is no latent content, that rather than metaphor or symbol, dreams consist entirely of what is manifest on the surface of the dream, not disguised and in need of decoding" (ibid.). It is noteworthy that Braun, like Jung, whose doubts about whether dreams are symbolic of repressed unconscious conflicts he quotes, believes nonetheless that dreams are psychologically meaningful.

It is also noteworthy that PMA, as extrapolated from dreaming, is dependent upon on a neural network that is present and fully functional even before birth, judging from in utero studies of REM activity, and that it continues throughout life. Hobson (2009) believes the activity that underlies dreaming is always running but ordinarily suppressed. Studies of myelination of white matter indicate that the other areas of brain that support higher order symbolic thinking are rudimentary at birth and develop slowly over the first years of life (Paus et al., 1999). Hence it is reasonable to assume that thought develops from separate neural circuitry. MRI findings by Fiebach et al. (2003) indicate that imagery is initially encoded in sensory-perceptual-emotional areas of the brain and subsequently elaborated in higher centers, and words learned early in life are encoded in auditory and visual centers whereas words learned later are encoded in the inferior frontal cortex. This may help to provide a neurological basis for the psychological finding that formal elements of learned language and imagery can be employed concretely in primordial mental expression whereas more abstract and symbolic meanings are incorporated into thought.

The phenomenon of lucid dreaming suggests an apparently congenital neurobiological linkage between thought and PMA. Those data are summarized in Chapter 11. The finding that some persons have an innate crossover sensitivity could be an important clue to understanding the particular balance between nature and the particular interpersonal and socio-cultural circumstances in which a person grows up in determining whether the outcome is exceptional ability or psychotic pathology.

Attachment, implicit knowledge, affect and emotion

Neuroscientific studies of the relationship between brain functioning, attachment behavior and implicit or procedural learning and knowledge are summarized in Chapter 4. I have noted how PMA is distinguished from thought insofar as it is based on somatic affect rather than mentally represented emotion. In 1911 Bleuler noted some of the peculiarities of affect and emotion in schizophrenia. The absence of emotional awareness was identified and named alexithymia by Sifneos (1975). It is described in detail a bit earlier by De M'Uzan (1974). It means there are no words for emotions. Panskepp's (1998, 2003) studies on affect in dreaming suggest that PMA is driven by the centers in the limbic system responsible for diffuse global psychosomatic affect rather than those in the prefrontal cortex which identify and process specific emotions. Fellous (1999), Lane (2000), Schore (2003, 2005) and Lane and Garfield (2005) have begun to outline the neuroanatomical basis of the important distinctions between affect and emotion that underlie the difference between thought and the implicit or unconscious processes that relate to PMA. A rudimentary neuro-anatomical model of emotional awareness that distinguishes between implicit (affective, unconscious) and explicit (conscious, thoughtful emotional awareness) processes can now be formulated (Lane, 2000). The lowest levels are called background feelings and focal attention to feelings. These levels subsume reflexive sensory-motor-enactive behaviors and enable crude distinctions between globally positive and globally negative states (Rolls, 1996). Background feelings seem to involve the ventral medial frontal lobe including structures involved in mapping of somatic states – ventral striatum, basal ganglia thalamus, hypothalamus and amygdala (Cahill and McGaugh, 1998; LeDoux, 1996). This concept seems to correlate with the affect-driven mind of PMA. The highest level, reflective awareness of feelings, is an aspect of thought, and requires the participation of the medial prefrontal cortex and paralimbic structures including the anterior cingulate cortex, insula, temporal pole and orbitofrontal cortex.

Schizophrenia

Freud (1900, 1940), Jung (1945) and Bleuler (1911) are among many who have suggested a relationship between dreaming and psychosis, so it is logical to wonder whether there is a relationship between the neural circuitry involved in dreaming and in schizophrenia, and to speculate about how images of the schizophrenic mind differ from those of "normal" subjects.

The problems in recording and making sense of the cerebral activity patterns of schizophrenic subjects are formidable. Is schizophrenia a unitary disorder to begin with? How have the subjects been diagnosed? What subtypes are being studied? Positive or negative symptoms? In what phase of illness are they? Are particular signs and symptoms being studied, such as hallucinations or delusions? How does one take into account the nature of the relationship with the experimenter and the effects of experimental expectations on the subject? Given the level of cooperation required for a neuroimaging study and the confining space in which it takes place, is it possible to study truly ill persons? Can such persons be relied upon to report accurately whether and when they are hallucinating? Most subjects nowadays are likely to be medicated, so how is one to take into account the effects of drugs? Some studies measure persons in a resting state or doing rote tasks, and some present tasks intended to be emotionally stimulating or challenging of cognitive skills. Finally, in making comparisons with findings during dreaming, it is important to keep in mind that wakefulness involves sensory-perceptual contact with the outside world and motor functioning, functions that are inhibited in dreaming. Much of the summary that follows is taken from the excellent volume edited by Lawrie *et al.* (2004). PET and sPET research is summarized in a chapter by Heinz, Romero and Weinberger (2004) and fMRI research is summarized in a chapter by Honey *et al.* (2004).

A number of studies focus on hallucinations; some simply measure metabolic activity during reported hallucinating while others assign various cognitive performance tasks to the person who is hallucinating. Neural activity accompanying schizophrenic hallucinations would seem especially fruitful data to compare with such activity during dreaming. It should be kept in mind that the hallucinations are usually auditory, whereas dreams are predominantly (but not exclusively) visual. We would not expect to find anything like a perfect correlation between findings in dreaming and in schizophrenia if for no other reason than schizophrenics are studied in the waking and potentially active state whereas dreamers are asleep in a phase where motor activity is inhibited; also, in schizophrenia the environment-sensing elements of sensory-perceptual systems are active whereas in sleep they are not.

Both dreaming and schizophrenic delusions and hallucinations involve activity of speech centers in the temporal and occipital cortices, which produce sensory-perceptual experiences. There is broad consensus in studies of auditory hallucinators that during periods of hallucination there is increased activation of such areas – inferior frontal and left and medial temporal cortices including the left auditory cortex. And there is increased activation of Broca's motor-speech area, suggesting that the speech that is "heard" is originating from the subject. This is consistent with studies of subvocal speech and subtle lip and mouth movements.

Along with sensory-perceptual actualization of internal states (hallucination) PMA creates holistic experiences that do not distinguish internal from external activity. In dreaming and schizophrenia there seems to be a pattern of relative activation and quiescence within the parietal lobes that could be related to functions of self–object differentiation and could lead to the inaccurate perception of the locus of action as external rather than internal. Specifically, there is increased activation of limbic and paralimbic areas including thalamus, hippocampus, cingulate gyrus, right middle temporal gyrus and orbitofrontal cortex. There is associated diminution of activity in the areas that ordinarily respond to, recognize, monitor and differentiate internal and external speech. For example, when persons who are hallucinating are assigned tasks involving reception of external speech, the areas that would normally respond – temporal, paralimbic, and cerebral cortex – are relatively inactive.

Frith *et al.* (2000) propose a way of understanding the neuroimaging findings in schizophrenia that is consistent with absence of self–object differentiation, a feature of primordial mental activity. During auditory hallucinating, there is inactivity of higher-order prefrontal cortical processing as well as inactivity of temporal-cortical areas that ordinarily process and distinguish internal from external speech. During delusions of reference there is increased activity in an area of the right parietal lobe associated with spatial processing that ordinarily responds to external stimulation, and diminution in prefrontal-cortical activity. In other words, that which is internally generated thought is misperceived as being external. Similar absence of integration (disconnection of normally active frontal-temporal circuits) has also been postulated as playing a part in auditory hallucinations (Lawrie *et al.*, 2002; Hubl and Dierks, 2004).

The relative activation of limbic, paralimbic and associated cortical structures during dreaming is consistent with findings among schizophrenics during uninterrupted periods of hallucinating of activation of structures including the cingulate gyrus, thalamus, hippocampus, amygdala, orbitofrontal cortex and left and lateral temporal cortices. Reciprocally, the limbic and paralimbic structures that should be activated when a person is expected to perform cognitive tasks are not active in schizophrenics or in dreamers. When persons with significant thought disorder are assigned cognitive meaning tasks they show a pattern of diminished activation in inferior frontal and superior temporal cortices (Kircher *et al.*, 2001).

The finding, replicated in study after study, that is common to schizophrenia and to dreaming is "hypo-frontality" (Andreasen, 1992; Andreasen *et al.*, 1997), diminished metabolic activity in the prefrontal cortical areas ordinarily associated with thought (higher cognitive processes, reflection, language and symbolization). The disconnection of limbic-paralimbic functioning from the prefrontal cortex and the general absence of activity in the prefrontal cortex would seem to underlie the absent capacity in schizophrenia to integrate affective experiences with a conscious reflective sense of self, and the inability to represent and be aware of feelings that are characteristics of PMA.

However preliminary and tentative these findings in schizophrenia may be, they suggest a process similar to that underlying dreaming. Solms and Turnbull, who have studied dreaming and schizophrenia from the dual perspectives of psychoanalysis and neurology, assert that: "The functional anatomy of dreaming is therefore almost identical to that of schizophrenic psychosis, as revealed by functional imaging studies" (2002, p. 213). These same authors cite other convincing evidence, from the era of psychosurgical treatment of schizophrenia, half a century prior to the advent of neuroimaging technology, that the processes might be related. It was observed that prefrontal lobotomy or leucotomy (a technique that was eventually refined over years of human experimentation), involving ablation of the ventromesial part of the limbic structures of the frontal lobe, which yielded maximal relief of symptoms with minimal brain damage, caused cessation of dreaming as well. One of the post-operative indices surgeons came to depend on in their effort to predict the "success" of a lobotomy was whether or not dreaming had ceased.

What conclusions can be drawn from these studies? Evidence is insufficient to make convincing claims about the neural circuitry underlying any of these phenomena, much less to speculate about a circuitry common to all of them. I have omitted some opinions that lateralization of function is responsible for many of the phenomena of PMA – the old "right brain–left brain" idea – because they are quite controversial. However, integrating the findings about dreaming and schizophrenia there seems to be some consensus.

- The phenomenology of PMA is driven by the centers responsible for diffuse global psychosomatic affect rather than those responsible for particular identifiable emotions.
- PMA makes use of parts of brain responsible for holistic processes that do not differentiate the person from the world and the other.
- PMA it is dominated by sensory-perceptual elements of brain.
- PMA does not make much use of the areas of prefrontal cortex necessary for symbolic reflective thought.
- PMA involves a disconnect between emotional and higher cognitive centers that is suggestive of lack of integration.

While these findings do not prove or disprove the existence of PMA they are highly suggestive. It seems likely that there is no single neural circuit that is responsible for all these disparate phenomena but there may be broad similarities. Studies of shamans, persons in trance and on mind-altering drugs would be useful, along with further studies of infants, bonding between parents and infants, and psychosis.

Chapter 17

Analogy and transformation in human systems

General Systems Theory was proposed in the 1920s and 1930s by a diverse collection of individuals accomplished in such seemingly unrelated fields as biology, physics, psychology, philosophy, and even literature (Drack *et al.*, 2007). Some of these illustrious names include Ludwig von Bertalanffy (1952), Arthur Koestler, Neils Bohr, Werner Heisenberg, Heinz Werner and Fritz Perls. The German biologist Paul Weiss, whose 1922 doctoral thesis on butterflies was translated into English in 1959, may have been the first to publish in the field. He articulated some of its axioms with a clarity that has not been surpassed. In what might be taken as a commentary on Crick's (1993) position that humans are nothing more than a collection of biological parts, were it not written much earlier, Weiss writes that:

> The study of parts – analytical information about parts – paid off magnificently as long as we indulged primarily in learning more and more about less and less, relying on the ingrained conviction that from the parts of that diminutival knowledge we would be able to reconstruct, "synthesize" (at least in our mind) the typical patterned order of the phenomenon that we had deliberately disordered in our analytical procedure as if we could resurrect the phoenix from its ashes.
>
> (1977, p. 254)

Neils Bohr (1937) states succinctly that the linear reductive study of life, taken to its extreme, literally destroys its subject. Weiss writes that "all living phenomena consist of group behavior" (1969, p. 8) and he adds that "the ordered state (organization) of a living entity can, therefore, not be conceived of as the blind outcome of microprecisely defined serial cause-effect chain reactions, as in an assembly line" (1977, p. 29), and that "hierarchical concepts of organization. . . imply some sort of discontinuity encountered as one crosses interfaces between lower and higher orders of magnitude" (1969, p. 8). In recent decades Systems Theory has evolved into what was initially called Chaos Theory and is now sometimes referred to as Complexity Theory. In his classic 1967 paper *How Long is the Coast of*

Britain? Mandelbrot demonstrated the difference between different systems and their scales. For example, measurements taken at a macroscopic systems level from a photo taken from space are very different from measurements taken at a sub-microscopic level and the two cannot be related by linear processes. He concluded that the different systems and their scales are in an analogical relationship with one another.

The knowledge gained from these theories has not been extensively applied to human psychosocial affairs. Within psychiatry and psychoanalysis the work of Meyer, Freud and Engel on understanding human systems and their relationships (reviewed in Chapter 17) focused particularly on the relationship between the body and the mind, and they struggled with whether or not to accept linear reductionist assumptions.

Embedded in the effort I have made to model primordial mind and its relationships to thought and to examine the variety of phenomenology that it leads to is the assumption that human phenomena "exist" at a number of systems levels that are related to one another. Genetic endowment is related to the workings of the brain is related to the workings of the mind is related to the patterning of individual and social human relationships is related to patterns of culture. I believe it is equally valid to reverse this bottom-up statement and make a top-down statement, starting with culture and working down to individual mind and possibly through the experimentally verified concept of neural plasticity, to the functioning of brain as well. These are the separate but related systems that comprise human phenomena. Linear causal reasoning may be useful within a single system; however, it does not apply across systems. I have described the theoretical confusion that results when this distinction is not made clear. One example is models of dreaming and psychosis that assume these phenomena can be understood by the symbolic semantics of thought.

In 1993 and 1996 I proposed a model called systems in transformation theory, predicated on the assumption that human phenomena do not "exist" at any single level but manifest themselves simultaneously at multiple levels: constitutional, neurobiological, intrapsychic, interpersonal, social and cultural. These phenomenal levels have an analogical rather than a linear causal relationship with one another. Each level requires a separate conceptual system. In modeling the relationship between primordial mind and thought I proposed that these qualitatively different systems can be related to one another by analogy and transformation. That is, each expresses meaning, but in a different way. The meaning is transformed when one goes from one system to the next, but it is analogous. It is possible to use analogical reasoning to express the meaning of PMA-based phenomena in thought. I would like to use the principles of analogy and transformation that help us to understand the relationship between primordial mind and thought in a larger context consisting of all the systems levels that describe human phenomena.

Chapter 18

Conclusion

I have presented a model of primordial mind and demonstrated the multiplicity of phenomena that result from its expression in a variety of relationships to thought. As qualitatively different systems of mind the two are related by analogy and not by the linear causality that applies when one is working within a single system, based on the assumption that all mental activity is a subset of symbolic representational thought. This two-system model of mind based on analogical principles and transformations of meaning is nested within a larger multi-system model consisting of genetic endowment, brain, mind, interpersonal relationships, social structure and culture.

In constructing this model I have drawn on important contributions to the study of mind from the fields of psychology, cultural anthropology, linguistics, neuroscience, and of course my primary field of psychoanalysis. Without the wisdom and groundbreaking work of my predecessors the book could not have been written. From psychoanalysis I began with Freud's description of the primary process and dreaming, which I consider the bedrock or foundation for all subsequent efforts to comprehend primordial mind. He is not given sufficient credit for this revolutionary discovery, which he made very early in his own career, perhaps in part because he turned away from it to what he seemed to consider more important ideas. Klein proposed a model of primordial mind in psychosis, although she couched it in an unrelated conceptual language and seemed unaware of the similarities between her work and Freud's model of the primary process. Although her concept of projective identification is based on a model of primordial mind as defensive rather than different, it eloquently portrays the concrete, affectively pressuring quality of PMA. Jung introduced a less pathological way of looking at primordial mind along with the idea of an unbiased dialectic between two equally important mental activities. He also related primordial mind to spiritual culture. Matte-Blanco developed further the idea of two mental processes that operate in tandem, one of which is difficult to comprehend directly and therefore to respect insofar as it differs from the "logic" with which we view the world. He and Bion used abstract concepts in an effort to avoid the problem of surplus or confusing meaning that plagues the models of Freud and Klein. The developmental psychologists Werner and Piaget demonstrated that it is possible to formulate primordial mind in a conceptual language that is more universal than idiosyncratic and does not imply that such a process is pathological. From linguistics and cultural anthropology I have learned about the lively debate between universalism and contextualism. Cultural anthropology has taught me to respect the difference and wisdom of indigenous non-western cultures and to be aware of how contextually embedded the western view of human beings and the cosmos is. Linguistics is another field immersed in debate between universalists and contextualists and from it I have also learned about the controversies about the relationship between language, thought and communication. Neuroscience has informed me about the importance of correlating theories about mind with findings about the brain. Out of these ideas, my clinical experience with psychotic persons, and acquaintance with Maori New Zealand healers I have proposed a model of primordial mind that is qualitatively distinctive from thought.

Primordial mental activity (PMA) is a normal way that mind works that is qualitatively different from thought. This mental function has a wider impact on human beings and human affairs than has generally been appreciated. It is both an expressive modality and a receptive or deep learning process. Meaning is generated and assimilated as a forceful sense of actual sensory-perceptual happening or belief. In the primordial cosmos, mind and the interpersonal and natural worlds are a holistic unity. PMA is existential rather than intrapsychic. It is enacted in the world rather than contemplated in the mind. It is driven by somatic sensation and affect creating sensations that are ominous, prescient and intuitive. PMA expresses meaning in a different way than thought. The meanings in the two systems can be related by analogy rather than by linear symbol decoding.

PMA is to be distinguished from another relatively recent formulation about unconscious mind known as implicit learning and knowledge. Implicit knowledge is the basic affective-somatic-motor reflex pattern that is learned through the initial interaction between infant and caregiver. PMA is the process through which implicit learning occurs and subsequently through which that knowledge is expressed in other relationships.

Because PMA draws on the same reservoir of language and learning as thought, its presence is easily camouflaged. It uses language differently from thought and communicates in a different way as well. Grammar and syntax are the same as in ordinary language, and morphology is similar for the most part, but meaning is conveyed impressionistically and concretely rather than symbolically and conceptually. Its presence is easily camouflaged from western thoughtful eyes by the fact that it can utilize the same reservoir of learning as thought. The mental activity that underlies language usage in PMA is holistic or unitary. The process is sensory-perceptual. Shapes, forms and word meanings are interchangeable rather than differentiated, comparative and contrasting. The center of experience and action is not a separate self but a collective. Time-related words are used, but the sense that underlies them is timeless, of the moment which is all moments. Narrative and integration originate collectively rather than personally and are driven by subjective affect rather than represented emotion and causal logic.

Although PMA is not recursive it is nonetheless the basis of a deep and powerful language of expression and learning. The debate within linguistics between universalism – the belief that there is but a single language prototype of which recursion is an invariant feature – and relativism – the belief that languages are a product of cultural context and need not have universal features – seems too narrowly conceived. Language does not appear to be a unitary entity. Moreover, language arises from mental activity, and if there is more than one kind of mental activity then the rules that apply to thought are valid within that context. Language may be different in form and substance as it is called upon to serve qualitatively different masters – thought or primordial mental activity.

Neuroscientific studies of dreaming, attachment behavior, implicit learning and schizophrenia suggest possible circuits that underlie PMA and distinguish it from thought. PMA seems to arise from affect-generating somatic sensing areas of brain as well as areas that are predominantly sensory-perceptual and that do not differentiate inner from outer. Areas of the prefrontal cortex involved in symbolic reflective thought are relatively inactive. The technology necessary to do these studies is relatively new, and the studies themselves are still in a preliminary stage, so much is yet to be learned.

From a developmental perspective, based on what we know of dreaming and of infancy, PMA is fully functional at birth and is the "normal" form of expression and learning in infancy, whereas thought is rudimentary and matures over the first decade of life. PMA does not transform into thought. Rather, under ordinary circumstances thought comes to have regulatory control over PMA and to play a significant integrating role that tends to be more suppressive in western culture and more utilitarian in spiritual cultures. In all cultures both mental processes, in a variety of relationships to one another, contribute to human behavior and interaction throughout life, leading to phenomena that are adaptive and socially constructive and to others that are not depending upon the socio-cultural context.

PMA-related phenomena are first evident in infant–parent bonding and in dreaming. In western culture PMA plays a large part in creativity, spirituality, and the spectrum of psychotic phenomenology, both individual and social, as well as in other everyday behaviors that are not so obvious. In spiritual cultures PMA, guided and interpreted by thought, is the fundamental mode of knowledge acquisition and plays a predominant role in social interaction.

The distinction between manifestations of PMA that society judges healthy and those labeled illness or pathology depends on several variables: the ratio of PMA to thought, the nature of the relationship between thought and PMA (whether integrated or dissociated), and the adaptive or maladaptive nature of the result as defined within the social-cultural context in which the behavior is manifest. An integrated relationship between rational thought and PMA is designed to benefit not only the individual in adapting to the community or social structure, but also the community structure itself. When this integration does not occur and the two forms of mental activity are more or less dissociated, or when thought capacity is relatively undeveloped, the result is disruptive to the social structure and the individual's adjustment to it, and hence is labeled psychosis.

Psychosis develops within a particular pathological family constellation that has distorted the infant's initial implicit learning by failure to meet basic psychological needs and by malignant admixtures of hostility, rejection, and distortion of meaning. Such caregiving also discourages development of thought and identification of emotions in their appropriate context. As a consequence thought, with its adaptive power, is relatively unavailable and is dissociated from the predominant disturbed manifestations of PMA. Psychosis most commonly manifests itself in late adolescence and early adulthood when social-cultural expectations are that the person establish a separate identity including work and a family of his or her own. At that time the maladaptive nature of the mental activity learned and fostered within the family becomes apparent.

In spiritual cultures the afflicted person is not labeled as "sick," merely different, not in synchrony with the community. Typically society provides help for the sufferer to heal and regain harmony with self and community by mastering the experiences of dissolution, voices and visions and learning to use them as sources of information about his or her place in the cosmos and the social order.

The relationships between creativity, extreme spiritual expressions such as trance, ecstasy and shamanism, and psychosis are complex, and depend on several variables including the relationship of PMA to thought, learned adaptive development within the nuclear family, subsequent cultural expectations and the capacity or incapacity of the person to adapt to them. A predominance of PMA in mental life is not of itself synonymous with any particular outcome – normality, psychosis or creativity. Creativity may result from dissociation of PMA from thought in a social setting in which the product is deemed remarkable by the community and the bizarre behavior of the creator is overlooked. Alternately, creativity can result from thoughtful controlled entry into PMA states for inspiration, then emergence and use of the result in a disciplined way so that the result is deemed creative by the community. In spiritual cultures some individuals are perceived as having special powers related to PMA. Through a combination of personal struggle and rigorous training they learn to negotiate controlled entry into and exit from states of trance and ecstasy and are designated shamans. They utilize the special information to which they are privy in the service of the community.

Two constitutionally determined special sensitivities – lucid dreaming and synesthesia (alone or in concert) – predispose some people toward PMA and to ease of crossover between PMA and thought. Depending on the childhood interpersonal and cultural background the presence of these sensitivities can become a vulnerability to psychosis or a special ability to integrate the two forms of mental activity in mature and creative ways.

There are important implications of what I have written. Most of us are insufficiently aware of how western contextual cultural bias limits and distorts theories of mind. We need to question the assumption that western epistemology is universally applicable, and to reconsider the nature of mind from a cross-cultural perspective. Such a task is not entirely possible for those of us who are limited to the perspective of logical thought. It is difficult to contemplate and formulate mind from within a western cultural context. Westerners are biased by the requirement of reducing phenomena to thought or judging them in relation to thought. The very concept of objectivity, which is a bastion of western perspective, is inherently biased when it comes to contemplating a way that mind works that is different. Western culture analyzes the world through the lens of science – logical, rational objectification. We cannot actually experience the world through "eyes" that are qualitatively different from our own. Phenomena of the other kind tend to pass unnoticed or be misinterpreted because they are not grounded in the idea of progress and it is easy to conclude that they are unsophisticated, primitive or otherwise inferior to western ways of thinking.

Another implication of this work is that theories of mind and its development that are based on analytic work with disturbed persons are likely to have inherent bias and limited validity when it comes to formulating general propositions about the nature of mind. There has been a tendency among psychoanalysts to view primordial mental activity in infancy and childhood, and in whatever form it lingers into adult life, as an abnormal or psychotic process and to see mind as inherently defensive against intense affective experiences and against the expectations of consensual social reality. Along with western cultural bias the result is an implicit assumption that primordial mind is a dark continent, inferior to rational logical thought; that it is primitive, immature and unrealistic, driven by untamed and dangerous passions, possessing the potential for loss of social control and reason itself – in short, fundamentally abnormal.

It is important to make a clear distinction between primordial mental activity and thought. This is difficult to do for reasons I have mentioned, namely that we are constrained to view PMA through the lens of thought. Much of this confusion has been about whether primordial mental activity is symbolic and communicative, or to say it differently, whether there is a way to receive and impart meaning that is different from thought but plays an equally prominent role in human affairs. Since most of the theories of primordial mind are psychoanalytic and are intended for use in the consulting room, some of the most obvious consequences of the confusion between primordial mental activity and thought are to be found in that setting. For example, Freud implied that dreams are a unique source of meaning when he wrote that they are the royal road to the unconscious. However, his inability to clarify the uniqueness of the primary process and a similar lack of clarity that has characterized subsequent contributions has led to a general perception of dreaming as just another of many roads involving repressed and symbolically distorted thoughts that can be decoded by a linear process of association. Klein's ideas about treatment of psychotic conditions are limited by the belief that primordial mental activity is reactionary – defensive against thought rather than being another way of learning and experiencing – and by a lack of clarity about whether or not the patient functioning in primordial mode can learn from inter-pretations couched in the language of symbolic thought.

The implicit cultural and pathological biases I note raise larger questions about the scope of psychoanalytic theory. Is it truly a universal theory of mind, and is it reasonable to expect it to be? Perhaps the debate between universalists and contextualists has come to psychoanalysis later than to other disciplines? Which propositions are fundamental and universal and which are only applicable to western culture at a given time and place in the history of civilization in general, and to persons in that culture with significant mental ills in particular? Awareness of some of these biases has already brought about fundamental changes. For example, all societies are not paternalistic and authoritarian. Phallocentrism and gender prejudice are not innate attributes of human beings. The tendency to see the person as a separate individual and the locus of action as intrapsychic does not adequately take into account the relational matrix and the collective cultural matrix. Perhaps the concept of psychic unconsciousness, long considered one of the bedrocks of psychoanalytic theory, also needs to be reconsidered and re-configured. What psychoanalysis looks upon as unconscious, a term synonymous with not thought, is actually quite visible if one looks for another form of expression that is different. Mind works in two different ways.

The idea that language is not restricted to thought, that it may reflect two different kinds of mental activity, and that there may be two different forms of communication as a result, might help to resolve the debate within linguistics as to whether there is a universal grammar common to all language. Piraha seems to be an example of a language that functions in a qualitatively different way.

In closing, some recommendations: More sophisticated, less prejudicial studies of the workings of mind in spiritual cultures and spiritually altered states are needed before such cultures vanish under the weight of western colonization. Studies using neuroimaging technologies will provide new insights and help refine psychological theories. Studies of constitutional sensitivity to PMA and to crossover between PMA and thought may help to clarify the nature of some of the pathways that lead to special abilities and to disabilities such as schizophrenia. Studies of shamans and persons in trance, and on mind-altering drugs will reveal new information about mind, as will further studies of infants and bonding between parents and infants. Before the humanistic psychosocial understanding of psychotic mind gets lost in the rush toward organic reductionism and pharmacological treatment, psychoanalysis needs to get back into this area, which it never wholeheartedly embraced and now has mostly abandoned.

I have attempted to demonstrate the ubiquity, power and importance in human affairs of a form of mental activity that is qualitatively different from thought. Primordial mental activity and thought, each with a particular neurological substrate and operating in a variety of relationships with one another in a context of interpersonal relationships and cultural expectations, combine to produce the richness of our human experience, meaning and social interaction.

References

Achterberg, J. (1987). The shaman: Master healer in the imaginary realm. In S. Nicholson (Ed.), *Shamanism*. Wheaton, IL: The Theosophical Publishing House (pp. 101–123).

Ainsworth, M. (1982). Attachment: Retrospect and prospect. In C. Parkes & J. Stevenson-Hinde (Eds), *The Place of Attachment in Human Behavior*. New York: Basic Books (pp. 3–30).

Ainsworth, M. D. S., Blehar, M. C., Waters, E., & Wall, S. (1978). *Patterns of Attachment: A Psychological Study of the Strange Situation*. Hillsdale, NJ: Lawrence Erlbaum Associates Inc.

Alkjamian, A., Demers, R., & Harnish, R. (1984). *Linguistics: An Introduction to Language and Communication*. Cambridge, MA: MIT Press.

Andreasen, N., Hoffman, R., & Grove, W. (1985). Language abnormalities in schizophrenia. In M. Mednick & M. Seeman (Eds), *New Perspectives in Schizophrenia*. New York: MacMillan (pp. 97–120).

Andreasen, N., Rezai, K., Alliger, R., Swayze, V., Flaum, M., & Kirchner, P. (1992). Hypofrontality in neuroleptic-naive patients and patients with chronic schizophrenia: Assessment with xenon 135 single photon-emission computed tomography and the Tower of London. *Archives of General Psychiatry*, 49, 943–958.

Andreasen, N., O'Leary, D., Flaum, M., Nopoulos, P., Watkins, G., Boles-Ponto, L., & Hichwa, R. (1997). Hypofrontality in schizophrenia: Distributed dysfunctional circuits in neuroleptic-naive patients. *Lancet*, 349, 1730–1734.

Arieti, S. (1966). Creativity and its cultivation: Relation to psychopathology and mental health. In S. Arieti (Ed.), *American Handbook of Psychiatry, Vol. 3*. New York: Basic Books.

Arieti, S. (1964). The rise of creativity: From primary to tertiary process. *Contemporary Psychoanalysis*, 1, 51–68.

Arieti, S. (1967). *The Intrapsychic Self*. New York: Basic Books.

Arieti, S. (1974). *Interpretation of Schizophrenia*. New York: Basic Books.

Arieti, S. (1976). *Creativity: The Magic Synthesis*. New York: Basic Books.

Beebe, B. & Lachmann, F. (2003). The relational turn in psychoanalysis: A dyadic systems view from infant research. *Contemporary Psychoanalysis*, 39, 379–409.

Berlin, B. & Kay, P. (1969). *Basic Color Terms: Their Universality and Evolution*. Berkeley, CA: University of California Press.

Bidois, E. (2009). Nga Tapuwae o Nga Tupuna. *Mauri Ora Korero Series, Part I*. DVD.

Bion, W. (1955). Language and the schizophrenic patient. In M. Klein, P. Heimann, & R. Money-Kyrle (Eds), *New Directions in Psycho-Analysis*. London: Tavistock Publications (pp. 220–239).

Bion, W. (1957). Differentiation of the psychotic from the non-psychotic personalities. *International Journal of Psycho-Analysis, 38*, 266–275.

Bion, W. (1959). Attacks on linking. *International Journal of Psycho-Analysis, 40*, 308–315.

Bion, W. (1962). *Learning from Experience*. London: Tavistock.

Bion, W. (1967). *Second Thoughts*. London: William Heinemann Medical Books.

Bion, W. (1970). *Attention and Interpretation: A Scientific Approach to Insight in Psycho-Analysis and Groups*. London: Tavistock.

Bion, W. (1992). *Cogitations*. London: Karnac.

Bleuler, E. (1911). *Dementia Praecox or the Group of Schizophrenias* (J. Zinkin, Trans.). New York: International Universities Press, 1950.

Blum, H. P. (2004). Separation-individuation theory and attachment theory. *Journal of the American Psychoanalytic Association, 52*, 535–553.

Bobon, J. (1962). *Psychopathologie de l'expression*. Paris: Masson.

Bohr, N. (1937). Causality and complementarity. *Philosophy of Science, 4*, 289–298.

Bollas, C. (1987). *The Shadow of the Object: Psychoanalysis of the Unthought Known*. London: Free Association Books.

Bosher, A. (1974). African apprenticeship. *Parapsychology Review, 5*, 1–27.

Boston Change Process Study Group (BCPSG) (2007). The foundational level of psychodynamic meaning: Implicit process in relation to conflict, defense and the dynamic unconscious. *International Journal of Psycho-Analysis, 88*, 843–860.

Bourguignon, E. (1973). Introduction: A framework for the comparative study of altered states of consciousness. In E. Bourguignon (Ed.), *Religion, Altered States of Consciousness, and Social Change*. Columbus, OH: Ohio State University Press (pp. 3–38).

Bourne, V. J. & Todd, B. K. (2004). When left means right: An explanation of the left cradling bias in terms of right hemisphere specializations. *Developmental Science, 7*, 19–24.

Bowlby, J. (1969). *Attachment and Loss, Volume I: Attachment*. London: Hogarth Press and the Institute of Psycho-Analysis.

Boyer, L. B., Klopfer, F., & Kauai, H. (1964). Comparisons of the shamans and pseudoshamans of the Apaches of the Mescalero Indian reservation: A Rorschach study. *Journal of Projective Techniques, 28*, 173–180.

Brakel, L. (2004). The psychoanalytic assumption of the primary process: Extra-psychoanalytic evidence and findings. *Journal of the American Psychoanalytic Association 52*, 1131–1161.

Brakel, L., Shevrin, H., & Villa, K. (2002). The priority of primary process categorizing: Experimental evidence supporting a psychoanalytic developmental hypothesis. *Journal of the American Psychoanalytic Association, 50(2)*, 483–505.

Braun, A. (1999). The new neuropsychology of sleep: Commentary. *Neuropsycho-analysis 1*, 196–201.

Braun, A., Balkin, T., Wesensten, N., Gwadry, F., Carson, R., Varga, M., Baldwin, P., Belenky, G., & Herscovitch, P. (1998). Dissociated patterns of activity in visual cortices and their projections during rapid eye movement sleep. *Science*, *279*, 91–95.

Bretherton, I. (1987). New perspectives on attachment relationships: Security, communication and internal working models. In J. Osofsky (Ed.), *Handbook of Infant Development*. New York: Wiley (pp. 1061–1100).

Bretherton, I. (1995). Internal working models: Cognitive and affective aspects of attachment representations. In D. Cicchetti & S. Toth (Eds), *4th Rochester Symposium on Developmental Psychopathology on "Emotion, Cognition, and Representation"*. Hillsdale, NJ: Lawrence Erlbaum.

Bretherton, I., Bates, E., Benigni, L., Camaioni, L., & Volterra, V. (1979). Relationships between cognition, communication, and quality of attachment. In E. Bates, L. Benigni, I. Bretherton, L. Camaioni, & V. Volterra (Eds), *The Emergence of Symbols*. New York: Academic Press.

Breuer, J. & Freud, S. (1893). On The Psychical Mechanism of Hysterical Phenomena: Preliminary Communication from Studies on Hysteria. *SE2* (pp. 1–17).

Britton, R. (1989). The missing link: Parental sexuality in the Oedipus complex. In R. Britton, M. Feldman, & E. O'Shaugnessy (Eds), *The Oedipus Complex Today: Clinical Implications*. London: Karnac Books (pp. 83–101).

Brook, A. (1997). *Kant and the Mind*. London: Cambridge University Press.

Bucci, W. (2000). Pathways of emotional communication. *Psychoanalytic Inquiry*, *21*, 40–70.

Burnham, D. (1955). Some problems in communication with schizophrenic patients. *Journal of the American Psychoanalytic Association*, *3*, 67–81.

Cahill, L. & McGaugh, J. L. (1998). Mechanisms of emotional arousal and lasting declarative memory. *Trends in Neurosciences*, *21*, 294–299.

Cameron, N. (1944). Experimental analysis of schizophrenic thinking. In J. S. Kasanin (Ed.), *Language and Thought in Schizophrenia*. New York: W. W. Norton (pp. 50–64).

Cameron, N. (1963). *Personality Development and Psychopathology*. Boston: Houghton Mifflin.

Cavallero, C., Cicogna, P., Natale, V., Occhioneero, M., & Zito, A. (1992). Slow wave sleep dreaming. *Sleep*, *15*, 562–566.

Chaika, E. (1990). *Understanding Psychotic Speech*. Springfield, IL: Charles C. Thomas.

Chaika, E. & Lambe, R. (1985). The locus of dysfunction in schizophrenic speech. *Schizophrenia Bulletin*, *11*, 8–15.

Chomsky, N. (1957). *Syntactic Structures*. The Hague: Mouton.

Chomsky, N. (1965). *Aspects of the Theory of Syntax*. Cambridge, MA: MIT Press.

Chomsky, N. (1975). *Reflections on Language*. New York: Pantheon Books.

Chomsky, N. (1986). *Knowledge of Language: Its Nature, Origin and Use*. New York: Praeger.

Clyman, R. (1991). The procedural organization of emotions: A contribution from cognitive science to the psychoanalytic theory of therapeutic action. *Journal of the American Psychoanalytic Association*, *39*(Suppl.), 349–383.

Colapinto, J. (2007, April 16). The interpreter. *New Yorker*, 118–137.

Coleman, R. & Smith, M. (2006). *Working with Voices II: Victim to Victor*. London: P&P Press.

Crick, F. (1993). *The Astonishing Hypothesis: The Scientific Search for the Soul*. New York: Charles Scribner's Sons.

Cytowic, R. (2002). *Synesthesia: A Union of the Senses*. Cambridge, MA: MIT Press.

De M'Uzan, M. (1974). Psychodynamic mechanisms in psychosomatic symptom formation. *Psychotherapy and Psychosomatics*, *23*, 103–110.

Devereaux, G. (1953). *Psychoanalysis and the Occult*. New York: International Universities Press.

Devereux, G. (1958). Cultural thought models in primitive and modern psychiatric theories. *Psychiatry*, *21*, 359–374.

Dimberg, U. & Petterson, M. (2000). Facial reactions to happy and angry facial expressions: Evidence for right hemsphere dominance. *Psychophysiology*, *37*, 693–696.

Dor, J. (1998). *Introduction to the Reading of Lacan: The Unconscious Structured Like a Language*. New York: Other Press.

Drack, M., Apfalter, W., & Pouvreau, D. (2007). On the making of a system theory of life: Paul A. Weiss and Ludwig von Bertalanffy's conceptual connection. *Quarterly Review of Biology*, *82*, 349–373.

Dylan, B. (2003/1964). *Eleven Outlined Epitaphs*. Cologne: Kiepenheuer & Witch GmbH.

Ehrenzweig, A. (1953). *The Psycho-Analysis of Artistic Vision and Hearing*. London: Routledge & Kegan Paul.

Ehrenzweig, A. (1967). *The Hidden Order of Art*. Berkeley and Los Angeles, CA: University of California Press.

Eliade, M. (1964). *Shamanism: Archaic Techniques of Ecstasy*. New York: Pantheon.

Emde, R. (1983). The prerepresentational self and its affective core. *Psychoanalytic Study of the Child*, *38*, 165–192.

Emde, R. (1990). Mobilizing fundamental modes of development: Empathic availability and therapeutic action. *Journal of the American Psychoanalytic Association*, *38*, 881–913.

Emde, R., Biringen, Z., Clyman, R., & Oppenheim, D. (1991). The moral self of infancy: Affective core and procedural knowledge. *Developmental Review*, *11*, 251–270.

Engel, G. (1977). The need for a new medical model: A challenge for biomedicine. *Science*, *165*, 129–136.

Engel, G. (1980). The clinical application of the biopsychosocial model. *American Journal of Psychiatry*, *137*, 535–544.

Engels, H., Heynick, F., & van der Staak, C. (2003). Emil Kraepelin's dream speech: A psychoanalytic interpretation. *International Journal of Psycho-Analysis*, *84*, 1281–1294.

Everett, D. (2005). Cultural constraints on grammar and cognition in Piraha: Another look at the design features of human language. *Current Anthropology*, *46*, 621–646.

Everett, D. (2008). *Don't Sleep, there are Snakes: Life and Language in the Amazon Jungle*. New York: Pantheon Books.

Fabrega, H. & Silver, S. (1970). Some social and psychological properties of Zinacanteco Shamans. *Behavioral Science*, *15*, 471–486.

Fechner, T. (1871). *Vorschule der Aesthetik*. Leipzig: Breitkopf und Hartel.

Feldman, M. (1971). Physiological observations in a chronic case of "locked in" syndrome. *Neurology*, *21*, 459–478.

Fellous, J. M. (1999). The neuromodulatory basis of emotion. *Neuroscientist* (Summer), 1–15.

Ferro, A. (1995). Bion: Theoretical and clinical observations. *International Journal of Psycho-Analysis*, *86*, 1535–1542.

Fiebach, C., Friederici, A., Muller, K., Von Cramm, D. Y., & Hernandez, A. (2003). Distinct brain representations for early and late learned words. *NeuroImage*, *19*, 1627–1637.

Fisher, C. (1956). Dreams, images, and perceptions: A study of unconscious-preconscious relationships. *Journal of the American Psychoanalytic Association*, *4*, 5–48.

Fisher, C. & Paul, I. (1959). The effect of subliminal visual stimulation on images and dreams: A validation study. *Journal of the American Psychoanalytic Association*, *7*, 35–83.

Fitzgerald, F. S. (1936). The Crack-Up. *Esquire Magazine*.

Fonagy, P. (1999a). Points of contact and divergence between psychoanalytic and attachment theories: Is psychoanalytic theory truly different? *Psychoanalytic Inquiry*, *19*, 448–480.

Fonagy, P. (1999b). Memory and therapeutic action. *International Journal of Psycho-Analysis*, *80*, 215–223.

Fonagy, P. & Target, M. (1996). Playing with reality: I. Theory of mind and the normal development of psychic reality. *International Journal of Psycho-Analysis*, *77*, 217–233.

Fonagy, P. & Luyten, P. (2009). A developmental, mentalization-based approach to the understanding and treatment of borderline personality disorder. *Development and Psychopathology*, *21*, 1355–1381.

French, T. & Fromm, E. (1964). *Dream Interpretation: A New Approach*. New York: Basic Books.

Freud, S. (1891). *On Aphasia: A Critical Study*. (E. Stengel, Trans.). New York: International Universities Press, 1978.

Freud, S. (1895). Project for a scientific psychology. *SE1* (pp. 283–398).

Freud, S. (1900). The Interpretation of Dreams. *SE4/5*.

Freud, S. (1911a). Formulations on the two principles of mental functioning. *SE12* (pp. 213–226).

Freud, S. (1911b). Psychoanalytic notes on an autobiographical account of a case of paranoia (dementia paranoides). *SE12* (pp. 12–85).

Freud, S. (1915a). Repression. *SE14* (pp. 141–158).

Freud, S. (1915b). The unconscious. *SE14* (pp. 166–215).

Freud, S. (1917). A metapsychological supplement to the theory of dreams. *SE14* (pp. 222–235).

Freud, S. (1920). Beyond the pleasure principle. *SE18* (pp. 7–64).

Freud, S. (1923). The ego and the id. *SE19* (pp. 3–68).

Freud, S. (1933). *New Introductory Lectures on Psychoanalysis*. *SE22* (pp. 3–248).

Freud, S. (1940). An Outline of Psychoanalysis. *SE23*.

Frith, C., Blakemore, S.-J., & Wolpert, D. (2000). Explaining the symptoms of schizophrenia: Abnormalities in the awareness of action. *Brain Research Reviews*, *31*, 357–363.

Frosch, J. (1967). Delusional fixity, sense of conviction, and the psychotic conflict. *International Journal of Psycho-Analysis, 48,* 475–495.

Gallese, L., Fadiga, L., Fogassi, L., & Rizzolatti, G. (1996). Action recognition in the premotor cortex. *Brain, 119,* 593–609.

Galton, F. (1880). Visualized numerals. *Nature, 22,* 494–495.

Gerson, W. (1928). Schizophrene Sprachneubildung und schizophrenes Denken. *Z Ges Neurol Psychiat, 113,* 159–176.

Glass, J. (1981). Facts and meaning: From the perspective of schizophrenic internality. *Contemporary Psychoanalysis, 17,* 118–135.

Goldstein, K. (1944). Methodological approach to the study of schizophrenic thought disorder. In J. S. Kasanin (Ed.), *Thought and Language in Schizophrenia.* New York: W. W. Norton (pp. 17–40).

Green, C. (1968). *Lucid Dreams.* London: Hamish Hamilton.

Greenberg, H. (1964). *I Never Promised You a Rose Garden.* New York: Holt, Rinehart & Winston.

Grigsby, J. & Hartlaub, G. (1994). Procedural learning and the development and stability of character. *Perceptual and Motor Skills, 79,* 355–370.

Grotstein, J. (2009). Dreaming as a "curtain of illusion": Revisiting the "royal road" with Bion as our guide. *International Journal of Psycho-Analysis, 90,* 733–752.

Halifax, J. (1979). *Shamanic Voices: A Survey of Visionary Narratives.* New York: Arkana.

Halifax, J. (1982). *Shaman: The Wounded Healer.* London: Thames & Hudson.

Harrow, M., Tucker, G., & Adler, D. (1972). Concrete and idiosyncratic thinking in acute schizophrenic patients. *Archives of General Psychiatry, 26,* 433–439.

Hauser, M., Chomsky, N., & Fitch, W. T. (2002). The faculty of language: What is it, who has it, and how did it evolve? *Science, 298,* 1569–1579.

Heinz, A., Romero, B., & Weinberger, D. (2004). Functional mapping with single-photon emission computed tomography and positron emission tomography. In S. Lawrie, D. Weinberger, & E. Johnstone (Eds), *Schizophrenia: From Neuroimaging to Neuroscience.* New York: Oxford University Press (pp. 167–212).

Hobson, J. (1999). The new neuropsychology of sleep: Implications for psychoanalysis. *Neuropsychoanalysis, 1,* 157–183.

Hobson, J. (2009). REM sleep and dreaming: Towards a theory of protoconsciousness. *Nature Reviews Neuroscience, 12,* 803–813.

Hobson, J., Pace-Schott, E., & Stickgold, R. (2000). Dreaming and the brain: Toward a cognitive neuroscience of conscious states. *Behavioral and Brain Sciences, 23,* 798–842.

Holt, R. (1967). The development of the primary process: A structural view. In R. Holt (Ed.), *Motives and Thought: Psychoanalytic Essays in Honor of David Rapaport.* New York: International Universities Press.

Holt, R. (1976). Freud's theory of the primary process: Present status. *Psychoanalysis and Contemporary Science, 5,* 61–99.

Holt, R. (2002). Quantitative research on the primary process: Method and findings. *Journal of the American Psychoanalytic Association, 50,* 457–482.

Honey, G., McGuire, P., & Bullmore, E. (2004). Functional magnetic resonance imaging (fMRI). In S. Lawrie, D. Weinberger, & E. Johnstone (Eds),

Schizophrenia: From Neuroimaging to Neuroscience. New York: Oxford University Press (pp. 237–292).

Hoppal, M. (1987). Shamanism: An archaic and/or recent system of beliefs. In S. Nicholson (Ed.), *Shamanism*. Wheaton, IL: The Theosophical Publishing House, 1987 (pp. 76–100).

Houston, J. (1987). The mind and soul of the shaman. In S. Nicholson (Ed.), *Shamanism*. Wheaton, IL: The Theosophical Publishing House (pp. vii–xiii).

Hubl, D. & Dierks. T. (2004). Visualizing the cerebral alterations that underlie auditory hallucinations in schizophrenia. In C. McDonald, K. Shulze, R. Murray, & P. Wright (Eds), *Schizophrenia: Challenging the Orthodox*. London: Taylor & Francis (pp. 7–16).

Isaacs, S. (1948). The nature and function of phantasy. *International Journal of Psycho-Analysis, 29*, 73–97.

Jakobson. R. (1956). Two aspects of language and two types of aphasic disturbances. In L. Waugh & M. Monville-Burston (Eds), *On Language*. Cambridge, MA: Harvard University Press (pp. 115–133).

Jamison, K. R. (1997). *An Unquiet Mind: A Memoir of Moods and Madness*. New York: Vintage Books.

Johnston, M. & Holzman, P. (1979). *Assessing Schizophrenic Thinking: A Clinical and Research Instrument for Measuring Thought Disorder*. San Francisco, CA: Jossey-Bass.

Jones, E. (1916). The theory of symbolism. In *Papers on Psycho-Analysis*. London: Ballière, Tindall & Cox, 1948 (pp. 87–144).

Jung, C. G. (1906). *The Psychology of Dementia Praecox*. New York/Washington: Nervous and Mental Disease Publishing Company, 1936.

Jung, C. G. (1954). The practical use of dream-analysis. In *Collected Works, Vol. 16* (R. F. C. Hull, Trans.). New York: Bollingen Foundation. Pantheon Press (pp. 139–162).

Jung, C. G. (1956). Two kinds of thinking. In *Symbols of Transformation, Collected Works, Vol. 5* (R. F. C. Hull, Trans.). New York: Bollingen Foundation/ Pantheon Books. Reprinted in V. S. de Laszlo (Ed.), *The Basic Writings of C. G. Jung*. New York: Random House, 1959 (pp. 10–36).

Jung, C. G. (1959a). Synchronicity: An acausal connecting principle. In *The Structure and Dynamics of the Psyche, Collected Works, Vol. 8* (R. F. C. Hull, Trans.). New York: Bollingen Foundation/Pantheon Books.

Jung, C. G. (1959b). On the nature of dreams. In *The Structure and Dynamics of the Psyche*. In *Collected Works, Vol. 8* (R. F. C. Hull, Trans.). New York: Bollingen Foundation/Pantheon Books. Reprinted in V. S. de Laszlo (Ed.), *The Basic Writings of C. G. Jung*. New York: Random House (pp. 363–379).

Jung, C. G. (2009). *The Red Book* (S. Shamdasani, Ed. & Trans.). New York: W. W. Norton & Co.

Kant, I. (1781). *Critique of Pure Reason* (W. S. Pluhar, Trans.). Indianapolis/ Cambridge: Hackett Publishing Company, 1996.

Kant, I. (1798). *Anthropology from a Pragmatic Point of View* (R. B. Louden, Trans.). New York: Cambridge University Press, 2006.

Kanzer, M. (1955). The communicative function of the dream. *International Journal of Psycho-Analysis, 36*, 260–266.

Katan, M. (1939). A contribution to the understanding of schizophrenic speech. *International Journal of Psycho-Analysis, 20,* 353–362.

King, P. & Steiner, R. (1991). *The Freud–Klein Controversies 1941–1945.* London: Tavistock/Routledge.

Kircher, T., Bulimore, E., Brammer, M., Williams, S., Broome, M., Murray, R., & McGuire, P. (2001). Differential activation of temporal cortex during sentence completion in schizophrenic patients with and without formal thought disorder. *Schizophrenia Research, 50,* 27–40.

Klein, M. (1926). The psychological principles of early analysis. In *The Writings of Melanie Klein.* London: Hogarth Press/Institute of Psycho-Analysis, 1975 (pp. 128–138).

Klein, M. (1930). The importance of symbol-formation in the development of the ego. In *Love, Guilt and Reparation and Other Works 1921–1945.* London: Hogarth Press, 1975 (pp. 219–232).

Klein, M. (1935). A contribution to the psychogenesis of manic-depressive states. In *Love, Guilt and Reparation and Other Works 1921–1945.* London: Hogarth Press, 1975 (pp. 262–289).

Klein, M. (1937). Love, guilt and reparation. In *Love, Guilt and Reparation and Other Works 1921–1945.* London: Hogarth Press, 1975 (pp. 306–343).

Klein, M. (1946). Notes on some schizoid mechanisms. In *Envy and Gratitude and Other Works 1946–1963.* London: Hogarth Press (pp. 1–24).

Klein, M. (1958). On the development of mental functioning. *International Journal of Psycho-Analysis, 39,* 84–89.

Klein, M. (1975a). *Love, Guilt and Reparation and Other Works 1921–1945.* London: Hogarth Press.

Klein, M. (1975b). *Envy and Gratitude and Other Works, 1946–1963.* London: Hogarth Press.

Kohut, H. (1971). *The Analysis of the Self.* New York: International Universities Press.

Kohut, H. (1977). *The Restoration of the Self.* New York: International Universities Press.

Kolberg, C. (2009). Experiences of acute psychosis – What may be helpful? Paper presented at ISPS conference, Copenhagen, June 19.

Kracke, W. (1999). A language of dreaming: Dreams of an Amazonian insomniac. *International Journal of Psycho-Analysis, 80,* 257–271.

Kraepelin, E. (1896). *Dementia Praecox and Paraphrenia* (R. M. Barclay, Trans.). Edinburgh: E. & S. Livingstone, 1919.

Kraepelin, E. (1906). *Über Sprachstörungen im Träume.* Leipzig: Engelmann Verlag.

Krippner, S. (2002). Conflicting perspectives on shamans and shamanism: Point and counterpoints. *American Psychologist, 57,* 962–977.

Kris, E. (1952). *Psychoanalytic Explorations in Art.* New York: International Universities Press.

Kroeber, A. (1940). Psychotic factors in shamanism. *Character and Personality, 8,* 204–215.

Krystal, H. (1978). Trauma and affects. *Psychoanalytic Study of the Child, 33,* 81–116.

LaBerge, S. (1980). *Lucid Dreaming: An Exploratory Study of Consciousness During Sleep.* PhD thesis, Stanford University.

LaBerge, S. (1985). *Lucid Dreaming*. Los Angeles, CA: J. P. Tarcher.

LaBerge, S. (1990). Lucid dreaming: Psychophysiological studies of consciousness during REM sleep. In R. Bootzen, J. Kihlstrom, & D. Schacter (Eds), *Sleep and Cognition*. Washington, DC: American Psychological Association (pp. 109–126).

LaBerge, S. (2000). Lucid dreaming: Evidence and methodology. *Behavioral and Brain Sciences*, *23*, 962–963.

Lacan, J. (1953). The function and field of speech and language in psychoanalysis. In *Ecrits: A Selection* (A. Sheridan, Trans.). New York: Norton, 1977 (pp. 30–113).

Lacan, J. (1968). *The Language of the Self: The Function of Language in Psycho-analysis* (A. Wilden, Trans.). Baltimore, MD: Johns Hopkins Press.

Lambrecht, I. (1998). *A Psychological Study of Shamanic Trance States in South African Shamanism*. PhD thesis, University of the Witwatersrand, Johannesburg.

Lambrecht, I. & Lampshire, D. (2009). Screaming in Whispers: A Dialogue about Voices. Paper presented at ISPS conference, Copenhagen, June 19.

Lampshire, D. (2009). Lies and lessons: Ramblings of an allegedly mad woman. *Psychosis*, *1*, 178–184.

Lane, R. (2000). Neural correlates of conscious emotional experience. In R. Lane, L. Nadel, G. Ahern, J. Allen, A. Kaszniak, S. Rapcsak, & G. Schwartz (Eds), *Cognitive Neuroscience of Emotion*. New York: Oxford University Press (pp. 345–370).

Lane, R. D. & Garfield, D. A. (2005). Becoming aware of feelings: Integration of cognitive-developmental, neuroscientific, and psychoanalytic perspectives. *Neuro-Psychoanalysis*, *7*, 5–30.

LaPlanche, J. & Pontalis, J.-B. (1973). *The Language of Psycho-Analysis* (D. N. Smith, Trans.). New York: Norton.

Lawrie, S., Buechel, C., Whalley, H., Frith, C., Friston, K., & Johnstone, E. (2002). Reduced frontotemporal connection in schizophrenia associated with auditory hallucinations. *Biological Psychiatry*, *51*, 1008–1011.

Lawrie, S., Johnstone, E., & Weinberger, D. (2004). *Schizophrenia: From Neuroimaging to Neuroscience*. New York: Oxford University Press.

Lecours, A. & Vanier-Clement, M. (1976). Schizophasia and jargonaphasia: A comparative description with comments on Chaika and Fromkin's respective looks at "schizophrenic" language. *Brain and Language*, *3*, 516–565.

LeDoux, J. E. (1996). *The Emotional Brain: The Mysterious Underpinnings of Emotional Life*. New York: Simon & Schuster.

Linton, R. (1956). *The Nature of Culture*. Chicago, IL: University of Chicago Press.

Litowitz, B. (2007). Unconscious fantasy: A once and future concept. *Journal of the American Psychoanalytic Association*, *55*, 199–228.

Loewald, H. (1980). Primary process, secondary process, and language. In *Papers on Psychoanalysis*. New Haven, CT: Yale University Press (pp. 178–206).

Lorberbaum, J. P., Newman, J. D., Horwitz, A. R., Dubno, J. R., Lydiard, R. B., Hamner, M. B., Bohning, D. E., & George, M. S. (2002). A potential role for thalamocingulate circuitry in human maternal behavior. *Biological Psychiatry*, *51*, 431–445.

Lyons-Ruth, K. (1999). The two-person unconscious: Intersubjective dialogue, enactive relational representation, and the emergence of new forms of relational organization. *Psychoanalytic Inquiry*, *19*, 576–617.

Lyons-Ruth, K. (2003). Dissociation and the parent–infant dialogue: A longitudinal perspective from attachment research. *Journal of the American Psychoanalytic Association, 51*, 883–911.

McLaughlin, J. (1993). Work with patients: The impetus for self-analysis. *Psychoanalytic Inquiry, 13*, 365–389.

Mahler, M. S., Pine, F., & Bergman, A. (1975). *The Psychological Birth of the Human Infant: Symbiosis and Individuation*. New York: Basic Books.

Makari, G. J. (1994). In the eye of the beholder: Helmholtzian perception and the origins of Freud's 1900 theory of transference. *Journal of the American Psychoanalytic Association, 42*, 549–580.

Mandelbrot, B. (1967). How long is the coast of Britain? Statistical self-similarity and fractional dimension. *Science, 155*, 636–638.

Manning, J. T., Trivers, R. L., Thornhill, R., Singh, D., Denman, J., Eklo, M. H., & Anderton, R. H. (1997). Ear asymmetry and left-side cradling. *Evolution and Human Behavior, 18*, 327–340.

Maquet, P., Peters, J.-M., Aerts, J., Delfiore, G., DeGueldre, C., Luxen, A., & Franck, G. (1996). Functional neuroanatomy of human rapid-eye-movement sleep and dreaming. *Nature, 383*, 163–166.

Matte-Blanco, I. (1975). *The Unconscious as Infinite Sets: An Essay in Bi-Logic*. London: Duckworth.

Matte-Blanco, I. (1986). Understanding Matte-Blanco. *International Journal of Psycho-Analysis, 67*, 251–254.

Matte-Blanco, I. (1988). *Thinking, Feeling, and Being: Clinical Reflections on the Fundamental Antinomy of Human Beings and World*. London: Routledge.

Matthysse, S. (1987). Schizophrenic thought disorder: A model-theoretic perspective. *Schizophrenia Bulletin, 13*, 173–184.

Maurer, D. & Mondloch, C. (2006). The infant as synesthete? In M. Johnson & Y. Munakata (Eds), *Attention and Performance XXI: Process of Change in Brain and Cognitive Development*. Oxford: Oxford University Press (pp. 449–471).

Meltzer, D. (1976). Dream-narrative and dream-continuity. *Contemporary Psychoanalysis, 12*, 423–432.

Meltzer, D. (1984). *Dream-Life: A Re-Examination of the Psychoanalytic Theory and Technique*. Worcester: Clunie Press.

Meyer, A. (1958). *Psychobiology: A Science of Man*. Springfield, IL: Charles C. Thomas.

Mitchell, S. (1988). *Relational Concepts in Psychoanalysis*. Cambridge, MA: Harvard University Press.

Molnar-Szaracs, I., Gallese, V., Buccino, G., & Mazziotta, J. C. (2005). Grasping the intentions of others with one's own motor neuron system. *PLoS Biology, 3*, e79.

Moore, B. & Fine, B. (1990). *Psychoanalytic Terms and Concepts*. New Haven, CT: Yale University Press.

Muller, J. P. (2005). Approaches to the semiotics of thought and feeling in Bion's work. *Canadian Journal of Psychoanalysis, 13*, 31–56.

Muzur, A., Pace-Schott, E., & Hobson, A. (2002). The prefrontal cortex in sleep. *Trends in Cognitive Science, 1*, 475–481.

Nakashima Degarrod, L. (1989). *Dream Interpretation Among the Mapuche Indians of Chile.* Ann Arbor, MI: University of Michigan Dissertation Information Service.

Nasar, S. (2001). *A Beautiful Mind.* New York: Simon and Schuster.

Nemiah, J. (1978). Alexithymia and psychosomatic illness. *Journal of Clinical and Experimental Psychiatry, 39,* 25–37.

Nicholson, S. (Ed.) (1987). *Shamanism.* Wheaton, IL: The Theosophical Publishing House.

Nofzinger, E. A., Mintun, M. A., Wiseman, M. B., Kupfer, D. J., & Moore, R. Y. (1997). Forebrain activation in REM sleep: An FDG PET study. *Brain Research, 770,* 192–201.

Noll, R. (1983). Shamanism and schizophrenia: A state-specific approach to the schizophrenic metaphor of shamanic states. *American Ethnologist, 10,* 443–459.

Noll, R. (1985). Mental imagery: Cultivation as a cultural phenomenon: The role of visions in shamanism. *Current Anthropology, 26,* 443–451.

Noll, R. (1989). What has really been learned about shamanism? *Journal of Psychoactive Drugs, 21,* 47–50.

Noy, P. (1968). A theory about art and aesthetic experience. *Psychoanalytic Review, 55,* 623–645.

Noy, P. (1969). A revision of the psychoanalytic theory of the primary process. *International Journal of Psycho-Analysis, 50,* 155–178

Ogden, T. (1989). On the concept of an autistic-contiguous position. *International Journal of Psycho-Analysis, 70,* 127–140.

Ogden, T. (2004). An introduction to the reading of Bion. *International Journal of Psycho-Analysis, 85,* 285–300.

O'Shaugnnessy, E. (1995). Whose Bion? *International Journal of Psycho-Analysis, 86,* 1523–1528.

Pally, R. (2007). The predicting brain: Unconscious repetition, conscious reflection and therapeutic change. *International Journal of Psycho-Analysis, 88,* 861–888.

Panksepp, J. (1998). *Affective Neuroscience: The Foundations of Human and Animal Emotions.* New York: Oxford University Press.

Panksepp, J. (2003). At the interface of the affective, behavioral, and cognitive neurosciences: Decoding the emotional feelings of the brain. *Brain and Cognition, 52,* 4–14.

Paus, T., Zijdembos, A., Worsele, K., Collins, L., Blumenthal, J., Geidd, J., Rapoport, J., & Evans A. (1999). Structural maturation of neural pathways in children and adolescents: In vivo study. *Science 283,* 1908–1911.

Perry, J. (1974). *The Far Side of Madness.* Englewood, NJ: Spring Publications.

Peters, L. & Price-Williams, D. (1980). Towards an experiential analysis of shamanism. *American Ethnologist, 7,* 397–418.

Piaget, J. (1936). *The Origins of Intelligence in Children.* New York: International Universities Press, 1952.

Pinker, S. (1994). *The Language Instinct.* New York: William Morrow & Company.

Plato (1927). *Republic.* In I. Edwin (Ed.), *The Works of Plato* (B. Jowett, Trans.). New York: Random House.

Price-Williams, D. (1982). The waking dream in ethnographic perspective. In B. Tedlock (Ed.), *Dreaming: Anthropological and Psychological Perspectives.* Santa Fe, NM: School of American Research Press.

Ramachandran, V. & Hubbard, E. (2001). Synesthesia: A window into perception, thought and language. *Journal of Consciousness Studies*, *8*, 3–34.

Ramachandran, V. & Hubbard, E. (2005). Neurocognitive mechanisms of synesthesia. *Neuron*, *48*, 509–520.

Randall, P., Geekie, J., Lambrecht, I., & Taitimu, M. (2008). Dissociation, psychosis and spirituality: Whose voices are we hearing? In A. Moskowitz, I. Schafer, & M. J. Dorahy (Eds), *Psychosis, Trauma and Dissociation: Emerging Perspectives on Severe Psychopathology*. Chichester, UK: John Wiley. (pp. 333–345).

Ranote, S., Elliott, R., Abel, K. M., Mitchell, R., Deakin, J. F. W., & Appleby, L. (2004). The neural basis of maternal responsiveness to infants: An fMRI study. *NeuroReport*, *15*, 1825–1829.

Rapaport, D. (1951). Toward a theory of thinking. In D. Rapaport (Ed.), *Organization and Pathology of Thought*. New York: Columbia University Press (pp. 689–730).

Rapaport, D. (1960). *The Structure of Psychoanalytic Theory*. New York: International Universities Press.

Rapaport, D. (1961). Psychoanalysis as a developmental psychology. In *Collected Papers of David Rapaport*. New York: Basic Books.

Rayner, E. (1981). Infinite experiences, affects and the characteristics of the unconscious. *International Journal of Psycho-Analysis*, *62*, 403–412.

Rayner, E. & Tuckett, D. (1988). An introduction to Matte-Blanco's reformulation of the Freudian unconscious and his conceptualization of the internal world. In I. Matte-Blanco (Ed.), *Thinking, Feeling, and Being: Clinical Reflections on the Fundamental Antinomy of Human Being and World*. London and New York: Tavistock/Routledge.

Reich, S. (1992). Come Out. On *Early Works* [CD].New York: Nonesuch Records.

Robbins, M. (1969). On the psychology of artistic creativity. *Psychoanalytic Study of the Child*, *24*, 227–251.

Robbins, M. (1976). Borderline personality organization: The need for a new theory. *Journal of the American Psychoanalytic Association*, *24*, 831–853.

Robbins, M. (1980). Current controversy in object relations theory as outgrowth of a schism between Klein and Fairbairn. *International Journal of Psycho-Analysis*, *61*, 477–492.

Robbins, M. (1981a). The symbiosis concept and the commencement of normal and pathological ego functioning and object relations: I. Infancy. *International Review of Psycho-Analysis*, *8*, 365–377.

Robbins, M. (1981b). The symbiosis concept and the commencement of normal and pathological ego functioning and object relations: II. Developments subsequent to infancy and pathological processes. *International Review of Psycho-Analysis*, *8*, 379–391.

Robbins, M. (1993). *Experiences of Schizophrenia*. New York: Guilford.

Robbins, M. (1996). *Conceiving of Personality*. New Haven, CT: Yale University Press.

Robbins, M. (2002). The language of schizophrenia and the world of delusion. *International Journal of Psycho-Analysis*, *83*, 383–405.

Robbins, M. (2004). Another look at dreaming: Disentangling Freud's primary and secondary process theories. *Journal of the American Psychoanalytic Association*, *52*, 355–384.

Robbins, M. (2008). Primary mental expression: Freud, Klein and beyond. *Journal of the American Psychoanalytic Association, 56*, 177–202.

Robertson, J. (1971). Young children in brief separation – A fresh look. *Psychoanalytic Study of the Child, 26*, 264–315.

Rolls, E. T. (1996). The orbitofrontal cortex. *Philosophical Transactions of the Royal Society of London, 351*, 1433–1444.

Sandler, J. & Freud, A. (1983). Discussions in the Hampstead Index of *The Ego and the Mechanisms of Defense*. *Journal of the American Psychoanalytic Association, 3*(S), 19–146.

Sapir, E. (1921). *Language*. New York: Harcourt Brace & World.

Schilder, P. (1914). Wahn und Erkenntnis. *Mono. Ges. Geb. Neurol. Psychiat*. Berlin: Springer.

Schilder, P. (1942). *Mind: Perception and Thought in Their Constructive Aspects*. New York: Columbia University Press.

Schmidt, M. (1987). Crazy wisdom: The shaman as mediator of realities. In S. Nicholson (Ed.), *Shamanism*. Wheaton, IL: The Theosophical Publishing House, 1987 (pp. 62–75).

Schore, A. (1997). A century after Freud's Project: Is a rapprochement between psychoanalysis and neurobiology at hand? *Journal of the American Psychoanalytic Association, 45*, 841–867.

Schore, A. (2003). *Affect Dysregulation and Disorders of the Self*. New York: W. W. Norton.

Schore, A. (2005). A neuropsychoanalytic viewpoint: Commentary on paper by Steven H. Knoblauch. *Psychoanalytic Dialogues, 15*, 829–854.

Scorsese, M. (Dir.) (2005). *No Direction Home*. DVD. Paramount Studios.

Searles, H. (1962). The differentiation between concrete and metaphorical thinking in the recovering schizophrenic patient. In *Collected Papers on Schizophrenia and Related Subjects*. New York: International Universities Press, 1965 (pp. 560–583).

Searles, H. (1965). *Collected Papers on Schizophrenia and Related Subjects*. New York: International Universities Press.

Seeman, M. (1970). Analysis of psychotic language: A review. *Diseases of the Nervous System, 31*, 92–99.

Segal, H. (1950). Some aspects of the analysis of a schizophrenic. *International Journal of Psycho-Analysis, 31*, 268–278.

Segal, H. (1952). Psychoanalytic approach to aesthetics. *International Journal of Psycho-Analysis, 33*, 196–207.

Segal, H. (1956). Depression in the schizophrenic. *International Journal of Psycho-Analysis, 37*, 339–343.

Segal, H. (1957). Notes on symbol formation. *International Journal of Psychoanalysis, 38*, 39–45.

Segal, H. (1978). On symbolism. *International Journal of Psycho-Analysis, 59*, 315–319.

Segal, H. (1979). *Melanie Klein*. New York: Viking Press.

Shelton, R. (1987). *No Direction Home: The Life and Music of Bob Dylan*. London: Penguin Books.

Shevrin, H. & Fisher, C. (1967). Changes in the effects of a waking subliminal stimulus as a function of dreaming and nondreaming sleep. *Journal of Abnormal Psychology*, *72*, 362–368.

Sieratzki, J. & Woll, B. (1996). Why do mothers cradle babies on their left? *Lancet*, *347*, 1746–1748.

Sifneos, P. (1975). Problems of psychotherapy of patients with alexithymic characteristics and physical disease. *Psychotherapy and Psychosomatics*, *26*, 65–70.

Silberer, H. (1951). On symbol-formation. In D. Rapaport (Ed.), *Organization and Pathology of Thought: Selected Sources*. New York: Columbia University Press (pp. 208–233).

Silverman, J. (1967). Shamans and acute schizophrenia. *American Anthropologist*, *67*, 21–31.

Simner, D., Sagiv, N., Molvenna, C., Tsakanikos, E., Witherby, S., Fraser, C. . . . Ward, J. (2006). Synesthesia: The prevalence of atypical cross-modal experiences. *Perception*. *35*, 1024–1033.

Solms, M. (1997). *The Neuropsychology of Dreams: A Clinico-Anatomical Study*. Mahwah, NJ: Lawrence Erlbaum.

Solms, M. & Turnbull, O. (2002). *The Brain and the Inner World*. New York: Other Press.

Spillius, E. (1988). *Melanie Klein Today: Volume I: Mainly Theory*. London: The New Library of Psychoanalysis/Routledge.

Squire, L. (1986). Mechanisms of memory. *Science*, *232*, 1612–1619.

States, B. (1992). The meaning of dreams. *Dreaming*, *2*, 1–13.

Stein, M. (1998). *Jung's Map of the Soul*. Chicago, IL: Open Court.

Steiner, J. (1987). The interplay between pathological organizations and the paranoid-schizoid and depressive positions. *International Journal of Psycho-Analysis*, *68*, 69–80.

Sterba, R. (1940). The problem of art in Freud's writings. *Psychoanalytic Quarterly*, *9*, 256–268.

Stern, D. B. (1989). The analyst's unformulated experience of the patient. *Contemporary Psychoanalysis*, *25*, 1–33.

Stern, D. N. (1985). *The Interpersonal World of the Infant*. New York: Basic Books.

Stern, D. N., Sander, L. W., Nahum, J. P., Harrison, A. M., Lyons-Ruth, K., Morgan, A. C., Bruschweilerstern, N., & Tronick, E. Z. (1998). Non-interpretive mechanisms in psychoanalytic therapy: The "something more" than interpretation. *International Journal of Psycho-Analysis*, *79*, 903–921.

Storch, A. (1924). *The Primitive Archaic Forms of Inner Experiences and Thought in Schizophrenics*. New York and Washington, DC: Nervous and Mental Disease Publication Company.

Stransky, E. (1905). *On Dementia Praecox*. Vienna: Vienna Medical Press.

Sullivan, H. (1953a). *Schizophrenia as a Human Process*. New York: W. W. Norton.

Sullivan, H. (1953b). *The Interpersonal Theory of Psychiatry*. New York: Norton.

Swados, E. (1991). *The Four of Us*. New York: Farrar, Strauss & Giroux.

Symington, J. & Symington, N. (1996). *The Clinical Thinking of Wilfred Bion*. New York: Routledge.

Tausk, V. (1933). On the origin of the "influencing machine" in schizophrenia. *Psychoanalytic Quarterly*, *2*, 519–556.

Tien, A. Y. (1991). Distributions of hallucinations in the population. *Social Psychiatry and Psychiatric Epidemiology*, 26, 287–292.

Tomasello, M. (1999). *The Cultural Origins of Human Cognition*. Cambridge, MA: Harvard University Press.

Trevarthen, C. (1980). The foundations of intersubjectivity: Development of interpersonal and cooperative understanding in infants. In D. Olson (Ed.), *The Social Foundation of Language and Thought*. New York: W. W. Norton (pp. 316–342).

Tzourio-Mazoyer, N., De Schonen, S., Crivello, F., Reutter, B., Aujard, Y., & Mazoyer, B. (2002). Neural correlates of woman face processing by 2-month-old infants. *NeuroImage*, 15, 454–461.

Urban, G. (1986). Semiotic functions of macro-parallelism in the Shokleng origin myth. In J. Scherzer & G. Urban (Eds), *Native South American Discourse*. Berlin: Mouton (pp. 15–58).

van Eeden, F. (1913). The study of dreams. *Society for Psychical Research*, 26.

Vitebsky, P. (2001). *The Shaman*. London: Duncan Baird.

von Bertalanffy, L. (1952). *Problems of Life*. New York: John Wiley & Sons.

Von Domarus, E. (1944). The specific laws of logic in schizophrenia. In J. Kasanin (Ed.), *Language and Thought in Schizophrenia*. New York: Norton (pp. 104–114).

Voss, V., Holzmann, R., Tuin, I., & Hobson, J. A. (2009). Lucid dreaming: A state of consciousness with features of both waking and non-lucid dreaming. *Sleep*, 12, 1191–2000.

Vygotsky, L. S. (1934a). *Thought and Language*. Cambridge, MA: MIT Press, 1962.

Vygotsky, L. S. (1934b). Thought in schizophrenia. *Archives of Neurology and Psychiatry*, 31, 1063–1077.

Waldhorn, H. (1967). The place of the dream in clinical psychoanalysis. In B. Fine, E. Joseph, & H. Waldhorn (Eds), *Indications for Psychoanalysis. Kris Study Group Monograph 2*. New York: International Universities Press (pp. 52–106).

Walker, E. & Lewine, R. (1990). Prediction of adult-onset schizophrenia from childhood home movies of the patient. *American Journal of Psychiatry*, 147, 1052–1056.

Walsh, R. (1990). *The Spirit of Shamanism*. New York: J. P. Tarcher.

Walter, M. & Fridman, E. (2004). *Shamanism: An Encyclopedia of World Beliefs, Practices and Cultures*. Santa Barbara, CA: ABC-CLIO.

Ward, J. & Simner, D. (2005). Is synesthesia an X-linked dominant trait with lethality in males? *Perception*, 34, 611–623.

Ward, J., Huckstep, B., & Tsakanikos, E. (2006). Sound-color synesthesia: To what extent does it use cross-modal mechanisms common to us all? *Cortex*, 42, 264–280.

Watt, D. F. (1990). Higher cortical functions and the ego: Explorations of the boundary between behavioral neurology, neuropsychology, and psychoanalysis. *Psychoanalytic Psychology*, 7, 487–527.

Weiss, P. (1959). Animal behaviour as system reaction: Orientation toward light and gravity in the resting postures of butterflies (Vanessa). *General Systems: Yearbook for the Society of General Systems Research* (pp. 19–44).

Weiss, P. (1969). The living system: Determinism stratified. In A. Koestler & J. Smithies (Eds), *Beyond Reductionism*. New York: Macmillan (pp. 3–55).

Weiss, P. (1977). The Systems of Nature and the Nature of Systems: Empirical Holism and Practical Reductionism Harmonized. In K. Schaefer, H. Hensel, & R.

Brady (Eds), *Toward a Man-Centered Medical Science*. Mt. Kisco, NY: Futura (pp. 17–64).

Werner, H. (1948). *Comparative Psychology of Mental Development*. New York: International Universities Press.

Werner, H. (1957). The concept of development from a comparative and organismic point of view. In D. Harris (Ed.), *The Concept of Development*. Minneapolis, MN: University of Minnesota Press (pp. 125–148).

Werner, H. & Kaplan, B. (1963). *Symbol Formation: An Organismic-Developmental Approach to Language and the Expression of Thought*. New York: John Wiley & Sons.

White, W. A. (1925). *Schizophrenia (Dementia Praecox)*. New York: Paul B. Hoeber.

Whorf, B. (1956). *Language, Thought and Reality*. Cambridge, MA: MIT Press.

Winkelman, M. (1990). Shaman and other "magico-religious healers:" A cross-cultural study of their origins, nature and social transformation. *Ethos, 18*, 308–352.

Winkelman, M. (1992). Shamans, priests and witches: A cross-cultural study of magico-religious practitioners. In *Anthropological Research Papers Number 44*. Tempe, AZ: Arizona State University.

Winnicott, D. W. (1965). *The Maturational Processes and the Facilitating Environment*. New York: International Universities Press.

Winnicott, D. W. (1971). *Playing and Reality*. London: Tavistock.

Index

Locators in *italic* refer to figures/tables
Locators for headings which also have subheadings refer to general aspects of the topic only
PMA is an abbreviation of primordial mental activity